Pandemic Urbanism ——————————

Pandemic Urbanism ————

Infectious Diseases on a Planet of Cities

S. Harris Ali, Creighton Connolly, & Roger Keil

polity

First published in 2023 by Polity Press

Polity Press
65 Bridge Street
Cambridge CB2 1UR, UK

Polity Press
111 River Street
Hoboken, NJ 07030, USA

ISBN-13: 978-1-5095-4983-2
ISBN-13: 978-1-5095-4984-9 (pb)

A catalogue record for this book is available from the British Library.

Library of Congress Control Number: 2022940785

Typeset in 11.5 on 15 pt Adobe Jenson Pro
by Fakenham Prepress Solutions, Fakenham, Norfolk NR21 8NL
Printed and bound in Great Britain by CPI Group (UK) Ltd, Croydon

The publisher has used its best endeavours to ensure that the URLs for external websites referred to in this book are correct and active at the time of going to press. However, the publisher has no responsibility for the websites and can make no guarantee that a site will remain live or that the content is or will remain appropriate.

Every effort has been made to trace all copyright holders, but if any have been overlooked the publisher will be pleased to include any necessary credits in any subsequent reprint or edition.

For further information on Polity, visit our website:
politybooks.com

Contents

Acknowledgements

This book is largely a collection of our thoughts and our research over the time of the COVID-19 pandemic, but it has its origin in prior collaboration by its authors. Towards the end of the SSHRC-funded Major Collaborative Research Initiative *Global Suburbanisms: Governance, Land and Infrastructure*, which was hosted by York University's City Institute and led by Roger Keil, we identified three areas for future research, with extended urbanization and infectious disease and public health as one of them. We held a workshop and wrote a position paper in 2018 which was the basis of a(n unsuccessful) research funding application with the title "Urbanizing Life: Health and Disease in an Age of Global Exposure" in 2019. We would like to thank our participating colleagues for their input, and the staff of *Global Suburbanisms*, especially Lucy Lynch and Cara Chellew, for their support.

The ideas paper that served as the impetus for this initiative was first published by the authors of this book as "Extended urbanisation and the spatialities of infectious disease: demographic change, infrastructure and governance" in the journal *Urban Studies* in early 2020 (https://doi.org/0.1177/0042098020910873), and parts of this paper found their way into the current volume. Following the publication of this paper, one of the most read and downloaded in the journal over two pandemic years, the folks putting together the podcast *The Urban Political* afforded us an early opportunity to speak about the paper's subject matter to their audiences. We thank them for putting our work on the map early in the pandemic when it mattered. Hyun Bang Shin at LSE also provided a platform for us to share and workshop our ideas early in the pandemic, through inviting us to participate in a much-publicized webinar and blog on COVID-19. Creighton Connolly shared insights developed from these forums in the edited collection *COVID-19 in Southeast Asia*, published by LSE Press (2022).

Equally, we previously collaborated in the IDRC-sponsored project *Improving Ebola Containment Through Community Based Initiatives*, led by Harris Ali. This book has benefited from this project in many ways, including highlighting for us the need for a renewed focus on the plight of the Global South in dealing with infectious disease threats, and providing lessons to us all in how such now-globalized threats can be addressed. In this connection, Harris Ali would like to thank his co-investigators in this project, Dr. Mosoka Fallah and Dr. Joseph M. Macarthy, as well as the excellent staff in the respective organizations they led: the Community Based Initiative (CBI) in Monrovia, Liberia, and the Sierra Leone Urban Research Centre (SLURC) in Freetown, Sierra Leone. He would also like to thank the people on the project team, including Laura Skrip, Pablo Idahosa, Axel Lehrer, Michaela Hynie, Robin Bloch, Ellie Perkins, and of course his long-time friend, colleague, and co-author Roger Keil, as well as the wonderful research assistants from the sociology department at York University: Kathryn Wells, Stefan Treffers, and Jarrett Rose, and Lucy Lynch from the Faculty of Environment and Urban Change. Finally, Harris Ali would like to thank the IDRC for their generous funding, and in particular a debt of gratitude is owed to Dr. Samuel Oji Oti – Senior Program Specialist – for his valued advice and support.

There are many with whom we have corresponded and learned from over the past two years, too many to mention here. During the two decades before 2020, the scholarly community of those who spoke of impending threats that were emerging at the interface of cities and infectious disease was small by comparison. It has grown since. Even on the brink of this planetary pandemic, talking about disease and cities was considered a niche interest, a topic for specialists. In this light, Roger Keil wants to thank Fulong Wu and John Tomaney at the Bartlett School, UCL, for inviting him to give the Sir Peter Hall lecture in June 2019, where he first presented some of the ideas that seeded this book. He is also grateful to Paul Maginn and his colleagues at the University of Western Australia in Perth, who gave him the opportunity to present on "Perforated Boundaries: Emerging Constellations of Disease in an Era of Extended Urbanisation" at the University's Public Policy Institute in November 2019. A special nod goes to Michele Acuto, who bought Roger Keil a coffee and invited him to talk on the topic at their *Cities, Coffee, Chats* series, Connected Cities Lab, University of Melbourne, in December of 2019, just weeks before the world started to learn about COVID-19. Further, Roger Keil wants to thank the journal *disP* for giving him the chance to write four columns for it during the first pandemic year of 2020, which gave him a regular outlet for his original thoughts on the pandemic. Some writing from these columns was used in chapters of this book.

These are the people we want to express our gratitude to for collabo-ration and joint research, as the crisis around COVID-19 continues to unfold and the ensuing trauma requires our continued post-pandemic attention: Raphael Aguiar, Aria Ahmad, Ahmed Allahwala, Samantha Biglieri, Hillary Birch, Robin Bloch, Neil Brenner, Chiara Camponeschi, Lorenzo De Vidovich, Mosoka Fallah, Phil Harrison, Sean Hertel, Julian Iacobelli, Maria Kaika, Brent Kaup, Axel Lehrer, Tait Mandler, Joseph McCarthy, Colin McFarlane, Daniel Mullis, James Orbinski, Jay Pitter, Xuefei Ren, Dallas Rogers, AbdouMaliq Simone, Stefan Treffers, Yannis Tzaninis, Murat Üçoğlu, and Jianhong Wu. At one further remove, during COVID-19 and beyond, we have always been ready to learn from the wise media interventions of Jason Kindrachuk, Scott Knowles, and Ed Yong.

Lastly, we want to express our appreciation to Jonathan Skerrett, Senior Commissioning Editor at Polity, for seeing the potential in our book, and helping us through the proposal and writing process. Assistant Editor Karina Jákupsdóttir kept us on track throughout, Rachel Moore and Fiona Sewell provided professional editing, and Judy Dunlop's assistance in creating the index for this volume was also invaluable. Finally, Amanda Kivlichan helped us in the closing days of finishing this manuscript with her keen editing skills.

In closing, we thank our loved ones and "quaranteams" who afforded us the opportunity, during a period that required attention to care of others and ourselves, to carve out time to finish this work. We hope the readers will see value in the outcome.

S. Harris Ali, Creighton Connolly, and Roger Keil
Toronto and Hong Kong, July 2022

1 | Introduction: Emerging Infectious Disease and the "Urban" Condition

This is a book for our urban age. It sits at the crossroads of global – some would say planetary – urbanization and the emergence of new infectious diseases. Here we consider the socio-spatial logic of the urban environment and how that can influence the course of and response to epidemics. COVID-19 has demonstrated to the world how quickly contagion can spread through the networks of trade, tourism, and technologies, and through what we will later refer to as the political ecologies of extended urbanization. Epidemiologists had warned of an outbreak like the COVID-19 pandemic for a generation (Coker et al., 2011; Yong, 2018). What had been hypothetical before 2020 is now experiential: COVID-19 has been the first pandemic of the urban century and has affected cities around the globe. Now that the "monster has entered," to paraphrase Mike Davis (2020), we can be certain that it is not the last one to come around. Understanding how a majority urban world can survive under the onslaught will be a crucial piece in our collective response in the future.

COVID-19 hit at a time when cities – understood here in the first instance in the most general sense, which we will complicate later in this chapter and throughout this book – were enjoying a period of optimism and emphatic positivity. In the new century, economic success, creative economies, and smart urbanism ostensibly had lured people "back" into the urban centre for work, life, and play. High densities were considered preconditions for hip and healthy lifestyles, free of the automobile, and virtuous allies in the struggle against the climate emergency. COVID-19 called some of that optimism into question, at least for a while. The pandemic reordered the ways we have been thinking about and acting in cities. In this sense, the pandemic has simultaneously refracted and recast urbanization. Like the financial crisis, Occupy Wall Street, the Black Lives Matter protests, and the climate emergency, the pandemic offered us a glimpse into a different urban future: thinking of the city as an arena of everyday life, of urbanization as the process that makes such life possible, and of urbanism as a collective project of shaping city and urbanization. The pandemic was both a disaster and an opportunity for urban life, much as climate change has challenged cities to redo their fundamental ways of operating (Goh, 2021).

Disasters are always cascading and complex and tend to harm those that are most vulnerable while exposing the hotspots of systemic injustice (Frisina Doetter et al., 2021) – those who had been forgotten or taken for granted when times were good. When people were first ordered to stay at home, the advantages and conveniences of urban life were severely curtailed and were only partially replaceable by new technologies of communications such as Zoom. When the lockdown lifted and the outdoors became open for use, urbanists everywhere called upon urban dwellers to occupy the streets on foot and with bicycles and to reorganize life around the necessities of collective sharing of roads and public spaces (Aaditya and Rahul, 2021). In the shadow of the new mainstream urbanist mantra of "we are all in this together" lay the danger of the dissolution of the urban fabric itself (see Burton, 2021). The tissue of urban life became threadbare under pressure as the most vulnerable fell to the virus. Diversities revealed themselves to be cut through with class and race in ways that were hard to reconcile with the official dogma of the open, creative, and multicultural city. *Access* to public space and *ownership* of private space became definitive markers of one's chance for survival in the pre-vaccine city. As cities – ostensibly places that should work for everyone – more recently pivoted towards reopening, they were called upon to improve the conditions of those who suffered most. We take up this discussion in the two final chapters of the book.

Cities have always been defined by their relationships with and response to disease. For most of human history, cities were particularly vulnerable to outbreaks and contagion due to a diverse set of socio-spatial factors, including those pertaining to mixed economies, high densities, connectivities across borders, and situatedness along distant trade routes (Bollyky, 2019). Of course, the plague outbreaks of the Middle Ages were largely urban in their impacts, but urban settlements were still somewhat insular and situated within a largely agrarian context in which the spatial distribution of cities was sparse and non-contiguous for the most part. In the industrial era, hygiene became the main concern of overcrowded working-class quarters as typhoid, cholera, tuberculosis, and other infectious diseases were recurring threats. As the twentieth century came around, scientific advances bolstered the prominence of the germ theory of disease and with that came an increased awareness of and more widespread emphasis on hygiene. With the protections offered by these developments, cities reversed their historical position as being the "natural" place of disease (due to filth, overcrowding, pollution, etc.) to become healthier than the countryside – at least in those urban environments where running water, sewage systems, and other hard infrastructures were working in conjunction with the newly adopted soft infrastructures associated with public health and social reform. In many cities, such technical, institutional, and socio-economic change was accompanied by changes in the built environment that literally or aesthetically brought more light and air, park and open space as well as other significant improvements to the built environment.[1]

Towards the end of the twentieth century, however, many of the new and accelerating waves of urbanization began to take place in informal settings, and many cities that were once flourishing in the industrial age started to deteriorate as deindustrialization intensified with the economic recessions and stagflation of the 1970s. Still, until HIV/AIDS started to ravage urban communities in the Global North, the existing belief was that infectious disease was the preserve of the underdeveloped world that had not yet undergone the epidemiological transition in which infectious disease threats diminished due to mass vaccination programmes and lessened population growth, leaving only those ailments associated with the Western "lifestyle" such as cancer and coronary heart disease. Infectious disease therefore was thought to be less of a concern to inhabitants of European and North American cities. The 1990s saw the beginning of a re-evaluation of this perspective due to the perceived threat of a global Ebola outbreak and the 1997 Hong Kong bird flu event (Sims et al., 2003).

A real threat to our now majority urban world came from the Severe Acute Respiratory Syndrome (SARS) epidemic of 2003 that hit many large, globalized urban centres, especially in East Asia, but also in Toronto, Canada (this is the subject of longer discussion in chapter 3 below). The West African Ebola virus disease epidemic of 2014/15 (covered at length in chapter 4) added to the concern, as it was the first of its kind that hit major cities such as Monrovia, Liberia, and Freetown, Sierra Leone. But a more universal and recognizable reality check occurred with COVID-19, which started to spread in a manner similar to SARS, in and through a network of global cities such as Wuhan, Madrid, Milan, New York, and London before ploughing its path through the social and spatial peripheries of those cities and becoming recognized as a universal problem by the international community (Biglieri et al., 2020; see chapter 5 for an extended discussion).

This pattern of infection seemed to confirm what scholars had predicted: extensive urbanization was playing an important role in the origin and spread of, and response to, epidemic outbreaks of emerging infectious disease (Connolly et al., 2021; chapter 2 below). From an urban geographic point of view, it was also important to see how the disease itself contributed, in a variety of ways, to our understandings of typical urban tropes like centrality, dispersion, density, urbanity, etc. (McFarlane, 2021; Mullis, 2021). While much early attention tended to be on the particular urban centres from where the disease seemed to have originated, and where it first went (Wuhan, Milan, Madrid, London, Seattle, New York, Detroit, Montreal, etc.), there was also much speculation regarding the massive urban informal settlements around the world where the virus was expected to hit particularly hard (Wilkinson, 2020). In the Global North, the lockdown was treated as a unique and new phenomenon; in the Global South, scholars and urban practitioners pointed to the different realities shaping urban life that made a clear line between a before, during, and after the pandemic more difficult to determine. Some observers noted that in the Global South, "lifeworlds … cannot be so clearly divided into 'before' and 'after' the pandemic, and … 'crisis' and the 'everyday' are not so neatly separable" (Bhan et al., 2020). In chapters 6 and 7, we discuss the dimensions of governance and urban planning with regard to the current and past infectious disease outbreaks in cities.

The association of cities with infectious disease has a long history, but we will argue and demonstrate in this book that today's world of "complete urbanization," especially in its form of extended urbanization – a typically characteristic pattern of settlement in the twenty-first century – changes the ways in which diseases emerge, spread, and are contained. As we elaborate at length in chapter 2, we refer to extended urbanization as development occurring at the peripheries of metropolitan cores and including a full range of non-city geographies that are now evident in the suburban (or post-suburban) zones and hinterland areas. Extended urbanization therefore refers to spaces where people work, for example in warehouses, factories, slaughter-houses, and oil fields, or places they occasionally travel to, such as airports or garbage dumps, or where they live, for instance in suburban residences or informal (slum) settlements. Notably, with the increasing gentrification of the metropolitan core areas, those referred to as the "precariat" in pre-pandemic times, and as "essential workers" during the pandemic, were forced to find places to live and work in exactly these zones of extended urbanization.

The socio-spatial configuration of extended urbanization in relation to work, residence, and travel, as we shall discuss later in the book, has significant implications for disease spread and response. This is particularly true in relation to the differential exposure and vulnerability to infectious disease for particular social groupings of people. In everyday life, the places where people live and work, and the infrastructural patterns that connect them, have been changing. In geopolitical terms, extended urbanization now connects any location to processes elsewhere (food, energy, labour), and in regional terms, it connects displacement and relocation of vulnerable populations from prime areas of investment (the "creative core") to urban peripheries, sometimes in informal settlements. Through such processes, permanent socio-spatial inequities are created across urban territories. Henri Lefebvre hypothetically framed these developments (2003) as "generalized" urbanization, where the urban is to be understood as a multi-scalar process of socio-spatial transformation.

From this perspective, the "urban" should no longer be equated with simply the city core as has been the conventionally held view. The "urban" should not be treated as a fixed, unchanging entity – as a universal form, settlement type, or bounded spatial unit ("the" city) that is being replicated across the globe following basic mechanisms of development (Scott and Storper, 2015). Rather, that which informs urban processes should be traced far beyond the physical boundaries of cities, and increasingly analysed as global or planetary phenomena (Brenner, 2014; Keil, 2018b) – an insight that we shall see has tremendous implications for understanding a global pandemic. Building on this broad conceptual framework, we see that at the core of our analysis stands the dialectics of infection in an era of complete urbanization: *we are getting exposed because we are too connected and then we are getting sick because we are not connected enough.* In other words: the reach of the urban footprint, the acceleration of connectivity, and the particular conditions of urban life together create the conditions for disease to proliferate.

Thus, increased and intensified connections between formerly disparate locations around the world, and between different groups within a city, have facilitated disease spread by providing opportunities for the disease to jump from locale to locale and from person to person. At the same time, increased societal polarization between groups within the city has meant that we were not readily able to immediately mobilize resources and mount a response that would beneficially improve everybody's chances of surviving the pandemic. Some, for example, will have less risk of exposure to COVID-19 because of their ability to self-isolate without the loss of income, while others lower in the social hierarchy are less able to protect themselves from exposure in the same manner. In sum, the increasing social, spatial, economic, and environmental disparities in the urban world have led to gross differences in the impact of outbreaks in different communities, the abilities to fight the disease, and the likelihood of surviving it. It is upon these issues emanating from both these processes – increased connectivity and increased social polarization between and within cities – that the bulk of the analysis in this book focuses.

INFECTIOUS DISEASES AND THE URBAN CONDITION

Anthony J. McMichael (2001) observes that, over the longue durée, significant shifts in the relationship between human beings and nature have always been accompanied by major outbreaks, epidemics, and pandemics. Inevitably, such shifts involved changes in the nature of interactions of humans with animals and the environment that were in turn due to the adoption of new settlement and mobility patterns. Such historic shifts included, for instance, the transition from societies based on hunting and gathering to settled livestock agriculture; military conquests pertaining to empire building and the movement of troops; and the establishment of trade channels such as the Silk Route – with each transition associated with a significant increase in infectious disease outbreaks of various kinds. Because of the dramatic increase in new and emerging diseases over a short period of time, McMichael (2001) hypothesizes that as we entered the new century, we were likely also to undergo a fourth great transition – one based on the inter-related processes of globalization and unprecedented urbanization. Since that time the number of people living in cities around the world has reached new heights. As early as 2007, the United Nations noted that more than half of the world's population lived in cities (UNFPA, 2007), and since then, the influence and impacts of urbanization in many different aspects of cultural, economic, and environmental life have intensified on a global scale, leading some to refer to this new phenomenon as planetary urbanization (Brenner, 2014).

Concerns about the relationship of the city to infectious disease is obviously not a recent development. Problems pertaining to urban settlement patterns and infectious disease date back to antiquity: epidemics of tuberculosis, smallpox, and the plague, for example, devastated cities of ancient empires from the beginning (Kelly, 2006; Woolf, 2020). Medieval cities became "burgeoning disease incubators" (Hassett, 2017: 204), and eventually Europeans would bring disease to the western hemisphere and beyond in deadly waves of colonization and settlement that have influenced the histories of New World societies dramatically since. In the European context, earlier efforts to deal with contagion included the practice of quarantining ships. First introduced in the port of Venice in the fourteenth century, this involved requiring the crew and cargo of newly arrived ships to remain on board for forty days to ensure that no infected person could enter the settled coastal area (Banta, 2001). Such a practice, however, disrupted international trade and financial transactions and led to tension between nation states as they dealt with imposed quarantine measures. Such international tension served as an impetus for diplomatic dialogue that led to increased formal attention to issues of international health in the realm of high politics, eventually culminating in the formation of the World Health Organization. Things changed again with the onset of industrialization.

Matthew Gandy (2006) observes that responding to infectious disease outbreaks was an integral element in the transformation of the modern city, especially in relation to the institutionalization of various urban infrastructure networks that mediated the relationship between the body and the city. While urban infrastructures of sanitation had already been part of urban life in ancient and medieval cities (Kelly, 2006: 67–71), the focus on infrastructure was necessary and unavoidable in the nineteenth century after the birth of the industrial city, spurred on by the receding of feudalism and the massive influx of people to cities to pursue work in the newly constructed factories. With rapid and dramatic population growth, the existing infrastructure of the industrial city simply could not support such numbers. For instance, the population of Manchester doubled within a decade, resulting in overcrowding and a significant increase in waste accumulation. The general state of existence at this time was a marked deterioration in urban living conditions punctuated by devastating infectious disease outbreaks. In this context, Gandy focuses particular attention on the development of water infrastructure and its relation to the prevention of cholera outbreaks.

At first, concern about urban disease outbreaks led to investigations and explanations based on the miasma theory. This approach attributed cholera epidemics to "bad air" emanating from the rotting of organic matter such as food and fecal waste (see UN Habitat, 2021). Later on, bacteriological explanations of disease came to dominate (Gandy, 2004). In effect, though, both perspectives contributed to the drive for sanitary reforms that called for a fundamental change in the structure of sanitation systems, such as using separate drainage systems so that the reflux of noxious sewer air would be prevented from entering back into homes (Gandy, 2004). With the implementation of these changes, the number of cholera outbreaks decreased. This led to the recognition of the link between contaminated water and ill health, which in turn served as the impetus for the physical reconstruction of cities based on explicitly public health criteria – a shift referred to by Gandy (2004) as the rise of the "bacteriological city." The enduring influence of sanitary reforms and the bacteriological city was dramatic and led London to become the first city to create a complex administrative structure that would coordinate modern urban services ranging from public transport to housing, clean water, and education. The success of the London model encouraged local governments of other European cities to follow suit.

In our present era, informed by globalization processes, anthropogenic environmental change, and an unprecedented level of planetary urbanization that have only intensified in the last quarter century, we may first ask if these conditions have prompted the introduction of new and emerging diseases as McMichael (2021) hypothesized. Second, if this is the case, we may ask, how can we then develop an analytical lens to study the socio-ecological processes on the basis of which these new and emerging diseases arise? In addressing the first question, we see that a great deal of evidence reveals that over the recent years there has been a disproportionate increase in the number of newly emerging infectious diseases, as well as outbreak, epidemic, and pandemic situations (Morens and Fauci, 2013), including COVID-19, Zika virus, Ebola virus disease, Middle East Respiratory Syndrome (MERS), Lassa fever, HIV/AIDS, hantavirus, Lyme disease, *E. coli* O157:H7, and Nipah virus. Also, on the rise are re-emerging diseases such as the Dengue virus and West Nile virus (Morens and Fauci, 2013).

"Emerging diseases" denotes new pathogens that appear in a population in a new region (Mayer, 2000), while "re-emerging diseases" refers to those disease agents that first appeared long ago, but have survived and persisted by adapting to human and environmental change (Morens and Fauci, 2013). To study the emergence and re-emergence of infectious disease, Jonathan D. Mayer (2000) builds on virologist Stephen Morse's (1993; 1995) concept of "viral traffic." Extending the concept to include other pathogens (and thus adopting the term "microbial traffic"), Mayer notes that the utility of the concept stems from the geographic implications of what is referred to as "traffic." Specifically, the notion of traffic draws attention to the movement and interaction of pathogens.

Mayer (2000) suggests that we focus on several mechanisms associated with microbial traffic, including (1) cross-species transfer, (2) spatial diffusion, (3) pathogenic evolution or changes in the structure and immunogenicity of earlier pathogens, and, importantly in the context of our book, (4) changes in the human–environment relationship. Notably, as we will discuss in greater detail in the following chapters, these mechanisms of microbial traffic are in fact interrelated and have profound implications for understanding the relationship between cities and infectious disease. Thus, for instance, it is important to consider how environmental change brought on by deforestation – pursued for various human-centred reasons, such as the lumber industry's demand for trees, the clearing of land for industrialized agriculture or for residential or commercial suburban development, or the loss of trees due to drought or wildfire induced by global climate change – may impact cross-species transfer (i.e., zoonotic spillover as the virus jumps from an animal to a human). As will be discussed in chapter 4, deforestation may in part help account for the onset and spread of the Ebola virus in West Africa.

Thus, as we shall discuss with reference to the relationship of disease onset and spread with urbanization, it is not sufficient to consider only the biophysical environment; equally important is the social environment. In this light, we can see that in reference to the urban environment, it is not just biophysical parameters such as the availability and density of human hosts that enable a disease outbreak. Equally important for facilitating disease transmission are the informal and formal social norms that govern human interactions, including most notably those pertaining to social organization and governance. For example, even though many of the public health directives aimed at breaking the chain of transmission during an outbreak – such as physical distancing (commonly referred to as *social* distancing), the donning of masks, washing hands, and even vaccination – are about creating a physical barrier between disease agent and host, the effectiveness of all such interventions is contingent on a wide range of social and political factors that govern individual behaviour and social interaction. For this reason, understanding the social and spatial logics that undergird an infectious disease event is integral to understanding how an outbreak occurs, and further, to developing effective strategies for response.

Notably, as will be discussed throughout this book, socio-spatial logics undergird the transformation of a localized outbreak into a regional epidemic and ultimately a global pandemic of the sort we are currently experiencing at the time of writing. In this regard, the concept of spatial diffusion may help us understand how COVID-19 spread amongst the so-called "essential workers" who laboured in warehouse distribution centres (examples include those from some of the world's largest transnational corporations, such as Amazon, FedEx, Apple, etc.), factories, and meatpacking plants, now situated in many suburban locales (Loreto, 2021: 273–98; MacGillis, 2021). The consideration of spatial diffusion may also help us to understand how COVID-19 spread was quite different in places of similar density, such as the wealthy high-rise condominium towers in the gentrified areas of Toronto compared to equally dense apartment towers occupied by renters in less gentrified areas (Pitter, 2020a). In the end, as we shall discuss in more detail later, it is not the density of the built environment per se that is critical to disease spread, but the density of relationships among humans, and of humans with the natural world. The consideration of spatial diffusion may also explain how Ebola in West Africa spread from slum areas to the more affluent areas, whereas COVID-19 spread in the reverse direction – from the more affluent to the less affluent areas. A consideration of spatial diffusion may also illuminate how SARS proliferated in 2003 through the networked connections between the global cities of Toronto, Hong Kong, and Singapore.

To grasp the spatial diffusion of disease in an outbreak, epidemic, or pandemic situation therefore requires a broader understanding of how the social and biophysical contexts have been changed by the conditions wrought by planetary and extended urbanization – such as the changing relationship between the suburbs and the city core, as well as between the suburbs and the surrounding natural environment, or the networked connections between global cities around the world. By adopting such a focus, we address what Mayer (2000) identifies as a foundational question of disease ecology, namely how changing human–environment relations and social activities can result in fundamental alterations in the interaction between people, the biophysical environment, and the broader social and economic context. In particular, as Mayer (2000) observes, one important analytical advantage of adopting this perspective is that it brings into relief the question of how disease emergence may result directly or indirectly from the unintentional consequences of human action. To shift such an analytic orientation to explicitly consider the relationship of planetary and extended urbanization with infectious disease, we suggest adopting a three-pronged approach based on how the various mechanisms of microbial traffic have been impacted by (1) socio-demographic influences (including those associated with social class and race/ethnicity), (2) infrastructure development (or lack of it), and (3) issues of urban governance and politics. We have selected these factors for special consideration in our analysis because of the role they play in other areas of urban studies.

POLITICAL ECOLOGIES OF DISEASE IN AN ERA OF PLANETARY URBANIZATION

We posit that particular landscapes themselves can be structured in a way that influences the likelihood of disease transmission. Some scholars working on the political ecology of health and disease have used landscape as an analytical lens to consider how various health discourses can become materialized in particular places (Mulligan et al., 2012; Parizeau, 2015). For example, Wald (2008: 2) has described how "the circulation of microbes materialises the transmission of ideas" regarding theories about how diseases spread and attitudes towards social change. In this way, disease is not only determined through biophysical factors, but also constructed out of a particular set of social and spatial relations which are mediated through the landscape. As we will discuss later in the book, processes of extended urbanization can increase vulnerability to infectious diseases – which are themselves rapidly evolving – as the risks and mode of transmission are often neither well understood by science nor properly regulated by government, particularly in informal peri-urban settlements common in the developing world.

A landscape political ecology perspective, in concert with other spatialized lenses such as urban political ecology (UPE), remains indebted to fundamental insights of disease ecology which posit that a disease outbreak does not simply materialize in a vacuum (Kaika et al., 2022; Keil, 2020c). Rather, as described by the classic epidemiological triad, an outbreak can only happen if a particular set of conditions is first met. Specifically, the disease agent (such as a pathogen, virus, bacterium, or parasite) and animal host must coincide in time and space. This is especially relevant with respect to viruses as they rely upon the machinery of the animal host cell to reproduce themselves. Critical to the spread of disease in this context is the presence of a conducive environment that can facilitate the travel of the disease agent to the host, thus helping to ensure the train of transmission. Conventionally, a conducive environment is conceived of exclusively in terms of biophysical or climatic factors such as humidity, acidity, temperature, and so on. But, as we shall argue in this book, the notion of environment should be expanded to include the social environment, most notably the socio-political dimensions of cities as discussed in relation to governance, socio-demographic influences, and infrastructure.

In this regard, we argue that the concept of urban political pathology (UPP) is useful for extending the insights of landscape political ecology specifically to the relationships of infectious disease and urbanization. David Fidler (2004b) originally developed the concept with respect to the SARS epidemic in 2003. He argued that SARS was the harbinger of a changing global landscape of health governance. While Fidler's attention was on the international system, we use the qualifier "urban" with "political pathology" to highlight both the role cities play in the overall architecture of global healthcare governance and how cities have responded to the COVID-19 pandemic. In both instances, we not only think of cities as municipalities or local governments, but also take into account the role of urban civil society and grassroots initiatives. Such a mobilization of the terminology of UPP builds on the existing literature from political ecology that is applied to the analysis of disease at various scales, especially in the urban context. It also recognizes urbanization's multifarious intersections and encounters with viruses and the sometimes fraught nature of human and non-human coexistence (Perng, 2020: 153).

Chapter 2, entitled, "Landscape Political Ecologies of Disease: Tracing Patterns of Extended Urbanization," is largely conceptual and focuses on how contemporary processes of extended urbanization, which include suburbanization, post-suburbanization, and peri-urbanization, contributed to increased vulnerability to infectious disease spread. Through a review of existing literature at the nexus of urbanization and infectious disease, we consider how this (potential) increased vulnerability to infectious diseases in peri-urban or suburban areas is in fact dialectically related to socio-material transformations on the metropolitan edge. The next three chapters apply our analytic framework to three case studies, each emblematic of particular aspects of microbial traffic in our present century. Our presentation in each of these chapters is guided by a general focus on how governance, socio-demographic influences, and infrastructure shape the microbial traffic and landscape political ecology of the infectious disease under consideration.

Chapter 3, "SARS and the Global City," sets up the specific relationship of urbanization and emerging infectious disease in the twenty-first century. Building on and extending our earlier work on SARS and urbanization, the chapter investigates how processes of globalization have affected the transmission of and response to SARS within the context of the global cities network. In particular, we make the case that it is vital to understand how various economic, political, and social shifts related to our globalized, networked society facilitated the movement of deadly pathogens. In a prelude to what the world experienced in the 2020 COVID-19 pandemic, the SARS crisis revealed a type of enduring tension between public health interventions and their effects on commerce. Specifically, this involved the controversies that arose when the World Health Organization (WHO) imposed travel bans and travel advisories on SARS-affected cities during the 2003 epidemic, resulting in considerable acrimony between nation states and the WHO. Similar tensions could also be seen even more recently in the debates over travel bans during the COVID-19 pandemic. Infectious diseases have posed response challenges for cities not only in terms of dealing with issues at the international level, but at the more local scale, within the city itself.

While SARS was a disease mostly felt in the advanced societies of the global cities network in the Global North and the surging urban centres of the East, in **chapter 4**, "Ebola and African Urbanization," we consider the spread of Ebola virus disease (EVD) in cities of the Global South, specifically in West Africa and the Democratic Republic of the Congo (DRC). In particular, we focus on the question of how Ebola went from a disease associated with isolated rural and remote outbreaks in Central and East Africa during the past decades to an urban-based epidemic phenomenon in West Africa in more recent times. We will explore possible answers to this question and consider other urban dimensions of disease spread in cities of the Global South more generally, and the capital cities of Freetown and Monrovia specifically. Further, we will also explore questions of how the spread of COVID-19 took place within these cities, with a particular focus on informal settlements. Of importance to that discussion is the fact that many of these informal settlements were situated in the peripheral areas of the city, or in other areas of the city that were under-serviced or contained undesirable environmental features that made them vulnerable to various risks (e.g., flood-prone swamplands, areas prone to falling rocks and mudslides or susceptible to land erosion from ocean tides, etc.).

This book is obviously motivated by the recent and ongoing experience of the urban world with the unprecedented COVID-19 pandemic. We give this story full attention in our **chapter 5**, "COVID-19 and Extended Urbanization," on COVID-19 and global urbanization. Here we follow the virus from its ostensible origin in Wuhan to the world's urban regions, with a focus on the place where two of us live and work, namely Toronto, Canada.

In **chapter 6**, "Health Governance on a Planet of Cities," we consider the question of how cities have responded to the COVID pandemic at the political level, particularly in relation to the role played by civil society and grassroots urban governance initiatives. As we will see, politics in municipalities, between cities and other jurisdictions, and between municipalities and civil society actors and local communities, will be crucial to understanding the role urban health governance plays in an increasingly urbanized and globalized society (Acuto, 2020).

In **chapter 7,** "Urban Planning and Infectious Disease Revisited," we focus on an important influence on life in the city, and especially during a pandemic, namely urban planning. The COVID-19 pandemic has highlighted both past successes and failures of planning as it revealed the fault lines of urban life's social and technical infrastructures. As the pandemic unfolded, the built, social, and institutional environments that had been put in place in prior periods of urban development and design were confronted with a mix of familiar and unfamiliar challenges: public space was not made for social distancing; institutional settings like care homes or educational facilities were ill prepared; and certain "forgotten densities" (Pitter, 2020a) in less privileged parts of town became pandemic hotspots. As the urban world moved from lockdown to reopening, urban planning and design provided prime discursive arenas in which experts and residents envisioned new forms of urban life that would catapult cities into a new socio-technological reality. We explore some of these issues in this chapter.

Our **chapter 8**, entitled "The City after the Plague," reflects on the key arguments advanced in the book and discusses the significance of the current pandemic for our global society. We also suggest some possible future avenues for urban researchers to develop new and better explanations for the relationships of extended urbanization and the spatialities of infectious disease along truly interdisciplinary lines.

2 | Landscape Political Ecologies of Disease: Tracing Patterns of Extended Urbanization

A landscape political ecology (LPE) framework can provide useful insights into the ways particular landscapes – understood as the physical ordering and social layering of the spatial environment – can facilitate the spread of infectious diseases and possible responses to them (see Lambin et al., 2010). As alluded to in the previous chapter, numerous social and ecological processes emerging over the past two decades, from globalization to tourism, climate change, and rapid urbanization, have generated a wide range of environmental stressors, pollutants, and toxins that have contributed to the increased spread of zoonotic disease (Carlson et al., 2022; Neuman et al., 2021). Further, as also noted in our introduction, the classical epidemiological triad that accounts for disease outbreak emergence is predicated upon the important role that the environment and landscape (always simultaneously material and social) play in facilitating the connection between the pathogen and the animal and human hosts that are central to disease spread. As these facilitating socio-ecological processes are experienced most acutely in cities, it has become increasingly clear – ever since the SARS pandemic – that urban areas are now at the front lines of infectious disease outbreaks and mitigation efforts.

In light of these developments, we argue that in order to understand the various (re-)emerging infectious disease outbreaks of the past two decades, we need to focus on the intersections of three processes: dynamics of population change; infrastructure (and especially mobility); and governance. There are certainly more specific factors that could be identified (e.g., deforestation and climate change; see Brenner and Ghosh, 2022; Treffers et al., 2021), but these are the three themes that have been most prominent in the literature on urbanization and infectious disease. We have kept these themes intentionally broad so as to capture as much as possible of the disparate work that exists on this topic. Moreover, we consider how these factors influence different phases of infectious disease management, from disease prevention to mitigation and control of outbreaks, and possible responses.

As we will demonstrate, these three empirical points of focus are well suited to a landscape political ecology approach and are crucial for identifying spatial patterns and political-economic arrangements that influence the spread of infectious disease. Such considerations are especially relevant in the context of ongoing, and accelerating, processes of "extended urbanization" we are experiencing today. Increased globalized urbanization, changing patterns of urbanization – including what Brenner and Schmid (2014) have called "extended urbanization" – have been linked with the acceleration of emerging infectious disease (see Brenner and Ghosh, 2022; Treffers et al., 2021). Historic patterns of disease transmission have been shown to parallel patterns of accelerated urbanization and associated ecological imbalance, uneven development, inadequate provision of hygiene and sanitation infrastructures, and of course vast social and economic inequalities (UN Habitat, 2021). These are all interconnected issues that urban and landscape political ecologists are uniquely positioned to examine.

In this chapter, we outline these processes but focus specifically on the changing patterns, dimensions, and forms of urbanization, and their specific junctures with emerging infectious disease (EID). We consider this work to be part not just of an empirical retracing of disease outbreaks to patterns of urbanization, but also of an intervention into the theory of both cities and disease. This is comprehensively expressed by Matthew Gandy (2022b: 215) for the COVID-19 pandemic:

> Thinking through the epidemiology of COVID-19 illuminates a series of conceptual disjunctures in relation to contemporary urbanisation and the possibilities for global modes of theorization. An emphasis on extreme topographies belies a certain kind of pandemic imaginary that traces connections between spillover sites such as remote caves, dense forests, or newly exploited pockets of biodiversity, to intermediate zones of zoonotic transfer such as "wet markets" for live animals, culminating in specific forms of human density such as overcrowded tenements, informal settlements or high-rise apartment complexes. But what kind of relations are occluded in this putative chain of infective proximity? Less clear in these representational tropes are the underlying connections between changes in agricultural practices, labour mobility, or other factors that constitute regional as well as global patterns of interconnection and corporeal precarity.

We will first establish some context for our main arguments in the book around extended urbanization and infectious disease, specifically the conceptual framework of landscape political ecology. We then outline why the relationship between extended urbanization and infectious disease is important to study, and how this can be understood through a landscape political ecology framework, particularly in peri-urban areas. Subsequently, we illustrate how these conceptual insights shine a light on how processes of extended urbanization have contributed to the emergence of the numerous infectious disease outbreaks of the past decade, while at the same time enabling us to understand how these processes confounded containment efforts adopted during the COVID-19 pandemic.

CHANGING URBAN GEOGRAPHIES OF HEALTH AND DISEASE

As noted above, the spatial structure and organization of the (expanding) built environment has significant implications for the emergence – and also potential mitigation – of infectious disease outbreaks. This is nothing new, as urban environments have been evolving to mitigate threats to the health and well-being of societies for thousands of years. As alluded to in our introductory chapter, this includes the public health reforms and technological changes in the "bacteriological city" during the twentieth century, which sought to reduce the incidence of disease (Gandy, 2006) – including changes involved in the creation of more open and green space to promote physical well-being and recreation, as well as improvement in waste management.

To date, the literatures on urbanization and globalization have focused primarily on economic, financial, cultural, information, and demographic flows to, from, and through cities and their regions (Brenner, 2014; Ren and Keil, 2017). More recently, there has been a growing academic and policy interest in connecting challenges of a majority urbanized world to questions of health and disease (Ali and Keil, 2008; Elsey et al., 2019; Moore et al., 2003; Wu et al., 2017). Meike Wolf (2016: 975) has proposed a number of "future challenges" of research into the "messy materialities" of (sub)urbanization and (emerging) infectious disease research. In summarizing her review of recent developments in the field, Wolf argues importantly that "a reconsideration of analytical categories of space, time, climate or nature – which are of equal importance to both the social sciences and public health – goes hand in hand with accounts that ramify different sites and aim to capture new paths of connection and association" (Wolf 2016: 976). Recognizing these emerging connections, we are specifically interested in new ways in which infectious disease is bound up with processes of *extended* urbanization, paying particular attention to the socio-ecological flows and disruptions leading to increased incidence of infectious disease in peri-urban or suburban areas, without reducing the notion of extension to mere peripheral growth, but seeing it as an overarching concept of urbanization today (Keil, 2020b).

Such processes of urban expansion are linked to the ubiquitous reordering of the global urban periphery, through complex processes of displacement of central populations to the margins and the creation of new functional centralities (jobs, infrastructures, densities) away from the traditional core. We use the term "extended urbanization" as a summary concept for these developments. The processes captured under this term, originally informed by the urban theory of Henri Lefebvre (2003), predict what he called "the complete urbanization" of society. This phenomenon is partially caused by the rapid growth of the human population and the expanding geographical reach of capitalist accumulation over the past century, which has created an "urban revolution" and an "urban society" at the planetary scale (see Keil, 2018a). Relatedly, various scholars have argued that we are now witnessing a process of planetary urbanization, which is premised upon expanding infrastructural networks and human settlements (Brenner, 2014).

In this broader context, we are specifically interested in what Lefebvre (2003) calls the spread of "the urban tissue" across the planet, which refers to the fluid relationships between urban and rural environments. Forms of extended urbanization – such as suburbanization – are an empirically recognizable process in this context. In many parts of the world, particularly in the Global South, "peri-urbanization" is the preferred term for extended urbanization (De Vidovich, 2019). Some scholars have called the current phase of urban extension post-suburbanization, which leads to an increasing complexity of structural form and daily life in the periphery of cities (Phelps and Wu, 2011; Charmes and Keil, 2015). In this context, "peripheral" can also refer to both the self-built structures and the informal communities that characterize much of today's urbanization without being necessarily spatially on the margins (e.g., refugee settlements, mining camps, and Indigenous reserves near urban centres) (Caldeira, 2017; Güney et al., 2019). Finally, "extended urbanization" refers to new and existing urbanization and urban settlement in the periphery of cities *and* relations that condition these spaces, but also reach beyond them (e.g., mines, factories, and infrastructures) (Keil, 2018a).

LANDSCAPE POLITICAL ECOLOGIES OF INFECTIOUS DISEASE

The term "landscape" has been used in cultural geography to refer to the appearance or physical characteristics of a certain place, with particular reference to the social, cultural, and political processes that shape these places (Cosgrove and Daniels, 1987; Mitchell, 1996). Landscapes are therefore understood as in flux and relational, created by interactions between both human and non-human actors. Landscapes are thus well suited for political ecological analysis because they are simultaneously cultural and "natural" (Batterbury, 2001). For example, "more-than-human geography" approaches have sought to rematerialize and reanimate landscapes by paying close attention to the ecologies of human and non-human actors through which a "vital topography" emerges (Barua, 2014: 916; see also Johnston, 2008; Lorimer, 2006). Tzaninis et al. (2020: 15) argue that focusing on the more-than-urban might therefore enable "new openings and possibilities for engagement between human and more-than-human worlds." Similarly, Kearns and Moon (2002: 611) have noted that landscape serves as a metaphor for "the complex layerings of history, social structure and built environment that converge in particular places." This can be seen in the infrastructural (dis)connections and changing nature–society interactions that are associated with urban expansion.

Landscape political ecology of health approaches – paying specific attention to interactions between urban, suburban, and rural landscapes – are important for their focus on the interaction between political interests, social institutions, and the human–non-human environment, which can bring about a greater systemic understanding of health and disease (see King, 2010; Jackson and Neely, 2015; Connolly et al., 2017). Given the interdisciplinary nature of health studies, political ecology is an ideal framework that facilitates the use of mixed research methods and incorporates a range of conceptual approaches (Robbins, 2004; King, 2010). This is because of its deep concern for human–environment relations, and its systematic study of the unequal distribution of socio-environmental harms and risks. More specifically, a landscape political ecology (LPE) perspective can be a useful orientation for examining the political ecologies of disease (Connolly, 2017). This is because both political ecology and health geographies draw on ideas of place and landscape and utilize an understanding of place as a socially (re)constructed phenomenon (see King, 2010).

The interdependence of environmental and social transformation becomes most apparent in urban landscapes where the metabolic transformation of nature is concentrated both in its physical form and in the production of socio-ecological consequences (Monstadt, 2009: 1933). The concept of landscape is therefore useful for studying processes of extended urbanization, given the hybrid nature of the term, which allows for blurring distinctions between the urban and the rural (see Connolly, 2022). This is one way in which (sub)urban political ecologies have moved beyond critiques of "methodological cityism," by exploring socio-ecological processes on the urban periphery and in the extended urban more generally (see Angelo and Wachsmuth, 2015; Connolly, 2019). Furthermore, we argue that a landscape political ecology perspective is crucial because the metabolic flows of air, water, pathogens, pollutants, and non-human species tend to move without any regard to municipal, regional, or national borders. As such, it is critical to develop modes of urban planning that work across municipal and national boundaries in order to mitigate the risk of the current and future pandemics.

URBANIZATION, SOCIAL MOBILITIES, DENSITY, AND INFECTIOUS DISEASE

Urbanization refers in the first instance to a combination of three aspects: socio-demographic change from rural to urban; economic industrialization and ultimately post-industrialization; and socio-cultural change (Friedmann, 2002; Lefebvre, 2003). Pandemic diseases rely on population growth in cities – driven primarily by rural–urban migration – as it enables the accelerated spread of disease (Coker et al., 2011). This is seen most clearly in rapidly urbanizing regions such as Africa and Asia, which have experienced recent outbreaks of Ebola and SARS, respectively. Projections by urban scholars hold that sub-Saharan Africa's urbanization rates are higher than anywhere else in the world as the urban population in the region "is expected to quadruple, from 295 million to 1.15 billion" (Angel et al., 2017: 169). Twelve million people now live in Kinshasa, capital of the DRC, which is three times the combined population of the cities affected by the 2014 Ebola outbreak in West Africa (Yong, 2018). Equally, regional towns in the DRC, where some of the Ebola cases have been recorded over the past decade, have also been expanding, some under the influence of conflict and war. While the ecological consequences of this expansion are beginning to be better understood, we are only starting to shed light on the impact of dramatic and massive (sub)urbanization on health and disease.

Urban density is one demographic factor which has been widely adopted in both popular and academic media to account for the severity of the COVID-19 pandemic in urban regions in places like New York City. However, research has shown that density alone cannot be a predictor of the spread of infectious diseases, which depends on other factors such as governance (health policy), socio-economic status, and adherence to social distancing measures (Keil, 2020a; Moos et al., 2020). Levels of development and the extent of access to public health infrastructure can play an important role (Florida, 2020). It is also important here to distinguish between "density" and "overcrowding": the former refers to high concentrations of people within an area and the latter to the lack of separation or space between people (often caused by inequalities). For instance, Asian cities like Hong Kong, Seoul, and Taipei are far denser than New York City but have had far fewer cases of COVID-19 per capita (see McFarlane, 2021).

Moreover, studies have shown that in some regions during the pandemic, per capita infection levels and mortality were lower in more densely populated city centres than in surrounding suburban or rural areas (UN Habitat, 2021). As a result, more distributed, decentralized population could lead to infectious disease becoming planetary, a process enabled through greater regional population mobility and transportation infrastructure. This indicates the importance of a landscape political ecology lens in examining urbanization and infectious disease, with a particular focus on the governance, infrastructure, and demographic factors that we emphasize throughout this book.

Research on urbanization is also beginning to consider how mobility patterns between urban, peri-urban, and rural areas influence infectious disease spread (see Herrick, 2014; Wolf, 2016). It should be noted that the first urban Ebola outbreaks happened in West Africa after almost four decades of rural outbreaks throughout the rest of Africa (WHO, 2015). Why, then, was there a change from rural to urban outbreaks after this time and in this particular region (i.e., West Africa)? One factor is the high degree of population movement on the continent, which is seven times higher than anywhere else in the world (WHO, 2015). This migration is driven by a myriad of social and political economic factors that force people to travel daily in search of food or work; social obligations to extended families with relatives living in different countries; the practice of returning to a native village to die and be buried near ancestors; and travel to traditional healers who have the trust of community members (WHO, 2015; Fallah et al., 2022). There are also the effects of civil war that have forced some family members to flee their home villages to other, usually more urban, areas, for relocation and resettlement.

Disease transmission in large urban populations can also be affected by heterogeneity in the health of urban dwellers, increased rates of contact, and mobility of people (Alirol et al., 2010). Rural-to-urban population movements, for instance, can substantially increase risk of transmission amongst newcomers who may not have previous exposure (immunization) (Alirol et al., 2010; Tong et al., 2015). It is also difficult to control migration between cities in many African countries, as Sierra Leone, Liberia, and Guinea each have 5,000 border crossing points (Wilkinson and Leach, 2015). Thus, the monitoring of rural–urban and inter-urban migration will be crucial to stopping the spread of disease in future outbreaks. Tong et al. (2015: 11029) further add that rural–urban migrants tend to be poorer and less educated than the permanent population in urban areas, live in lower-quality housing with inadequate sanitation, and have limited access to health services, and these factors also contribute to disease spread (see also Hynie, 2018). This is especially true because such migrants tend to settle in (often informal) places along the metropolitan edge (see figure 2.1). This can be problematic, as Wu et al. (2017: 21) have found that in many Chinese cities public health management has not kept pace with demographic changes in rapidly urbanizing areas.

As Wolf (2016: 965) has noted, infectious diseases are thus not so much a "natural" disaster, but emerge alongside social and spatial inequalities in housing, health education, or financial resources (see also Kotsila, 2017; Ali et al., 2022a). Studies of such processes are

Figure 2.1 Informal settlement area near Freetown, Sierra Leone

Source: S. Harris Ali

particularly well suited to an urban political ecology framework, which is useful for examining not only the "explosion" of urban societies but also the uneven and socially unjust power relations which amplify health inequalities in particular places, and underlines the issue of governance that we will deal with later (see Houston and Ruming, 2014; Parizeau, 2015; Ali and Rose, 2022). Understanding the root causes of disease emergence in urban areas will thus be essential to preventing additional rural-to-urban spread and to containing outbreaks within urban centres (Fallah et al., 2018: 280; Richards et al., 2015).

PANDEMIC URBANISM IN THE EXTENDED CITY: POLITICAL ECOLOGIES OF INFECTIOUS DISEASE

In a seminal text on urban political ecology, Erik Swyngedouw (2006) wrote that urbanization results in pushing the ecological frontier of a city outward as it expands. This is an urban political ecological process that produces a new urban and rural landscape, comprising new socio-natural relations. He argues that "the city's growth, and the process of nature's urbanisation are closely associated with successive waves of ecological transformation, socio-ecological organisation of metabolic processes ... and the extension of urban socio-ecological frontiers" (Swyngedouw, 2006: 114–15). Throughout this process, socio-natural entities from a variety of scales (local, regional, and national) are produced through political-economic practices and discourses related to civil engineering, economics, land speculation, geopolitical tensions, and the circulation of capital. Swyngedouw (2005) writes that the process of metabolic circulation underpinning urbanization is therefore deeply embedded in the political ecology of the local and national state, international divisions of labour, and power relations at different scales.

Socio-natural flows into and out of urban areas are often referred to by urban political ecologists as "urban metabolism," which includes biophysical, technical, social, and economic exchanges (Gandy, 2004; Loftus, 2006; Swyngedouw, 2006). The concept of urban metabolism refers to the process of material exchange and interaction between human beings and nature through which both entities are transformed (Foster, 2000; Swyngedouw, 2006). Indeed, as Heynen and colleagues previously noted: "natural or ecological conditions and processes do not operate separately from social processes" and cities "are themselves inherently natural and social" (Heynen et al., 2006: 3). Urban political ecologists have therefore sought to develop a framework for understanding the historically and geographically specific ways through which nature is urbanized. LPE approaches are crucial to comprehending the metabolic processes and socio-environmental implications bound up with extended forms of urbanization.

Urban political ecology approaches, as Gandy (2022a: 9) has adamantly maintained, have long located "the socioecological dynamics of urban space within a relational set of flows that extends beyond a bounded conceptualization of urban form." As Gandy (2022a: 29) notes, the focus of these studies has been on both "the urbanisation of nature" and "the nature of urbanisation" at a variety of spatial scales rather than a reified emphasis on the city as a spatial container. For instance, Lambin et al. (2010) have examined specifically how landscape attributes and land-use change can have a significant impact on re-emerging infectious diseases and/or zoonoses. Other authors have used a landscape lens to examine the interconnections between social and environmental systems (Fairhead and Leach, 1996; Walker and Fortmann, 2003; Ali, 2004). In this regard, Wald (2008: 2) has observed how interactions between microbes, bodies, and spaces have the tendency to blend together as they "animate the landscape and motivate the plot of the outbreak narrative."

Tzaninis and colleagues have also recently proposed a distinctive suburban political ecology lens which has considerable overlap with the perspective put forward here in our combined use of landscape and urban political ecologies (Tzaninis et al., 2020; Kaika et al., 2022). As Coker et al. (2011: 599) have elaborated, cities are home to "dynamic systems in which biological, social, ecological and technological processes interconnect in ways that enable microbes to exploit new ecological niches." Moreover, "the particular sociopolitical contexts and spatial configuration of urban regions have strong implications for how these various non-human natures are urbanised" (Connolly, 2019: 64). For these reasons, landscape political ecology thus becomes an extremely useful tool for understanding the political, social, economic, and cultural relationships between urban environments and public health.

In this context, political ecology is a useful framework for considering issues of governance, given that political economy and power are central to its analysis of the relationships between humans and their environment (Connolly, 2022; Kaup, 2018). For instance, King (2010: 42) has argued that political ecology of health frameworks can illustrate how key actors and institutions, as well as human–non-human relationships, can influence the transmission of disease and the ability of institutions to provide effective treatment. These frameworks can also help in understanding how various power relationships and government policies at a variety of scales can reinforce social inequalities that influence vulnerability to disease. These insights will be expanded upon in chapter 6, where we discuss the role of the city in planetary health governance.

One additional concept related to urban political ecology that scholars have used to theorize the relationship between disease and urban society is that of *biopolitics*, which refers to the ways in which health and disease have historically been closely associated with the modern (nation) state and its politics of governing (Bratton, 2021;

Figure 2.2 Animal market in Hong Kong
Source: Creighton Connolly

Braun, 2008; Collard, 2012; Sarasin, 2020). In particular, biopolitics describes how the state controls populations for various purposes, including ostensibly for the purpose of disease management. Examples include public health, town planning, and administration, which sought to "improve" the national population by eliminating risks to its future well-being (Braun, 2008). As Collard (2012) notes, biopolitical approaches examine how safe space is made, maintained, and unmade, and how non-humans (e.g., animals, bacteria, zoonoses) matter to the material and semiotic construction of "safety" and space. Biopolitics is related to urban political ecology, which also examines the ways in which governance decisions result in unequal and spatialized patterns of disease whereby particular spaces and population groups face a disproportionate burden of disease for various reasons. These are discussions that we will return to and elaborate on in chapter 6.

EXTENDED URBANIZATION AND EMERGING INFECTIOUS DISEASE

We put forward the thesis that processes of globalized extended urbanization have led to an increasing susceptibility to infectious disease, especially emerging infectious disease (EID), i.e., "an infectious disease whose incidence is increasing following its first introduction into a new host population" (Quammen, 2012: 43). Emerging diseases are those which have become more prevalent during the last quarter century, while new diseases are not only newly appearing ones, but also those that are spreading to new geographical areas (Mayer, 2000). Some examples of these include yellow fever, the Marburg virus, Legionnaires' disease, the Ebola virus, Lyme disease, hepatitis C, HIV/AIDS, hantavirus pulmonary syndrome, West Nile virus, and Severe Acute Respiratory Syndrome (Garrett, 1994; Heymann and Rodier, 1997; Drexler, 2002). At the same time, re-emerging diseases, or those thought to have been eradicated due to aggressive antibiotic and vaccination campaigns, have also begun to reappear with greater frequency in the population in recent years (for example, tuberculosis).

Zoonosis, in particular, which is "an animal infection transmissible to humans" (Quammen, 2012: 14), is seen as an important aspect of this vulnerability to EIDs. Notably, ecological pressures coupled with social and spatial change have led to new forms of disease spread that are likewise contributing to the rise of EID epidemics. These include changes in waterborne EID spread, as was the case with E. coli 0157:H7 (Ali, 2004); changes in food-borne EID transmission, as brought on by changes in global consumption patterns (Hoffman, 2014); and changes in the distribution of vector-borne diseases such as malaria, where the distribution of mosquitoes has been affected by global climate change (Epstein, 1998; Brisbois and Ali, 2010; Nading, 2014). In this light, Matthew Gandy has recently concluded that "zoonotic pathogens derived from animals are pivotal to the increasing prevalence of new and emerging diseases" and estimates that two thirds of human diseases are zoonotic in origin (2022b: 203). Gandy (2022b) traces such infections through various stages of urbanization and disease emergence over time and deploys the generative term "zoonotic city" to pinpoint the connection.

We posit that, while rapid and intensive forms of urbanization (densification) are seen as enabling factors for the spread of infectious disease (Munster et al., 2018), it is important to study extended urbanization because patterns of urban sprawl and expansion are more likely to lead to infectious disease outbreaks, as opposed to cities which are generally assumed to reduce incidence of infectious disease for inhabitants (see Wood et al., 2017). This is, in part, because urban expansion might expose suburban and ex-urban areas to higher levels of biodiversity (and disease sources) than are found in central urban areas (Kaup, 2018), and might connect urban dwellers (human and non-human) to new and expanded biophysical and political economic relationships around the globe. This is a thesis that has recently been supported by Brenner and Ghosh (2022: 1), who argue that "processes of planetary urbanisation are remaking the human and nonhuman geographies of *non-city* spaces, causing infectious pathogens to be unmoored from previously localized ecosystems and catapulted into broader territories of circulation."

(Sub)urbanization has also facilitated the expansion of human settlements into former rainforest areas, exposing humans to new possible sources of disease (see Yong, 2018; Treffers et al., 2021). Deforestation and human encroachment on wildlife habitats have increased interactions between wildlife, human beings, and livestock, thus heightening the potential for pathogens to cross the species barrier (Coker et al., 2011). As Yong (2018) has explained, patterns of human expansion have now established the general context for the spread of infectious disease due to zoonotic infection, noting that "wherever people push into wildlife-rich habitats, the potential for such spillover is high." Such processes have been facilitated by the greater and more rapid movement of people, exposing human populations to a host of microbes, insects, and other non-humans which were previously largely undisturbed by urbanization.

New (landscape) political ecologies of disease under conditions of extended urbanization also entail the diffusion of medical infrastructures, knowledges, and practices that have previously been associated with urban centres. While stark discrepancies in vulnerabilities, availability of, and access to health care persist in urban regions – something we will see with regard to how COVID-19 spread and how vaccine rollouts occurred unevenly (see chapter 5) – those in the peripheries of the urban world now also demand better health facilities and resources which can enable faster response times and enhance containment of disease outbreaks. In other words, the new and evolving global peripheries have been particularly susceptible to diseases that jump the animal-to-human species boundary (zoonosis); have seen the

Figure 2.3 Sign in Kowloon Park, Hong Kong
Source: Creighton Connolly

introduction of new disease vectors; and have been subject to dynamic changes to urban and spatial morphology as well as to transformations over time (Brisbois and Ali, 2010).

Based on Brent Kaup's (2021: 568) push towards decentring "examinations of health and disease away from densely populated urban centres and [drawing] greater attention to the social mechanisms driving ecological change and disease outbreaks," Gandy has equally proposed that a "critical reading of urban metabolic processes can illuminate multiple scales and temporalities of socio-ecological entanglement as part of an alternative perspective on the growing significance of zoonotic diseases" (2022b: 33). Contemporary patterns of extended urbanization fundamentally shift the vulnerability of cities to infectious diseases, in ways that differ from those that have historically been associated with urbanization.

Such patterns of urbanization – including connected processes of globalization and neoliberalization – can affect social and ecological conditions in ways that increase the statistical odds of microbial spread. This has resulted in a tripling of the total number of disease outbreaks per decade since the 1980s (Ali and Keil, 2007; Haggett, 1994; Mayer, 2000). Additionally, the most significant global disease outbreaks in recent years have originated in China and Africa, which are also amongst the most rapidly urbanizing regions (Alirol et al., 2010). Both SARS and Ebola originated in peri-urban regions before being carried and spread between major cities like Hong Kong, Toronto, or Kinshasa (Keil and Ali, 2007; Treffers et al., 2021). As such, how and why the proliferation of suburban or peri-urban areas is conducive to disease spread is an important question to explore.

While other approaches situate communicable disease as a function of social interactions, we focus on changing spatial factors that drive changing patterns of disease. This can be cast as part of a general concern with the spread of risk as associated with processes of peri-urbanization and suburbanization – developmental processes that are arguably the defining forms in which global urban society is taking shape in the twenty-first century. In this context, Bloch et al. (2013: 96) observed that "current urban growth patterns appear to have significantly amplified the exposure of urban populations to hazard risks, markedly but not exclusively those broadly characterised as the urban poor." Therefore, identifying areas where the convergence of risk factors is occurring with greatest intensity, and at the largest scales, is a logical first step in the development of a mitigation strategy (see, for example, Ali, 2010, in relation to the spread of tuberculosis amongst the homeless in Toronto).

Further, as we discuss in our case studies, the more intense spread of various infectious diseases occurred in certain areas, including the suburbs of global cities such as Toronto with reference to SARS (chapter 3); informal settlements on the margins of West African cities in the case of Ebola (chapter 4); and the spread of COVID-19 in suburban areas located both within and outside Toronto, where many "essential workers" lived and worked (chapter 5). Notably, these locales represented exactly those areas where the risk factors conducive to disease spread converged, including such factors as, to name a few, poor housing stock and infrastructure; low-income, crowded working conditions; and the inability to self-isolate because of financial necessity and the urgent necessity of tending to family responsibilities, such as caregiving for the elderly and young.

CONCLUSION

The massive increase of the global urban population over the past few decades has been concentrated primarily in ex-urban areas and across an extensive fabric of urban relationships and tissues, which has posed new challenges to the control of infectious disease. This rapid urbanization includes processes such as population growth and movement between urban, suburban, and rural areas, as well as infrastructure provision (e.g., water and sanitation) and land-use change. As we have noted, these processes are especially pronounced in (but not limited to) developing regions, which have also been the source of recent major outbreaks such as Ebola and SARS.

This chapter has introduced the usefulness of a landscape political ecology (LPE) framework to theorize the relationship between processes of extended urbanization and infectious disease, while also establishing part of the conceptual basis for the more empirical chapters that follow. As we have demonstrated, an LPE framing is more attentive to interactions along the urban periphery, which can be useful for examining these topics along interdisciplinary lines, given the holistic nature of the landscape concept and the diverse methodological approaches comprising political ecology. The attention to socio-ecological metabolisms also allows for understanding how zoonotic events and emerging infectious disease spread can be triggered by the expansion of urban settlements in previously forested or agricultural areas. Furthermore, as Coker et al. (2011) and others have cautioned, such transformations are producing new ecological niches for disease spread, meaning that ex-urban regions are likely to remain a hotspot for emerging infectious diseases into the foreseeable future. Political ecology approaches can thus help to identify the political-economic and biopolitical factors influencing the spread of disease through a range of spatial scales in an age of extended urbanization. This will require an interdisciplinary approach including geography, health sciences, sociology, and a wide range of other disciplines to identify the potential health risks posed by processes of extended urbanization, while also developing possible solutions to prevent and mitigate future disease outbreaks.

SARS and the Global City

In November 2002, the city of Foshan, located in the Guangdong province of China, experienced a mysterious outbreak of an unknown but highly contagious respiratory disease referred to at the time as "atypical pneumonia" (Booth and Stewart, 2005). Within a few weeks the disease spread to other cities within the country and most notably to Beijing (Kaufman, 2006). Little was known about the early stages of this mysterious illness, and what little was known was not shared by the Chinese central government. This was largely because collecting data on pneumonia (atypical or otherwise) was not mandatory, while any information about epidemics themselves was classified as a state secret (Saich, 2006). The alleged state secrecy and lack of epidemiological data sharing and communication resulted in the Chinese state being rebuked by the World Health Organization (WHO) for attempts at systematically covering up or denying the extent of the epidemic (Eckholm, 2006). As the rates of incidence and prevalence continued to climb, the extensive nature of the disease spread meant the burgeoning epidemic could no longer be hidden from public view. By late February 2003, based on reports received by the WHO's Global Alert and Response Network (GOARN) electronic surveillance system, the WHO dispatched a team to Guangdong, but were denied entry to the affected areas for two months (Heymann, 2004). By mid-March 2003, the mysterious illness was recognized by the WHO as a global threat and was given the designation

Severe Acute Respiratory Syndrome (SARS) (Knobler et al., 2004). By April, disease spread was no longer confined to China, with 1,320 confirmed cases and 50 deaths worldwide, and in June the case count dramatically escalated to 8,437 cases with 813 deaths in thirty-three countries (Wang et al., 2006; Murray, 2006). Due to the rapid mobilization and work of scientists around the world to identify the causative agent of the disease and develop laboratory methods for detection on that basis, coupled with the strict adoption of conventional public health outbreak measures such as isolation, quarantine, handwashing, and physical distancing in SARS-affected areas, the epidemic was brought under control in July 2003 (Wang et al., 2006).

The index case for the international spread of SARS was thought to be an elderly physician who had been treating patients with an unidentified virus in the city of Guangzhou. In late February 2003 the physician travelled to Hong Kong to attend a relative's wedding and stayed at the Metropole Hotel. Here the virus spread to eleven hotel guests who continued their respective travels to various cities around the world, including Toronto, Singapore, Taipei, and Hanoi, and to other parts of Hong Kong (Abraham, 2004). The exact mode of transmission within the hotel has not been conclusively determined, though it has been suspected that exposure occurred through a viral aerosol cloud that had lingered for some time in a hotel elevator or travelled through the ventilation system (NACSPH, 2003). The SARS epidemic helped shine light on how the international spread of a disease could so quickly propagate through the networked connections of major cities around the world. It also revealed the specific challenges faced by local and international responders when dealing with an epidemic in an age of planetary urbanization (Ali and Keil, 2008; 2006). In this sense, the international spread of SARS served as a dress rehearsal of sorts for what was to come with the COVID-19 pandemic in 2020.

The SARS 2003 epidemic revealed the physical and social manifestations of one of the more notable characteristics frequently associated with globalization, namely non-linear effects. Specifically, the epidemic showed in a vivid fashion how a seemingly isolated event, which would have had little consequence for the world in a previous era, could now have unexpected and disproportionate (i.e., non-linear) effects that were distant in time and space from when and where the event originated (Smith, 2003: 566). In this chapter we consider the role of global cities in facilitating just such a development with reference to disease spread. We begin with a general background discussion of the disease ecology involved in the spread of SARS coronavirus (SARS-CoV). We then discuss how the disease ecology of SARS was influenced by various social and cultural factors pertaining to animal–human relations and the nature of global cities – including a consideration of the role played by global city peripheries. This is followed by an examination of how the microbial traffic of SARS was influenced by various infrastructure systems, such as those of the built urban environment. Finally, we discuss the governance challenges presented by SARS in what is considered to be the first major infectious disease epidemic in the so-called post-Westphalian era.

As we relate the story of SARS in this chapter, two observations may be of note. First, in light of the much higher numbers of infections and deaths and the pandemic character of COVID-19, which is now a matter of experience to all readers of this book, the SARS epidemic may seem minor in significance and impact. Yet at the time, especially in the affected areas in East Asia and Canada, we saw the blueprint and patterns of response that have now become commonplace in more than two years of COVID-19. Second, in the early years of the century, when the urban population on the planet crept above the 50 per cent mark for the first time in history, the focus of globalized processes of urbanization was predominantly on the largest control centres of the urban world, especially global cities such as Hong Kong, Singapore, and Toronto. The global urban world at the time was, for better or for worse, mostly imagined as a world of global cities and demographic change. Through this lens, issues pertaining to mobility and governance of the globalized urban were restricted to the most technologically advanced, most powerful urban centres of the time. While at the same time scholars began to point to the analytic limits of this global cities perspective (Robinson, 2006), it was still widely accepted as a frame from which to understand the globalization of urbanization. In contrast to the focus on Southern urbanism that we will deploy in our discussion of Ebola in chapter 4, and planetary (sub)urbanization which will serve as the lens for chapter 5 and the story of COVID-19, we mainly discuss the relationships of urbanization and disease during SARS through the conceptual space of the global city (see also Keil, forthcoming).

THE MICROBIAL TRAFFIC OF SARS CORONAVIRUS (SARS-CoV)

Efforts at identifying the reservoir of SARS coronavirus (SARS-CoV) were challenging because structured and reliable epidemiologic studies to conclusively trace the origin of the virus were not conducted at the time the outbreaks were unfolding, due to problems alluded to above in relation to limitations in data collection and sharing. However, in the aftermath of the outbreaks, serologic surveys were performed. These revealed that live animal market traders and food handlers who were working during the outbreaks exhibited higher levels of antibodies against SARS-CoV than the control population, while the strains of viruses isolated from the animals in the markets were almost identical to the human isolates (Wang et al., 2006). Although different species were identified as being infected with a strain of SARS-CoV, including palm civet cats, racoon dogs, and ferret badgers, Wang et al. (2006) note that the subsequent experimental studies tended to focus on palm civet cats. Such an exclusive focus may have been because the rate of detection was higher in these animals or because the number of palm civet cats traded in the southern Chinese region exceeded those of other wildlife groups. For a variety of reasons, despite experimental results indicating a higher susceptibility of civet cats to SARS-CoV infection, and a wide presence of the virus in markets and restaurants during the time of the outbreaks, the civet cat itself is unlikely to have been the reservoir host but may have served as an intermediate host (Wang et al., 2006). What remains unknown is what the actual natural reservoir of SARS-CoV is, and how the virus entered into the civet cat population from that natural reservoir. Further complicating efforts to identify the natural reservoir for SARS-CoV was the legal and illegal trade of wild animals between China and other countries, which according to Wang et al. (2006) raised the possibility that the SARS-CoV reservoir may not have been necessarily native to China. At this time, there is some evidence, though still not conclusive, that suggests cave-dwelling horseshoe bats are the most likely reservoir (Normile, 2005).

The question of the true SARS-CoV reservoir, which we can only touch lightly upon in this book, pertains to the political ecology of the disease and speaks to many practical issues, such as those concerning the origins of the outbreaks, immunogenicity, vaccine efficacy, the ability to find permanent solutions, and so on. But to understand the socio-spatial logics involved in the spatial diffusion of the disease within the human population once the initial zoonotic spillover event has already occurred – at which point human-to-human transmission supersedes animal-to-human transmission as the dominant mode – we will have to expand our analytical lens to consider the relevant social and cultural dimensions implicated in the microbial traffic. It is to these dimensions we now turn.

THE SOCIAL AND CULTURAL CONTEXT OF THE DISEASE ECOLOGY OF THE SARS CORONAVIRUS (SARS-CoV)

We can see from the discussion above that in tracing the origins of the SARS epidemic, the microbial traffic of SARS-CoV was indeed influenced by a series of biologically and ecologically based factors, such as the interaction of different animal species, the existence of natural and intermediate viral reservoirs, bodily fluids of animals, pathogenic evolution, and so on. These biological variables and mechanisms represent, however, only one dimension involved in the emergence of an outbreak. Recall from chapter 2 that a disease outbreak does not occur in a vacuum. Rather, both material and social factors contribute to the production of an environment that is conducive to the disease agent and host coming together in time and space. For example, in the present case we alluded to the role of animal markets and food handlers in restaurants in facilitating the zoonotic transfer of SARS-CoV from the intermediate host of the civet cat to the human host. But to focus only on that biological connection, without considering the social context in which that connection was made, will not give a full picture of how the disease agent (i.e., SARS-CoV) and hosts (i.e., civet cats and humans) happened to coincide in the first place. In other words, we need to consider in more detail the socio-spatial aspects of the role played by animal markets and restaurants as places of human interaction in the emergence of the SARS epidemic. Such consideration has implications not only for understanding the potential for zoonotic spillover from the civet cat to human beings, but also in relation to human-to-human transmission – as vividly illustrated, for instance, by the community transmission of SARS in the Pasir Panjang Wholesale Market in Singapore in April 2003 that led to the quarantine of 2,500 people (Teo et al., 2008), as well as community transmission in the Amoy Gardens apartment complex in

Hong Kong in March 2003 that resulted in over 300 cases (discussed in detail below).

It is unlikely that people became infected by eating civets. Rather, the viral transfer from civets to humans was much more likely to have occurred as humans were engaged in the process of raising, slaughtering, and preparing the animals to be cooked. Civet is one of the main ingredients in the "exotic" wildlife dish "dragon-tiger-phoenix soup," for which wealthy Chinese in Guangdong province will pay large sums (Sample and Gittings, 2003). In this culinary preference we see a socio-demographic contextual variable at work. Some observers have noted that the dramatic economic growth of the free market economy in China has triggered a change in dietary preferences (Jackson, 2008). Notably, with the increased affluence associated with a burgeoning Chinese economy, a meat-based diet has become more popular as people are better able to afford meat products. Greater demand for fresh meat products has in turn led to larger numbers visiting animal markets, thus amplifying the potential for human–animal interactions of the type that facilitates disease transmission (Zhan, 2005). From there, the virus will be able to undergo community spread. The changing nature of animal markets and its connection to dietary change, and the role these both had in enhancing the potential for an epidemic, were noted by a laboratory scientist who played a key role in identifying SARS-CoV as the causative agent of the disease. In an interview in 2005 with two of the authors (Keil and Ali, 2011), this leading scientist noted that one of the implications of the increased demand for certain animal meat products was that there was now a constant and greater circulation of different animals in markets that were themselves becoming larger. In this context, animal markets served as amplifiers of microbial traffic by ensuring the continued and uninterrupted flow of viral hosts. The increased number of different types of animals not only increases the chance of inducing change in the pathogenic evolution, structure, and immunogenicity of a virus, but will also affect microbial traffic in other ways. Most notably, the changing nature and size of animal markets will affect the pathways of microbial traffic within the human population as well.

From a socio-spatial perspective the animal market is an interesting site. This is not only because it is a place where disease amplification and spread may occur for the reasons outlined above, but because the animal market represents a place that exists at the interface of the rural and the urban, or at least serves to bring the rural and urban together temporarily. In this light, the live animal market is a place where animals from outside the city – both those farmed in the outskirts of the city and those from the wild – are brought to a location in which urban and suburban dwellers converge with animals with which they would not normally have any interaction. The animal market itself can be physically located within a peri-urban area or in the downtown core, but the actual physical situatedness of the marketplace does not change the inter-zonal (i.e., rural–urban or rural–suburban nexus) character of the animal market, because we are referring to a relationally defined characteristic. We will return to the role of such inter-zonal spaces in a separate discussion below when we discuss the nosocomial transmission of SARS in suburban Toronto neighbourhoods, but for now, we can note that once the virus leaves the market and is able to be transmitted from human to human, the dynamics of the microbial traffic shifts markedly, as one would expect. It is such dynamics we now consider.

SARS AND THE GLOBAL CITY

Emblematic of the 2003 spread of SARS was the manner in which this disease circulated through the global cities network (Ali and Keil, 2008). The Global and World Cities (GaWC) group defines and classifies a global (or world) city in terms of meeting various required parameters that combine economic, political, and cultural power, infrastructural connectivity, and diverse, often transnational populations (GaWC, 2004; Taylor, 2004).[1] Notably, global cities serve as nodal points within the connected network that undergirds the global economy (Friedmann, 1995; Sassen, 2000; Ren and Keil, 2017 for an overview). Within this networked context, the more influential of these global cities serve as the command-and-control centres of the globalized economy coordinating various types of transnational flows between different cities, including those pertaining to: material and information (Castells, 1996), labour market and investment cycles (Scott, 2000), knowledge and policy transfers, cultural exchange (Flusty, 2004), and the transnational movement of people and airline passenger flow (Smith and Timberlake, 2002). The SARS 2003 outbreak highlighted the understanding that, in addition to the types of flows that maintain the functional operation of the global economy, pathogens may represent a type of flow that, somewhat unexpectedly, may also be directly associated with the globalized economy. Thus, we see the diffusion of SARS-CoV occurring through networked connections between various global cities such as Hong Kong, Singapore, and Toronto. In analysing patterns of microbial traffic within the global cities context, not only can we trace the international movement of SARS through the networked architecture of global cities, but we can examine how the nature and character of various aspects of the global city have influenced the disease spread within each of these global cities. This discussion is accordingly part of a theoretical exercise around the turn of the century, now in need of adjustment, to capture the landscape of global urbanization. We have focused on both of these dimensions of microbial traffic of SARS in previous work (Ali and Keil, 2012; 2010a; 2010b; 2008; 2007; 2017; Hooker and Ali, 2009; Salehi and Ali, 2006; Sanford and Ali, 2004), but here we update our earlier findings and select for special consideration those insights and findings that have particular relevance for understanding the microbial traffic of COVID-19 (discussed in chapter 5), with a special focus on Toronto as an illustrative case.

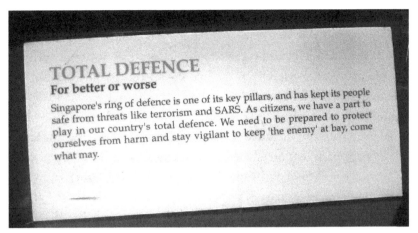

TOTAL DEFENCE
For better or worse

Singapore's ring of defence is one of its key pillars, and has kept its people safe from threats like terrorism and SARS. As citizens, we have a part to play in our country's total defence. We need to be prepared to protect ourselves from harm and stay vigilant to keep 'the enemy' at bay, come what may.

Figure 3.1 Sign in Singapore mass rapid transit station
Source: S. Harris Ali

SARS IN THE SUBURBS: THE SOCIO-DEMOGRAPHICS OF THE GLOBAL CITY

The networked relationships between global cities are often conceived of in terms of purely economic, communication, and resource flows. However, the diffusion of SARS-CoV through the global cities network revealed the importance of perhaps one of the more distinctive features of global cities, namely the ethnocultural and international diversity of their populations, and the significance of familial connections therein. In turn, this feature is associated with the familial and cultural linkages that weave together diaspora communities into an international network of ties. In what follows we shall discuss such connectivity between the global cities of Toronto and Hong Kong and the implications this had for the global spread of SARS.[2]

The index case for the Toronto outbreaks was the 78-year-old matriarch of a large extended family who contracted the illness during her stay at the Metropole Hotel in Hong Kong (Low, 2003). After returning to her family home in Toronto on 23 February 2003, she became ill and received ambulatory care at home until she passed away on 5 March 2003. Two days later her 44-year-old son became infected and was admitted to Scarborough Grace Hospital, where he succumbed to the disease on 13 March 2003. From this primary case, detailed contact tracing revealed the initiation of a chain of infection involving 128 cases, with 47 (37 per cent) of these consisting of hospital staff, 36 (28 per cent) of whom were patients in or visitors to this hospital (Varia et al., 2003). Epidemiological investigations revealed that Scarborough Grace Hospital was the epicentre of the first of two SARS epidemics experienced in various districts within Toronto but outside the central core of the city. Outbreaks in the first epidemic (13 March to 14 May 2003) were also faced in York Central Hospital in the suburb of Richmond Hill and West Park Health Care Centre in the Etobicoke area of the city (NACSPH, 2003). The epicentre of the second SARS epidemic (23 May to 30 June 2003) was North York General Hospital, with subsequent outbreaks at Sunnybrook Hospital, located within the North York area, and in a family clinic located in the Scarborough area of Toronto. The SARS outbreaks in Toronto were largely nosocomial (i.e., confined to the healthcare setting), with some limited community transmission in the general population originating from the healthcare setting. One example of the latter involved a chain of infection initiated by a member of a Philippines-based Roman Catholic group who had acquired SARS at Scarborough Grace Hospital (Krauss, 2003). This individual subsequently attended a Mass where hundreds gathered, with many participating in a religious retreat the next day. Within that religious group, there were twenty-nine probable and suspected SARS cases, in addition to the infection of one physician who was involved in treating the group.

Although the international spread of the disease may have occurred through the global cities network, once it arrived in a particular global city itself, the subsequent microbial traffic would then be influenced by the capillary networks of institutions and patterns of social contact uniquely present in that city. as well as the nature of the response that could be mounted. For instance, the unique history of Hong Kong, based on its colonial past and the ending of its leasing agreement with Britain in 1997 resulting in the return of political rule to China, contributed to a social and political context that was very different from the situation of Singapore. Although Singapore is also an island global city-state, like Hong Kong, Singapore's own unique colonial history and structure of governmental rule have contributed to what is referred to as an exceptionalist mindset based on a perennial "crisis mentality" (Ow, 1984; Teo et al., 2008). These different historically informed political and economic trajectories have resulted in different outbreak responses, which in turn influenced the microbial traffic of SARS in these two island global city-states (Ali and Keil, 2008). Similarly, the political, economic, and cultural history of Canada has uniquely influenced the microbial traffic of SARS in the City of Toronto. In this light, we turn to one aspect especially relevant to the nature of "urban" life in cosmopolitan global cities uniquely informed by a history of white settler colonialism (in contrast to the other forms of colonialism experienced in Hong Kong and Singapore) – namely, the rise of diasporic and multicultural communities.

THE IMMIGRANT SUBURB IN THE GLOBAL CITY

To ensure the required labour capacity necessary for rapid and expanding economic growth, as a British white settler colonial state, Canada has traditionally relied upon immigration, and this approach continues to the present day (Li, 2003). Notably, many newcomers have tended to settle in large cities, with Toronto being the chief recipient (Statistics Canada, 2011). In 2016, 51 per cent of Toronto residents self-identified as belonging to a visible minority group, making this city one of the most multicultural and multi-racial cities in the world (Statistics Canada, 2017). The settlement patterns of newcomers in Toronto have shifted over time, but in this century there is a much greater tendency for newcomers to settle in peripheral areas that border a central municipality – a trend referred to as "suburbanization of immigrants" (Statistics Canada, 2017). In part this trend was driven by escalating housing prices in major city centres that forced newcomers to find more affordable accom-modation in areas peripheral to the centre, creating "ethnoburban" areas where business and social ties were often in and among groups of newcomers from non-European countries, and mortgage credit schemes internal to those groups allowed for a debt-fuelled settlement pattern among certain groups of immigrants (Keil and Üçoğlu, 2021).

These settlement patterns have relevance for the situatedness of mobile diaspora communities that are connected globally through business and family ties. The epicentres of the SARS epidemic were situated in what were previously referred to as the Toronto boroughs of Scarborough and North York, in distinction from the inner-city core (referred to as "Old Toronto" in figure 3.2).[3] Moreover, the smaller outbreaks that arose were also located in these peripheral areas, such as in Markham, Vaughan, Etobicoke, and York.

The changing socio-demographics of diaspora communities and their locations within the global cities of Toronto, Singapore, and Hong Kong have particular relevance for understanding disease spread under the specific conditions of global urbanization at the turn of the century, but they also lay out the longer-lasting patterns for subsequent outbreak events such as the COVID-19 pandemic, discussed in chapter 5. These types of socio-demographic changes also have implications

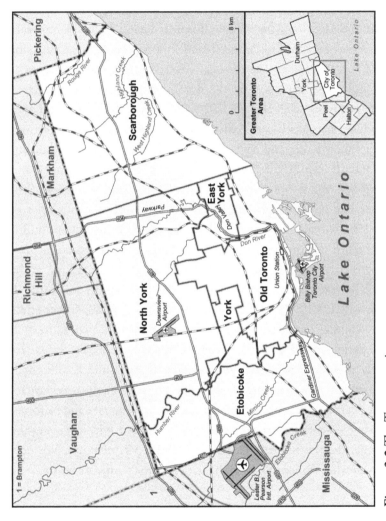

Figure 3.2 The Toronto region
Source: Wikimedia Commons

for other, often neglected aspects of outbreak reaction and response. Notably this includes the challenges stemming from xenophobic and racist reactions that accompany epidemics as certain groups come to be targeted as scapegoats by the dominant group. Anti-Chinese racism in relation to SARS was a big topic in Toronto during the 2003 outbreak, when restaurants in Chinatown stood empty and Asian-Canadians suffered everyday racism, as the blame for the disease was directed at China and those perceived by the dominant group to be associated with that country (Keil and Ali, 2008; 2006; Ali, 2008). The situation was serious in multicultural cities where the virus found its victims. In both Hong Kong and Singapore, scapegoating was observed. But in Toronto, it appeared to threaten the city's identity as an open and tolerant city. We wrote at the time that "[t]he main consequence of a disease like SARS might ultimately not be its impact as a killer of infected individuals, but its impact as a destroyer of the tenuous multicultural fabric of Toronto" (Keil and Ali, 2008: 154). It was no surprise that the racialization of the disease resurfaced in the beginning of the COVID-19 pandemic, and we will further pick up on this topic in relation to COVID-19 in chapter 5 below (Fang, 2020; Gover et al., 2020). Another important implication that we will also address in greater detail later is how the peripheral areas outside the city centre not only provide newcomers with residential space and accommodations in which they could affordably reside, but provide the necessary lot space for certain types of workplaces, such as warehouses and factories, that many "essential" workers continued to labour within during the pandemic, despite increased risk of COVID-19 infection. We now turn to another dimension of global cities, namely infrastructure.

SARS AND INFRASTRUCTURE

One of the key elements that defines a global city is the establishment of an advanced and reliable urban infrastructure. Such a networked infrastructure beneficially enables connectivity to the globalized economy by ensuring and maintaining the continued flow of goods and services. At the same time, however, the networked/connected quality of the infrastructure is predicated upon the assumption that all the sectors and components that are linked together are fully functioning. This increases the potential for catastrophe because the failure of any one component will lead to failure of the entire system, as we see today with supply-chain issues in the production and distribution of various goods. Thus, although the city economically (and otherwise) benefits from being connected to the world outside through infrastructure, it also becomes susceptible to threats originating from outside. For instance, the spread of SARS between global cities could not have happened without an established network of airports, which themselves were based on various infrastructures, ranging from airport runways to digital platforms for air traffic control, all working together to ensure, in this case, the flow of people (and inadvertently the flows of the virus as it travelled with those infected). But other types of infrastructure also influenced the spread of the virus. Two that were particularly influential with respect to microbial traffic during the SARS epidemic involved the water and sewage systems of apartment buildings, and information and communications infrastructures.

The importance of micro-infrastructures in the built environment in disease transmission has long been known in infectious disease research, as, for example, in the case of the transmission of Legionnaires' disease through the heating and ventilation system of a Philadelphia hotel in 1976 (Garrett, 1994). Building infrastructure was also implicated in the spread of SARS within the Amoy Garden private residential apartment complex located in Hong Kong (see figure 3.3).

The complex itself consisted of nineteen apartment towers (or blocks) that contained thirty-three stories each, together housing about 15,000 residents (McKinney et al., 2006). Over a three-day period in

Figure 3.3 Amoy Gardens apartment complex, Hong Kong
Source: Roger Keil

March 2003, 321 SARS cases were identified in this complex, with 99 of these cases occurring in one particular block. This community spread accounted for 18 per cent of all reported cases in Hong Kong. Investigations found that the interaction of the plumbing and ventilation systems in the apartment complex led to this outbreak: vertical drainage pipes were connected to multiple sanitary fixtures – toilets, sinks, bathtubs, and most notably floor drains – in the bathrooms in each of the units. Each of these bathroom fixtures was in turn fitted with a U-shaped pipe to trap water, thus sealing the connection between the fixture and vertical pipe. As is common practice, this was done to prevent sewer gases, insects, and rodents from climbing through the vertical pipes and entering the washrooms. To function properly the U-shaped tubes must be filled with water, but in one particular apartment block they were not filled, so there was no seal between the bathroom fixtures and the vertical sanitary downpipe. It was this channel opening that enabled the virus to enter into numerous bathrooms of the apartment complex – a route of transmission that was previously unknown.

In contrast to the role played by the conventional infrastructure of plumbing and ventilation, the SARS epidemic also revealed that more "sophisticated" or technologically advanced infrastructures, such as the digital platforms associated with information and communications infrastructures, likewise played an important role in influencing microbial traffic. In particular, digital infrastructure exerts an influence on microbial traffic by bolstering or impeding public health initiatives to contain the virus. Information and communication infrastructure may influence various aspects of the outbreak response, such as the degree to which epidemiological and clinical information is shared. In turn this impacts the effectiveness of various public health measures, ranging from those based on case investigation and contact tracing to vaccine development. For instance, despite the Chinese central government's efforts at containing online content about the outbreak in their midst, relatives and medical professionals in southern China were able to convey information about the disease to their extended family members, relatives, and other health professionals living in diaspora communities in Vancouver and Toronto. Such messaging could then be posted on online bulletin boards outside of China and be accessed by others. This was one way that information about the early outbreaks was picked up by Canada's Global Public Health Information Network (GPHIN), thereby leading to the early detection of SARS and ultimately enabling a better epidemiological response during the crucial early stages of the epidemic. At the international level, the 2003 SARS epidemic also demonstrated, for the first time, the importance of the information infrastructure for galvanizing the global scientific community in response to a common threat. The SARS crisis resulted in an unprecedented level of cooperation among the world's best research virologists and actually led to a novel approach to the workings of science and a definitive improvement on earlier patterns of laboratories working in isolation (Abraham, 2004). Coordinated by the WHO, the networks that formed to develop tools and standards for epidemic containment met daily by teleconference to share information and data in real time. This type of networking in turn brought front-line workers and international experts together in an unprecedented manner. The networked virtual teams of epidemiologists and laboratory clinicians led to other unprecedented achievements, including the discovery and characterization of the etiological agent of SARS-CoV within months, and the rapid development of the first generation of diagnostic tests (Knobler et al., 2004). In addition to the networking of experts facilitated by the digital infrastructure, such infrastructure also played a key role in detecting potential outbreaks.

SARS AND GOVERNANCE

Pandemic governance and response during SARS 2003 foreshadowed in many ways the pandemic politics of the COVID-19 emergency. As we will discuss at greater length in chapter 6, the virus that spread through the global city system in 2003 also showed the cracks of a global health governance order that was built on a Westphalian logic. At the same time, globalization, with the help of the virus, necessitated the emergence of post-Westphalian governance regimes that punctured the boundaries and sovereignty of the nation state from the side of both local and international politics. SARS came at the time when the WHO was in the process of drafting the International Health Regulations (IHR), which were ultimately introduced in 2005 as the organization's most important international legal instrument to govern the outbreak of epidemics. The logic of the IHR remained tied to the Westphalian-inspired relationship of nation states amongst each other and to the WHO (i.e., a relationship based on an overriding emphasis on protecting the sovereignty of nation states). Subsequently, the WHO recognized that the SARS crisis had shown the importance of large global cities in the coordination of outbreak response, while at the same time demonstrating the necessity of improving the communication between subnational, national, and international actors in times of crisis and emergency. As a consequence, the WHO initiated a process in 2008 to boost the understanding of the cities' role in the process of pandemic response and governance (WHO, 2009; see also WHO, 2016; 2018). The response to SARS was complicated by differing and competing jurisdictional responsibilities between the WHO and nation states, but also exposed fissures at subnational levels of governance, as, for example, in the relationship between the autonomously functioning Greater Toronto Airport Authority (GTAA), the federal government, and the local public health unit (Keil and Ali, 2007). The jurisdictional squabbles and lack of cooperation between different scales, and in particular across the public/private divide, clearly reveal how the "splintering" effects (Graham and Marvin, 2001) of privatization, vis-à-vis the reduced ability of the state to govern infrastructures such as those associated with airports and public health, make certain places particularly vulnerable to transboundary environmental and health threats such as disease outbreaks, particularly in light of *how* the world is interconnected today – the subject with which we conclude.

CONCLUSION

In many ways, with hindsight, the outbreak of SARS was a test run for the COVID-19 pandemic and the response to it almost twenty years later. The SARS crisis put to the test the very idea of infrastructural connectivity, which had previously been touted as an enabler of capital accumulation and economic growth in the nodal points of the network. Now, such infrastructural connectivity, the airports, the exclusive elite spaces, the popular immigrant quarters whose precarious and often racialized workforce supported both the global city economy and the luxury lifestyles of the elites, were potential sources of infection and disease. They also became distinct arenas of securitization and control inside the global city network (Ali and Keil, 2010b). To paraphrase Stephen Graham, the "master narratives" linked to idealized notions of globalized urban infrastructures were called into question and infrastructure was revealed to be a "precarious achievement" that was unsurprisingly prone to disruption and even failure (Graham, 2010: 9). In that sense, the SARS crisis prefigured both the catastrophic, cascading ruptures of Ebola crisis responses along various scales of West Africa and the Democratic Republic of the Congo that will be discussed in the next chapter and, ultimately, the dramatic failures of global infrastructures, especially in the cities of the Global North, during the COVID-19 crisis a few years later, which we will explain in greater detail in chapter 5. The world now knows that many lessons from 2003 were not learned. From the point of view of the subject matter of this book, SARS brought to light that we are now living in a networked world in which – at the time of the outbreak shortly after the turn of the millennium – a group of large financial centres or headquarter cities emerged as hubs of outsized importance in the emerging and rapidly restructuring global urban hierarchy (Ali and Keil, 2006). SARS was one of the first tests of that emergent network and of some of the hub cities to which that network's spokes directed flows of capital, labour, and information. Through SARS, this world of urban centrality was put on notice that not all flows through its connections were positive and growth-building. Those connectivities could carry a virus as well, thus highlighting the vulnerabilities that a network can also bring. Of course, even in 2003, globalizing urbanization was not confined to the rarefied club of global cities. Ordinary cities, even then, were part of the story (Robinson, 2006), and we will expand that story in subsequent chapters. In this chapter we focused on the spread of disease through some of the world's most advanced industrial and financial urban centres and extended urban areas; the next chapter deals with infectious disease in the least developed. With the COVID-19 pandemic (chapter 5), finally, we are dealing with both worlds because the two are today completely interconnected.

4 | Ebola and African Urbanization ——

In contrast to the spread of SARS through the international network of some of the most advanced capitalist cities of the world, Ebola virus disease (EVD), despite concerns about international spread, was largely confined to those areas of the world that did not have the advantages of stable governance and rigorous and well-funded health care. The limited nature of EVD spread is attributable to several factors (Quammen, 2014). First, EVD has typically been found to affect poorer people living in remote villages amid forested areas, who are simply not able to afford the price of air travel. Second, because EVD debilitates victims so quickly, those inflicted and exhibiting symptoms – which is the time individuals are most infectious – will be physically unable to travel long distances by plane. In this light, Quammen (2014: 110) notes that although Ebola is a slow-moving virus compared to others (such as SARS or COVID-19), the spread of EVD in West Africa "tell[s] us also about the ugly facts of poverty; inadequate health care, political dysfunction, and desperation in three West African countries, and of neglectful disregard of those circumstances over time by the international community."

It is in this light that in this chapter we examine the three countries most affected by the 2014–2016 EVD epidemic: Guinea, Liberia, and Sierra Leone. These three countries rank among the poorest in the world, with rising levels of rural impoverishment and rapid population growth heavily concentrated in urban informal settlements that are highly susceptible to disease spread (Howard, 2017;

Wilkinson, 2020). The material and social conditions existing in these (and other African) countries have implications for the disease ecology and microbial traffic of EVD, and for this reason we also bring into analysis the role and influence of (post)colonial rule in establishing a landscape political ecology in which infectious diseases may flourish. Further, we will consider how these structural factors also contributed to making the West African EVD epidemic rather exceptional in the sense that, unlike previous outbreaks of this disease that were limited to relatively remote and isolated locations in Central and East Africa, the West African EVD spread in part by entering the fully urbanized context of several major cities.

Notably, this urbanizing context of EVD spread includes particular features and forms that extended urbanization took in West Africa. This includes the dramatic increase in the number and size of informal settlements (also referred to as slum settlements), as well as recent human-induced environmental disruptions in the forest ecosystems situated at the peripheries of urban centres. To analyse the role of these developments in EVD spread and response through a landscape urban political ecology lens, we return to our focus on the interrelated factors of socio-demographic influences, governance issues, and infrastructural considerations. As such, we consider such socio-demographic factors as the role of social class in the relationship between informal settlement and urban centres, as well as in relation to rural–urban interactions. These factors in turn are affected by governance-related matters such as the displacement of people by civil war and a weak state. Further, as we shall also see, the failure of the government to mount an effective response in some instances led to a civil-society-based response predicated upon community participation in aspects of outbreak response previously not carried out by laypeople (such as involvement in active case investigation, contact tracing, disease surveillance, and providing for those quarantined). Lastly, it was feared that poor infrastructure networks (water, sewage, electricity) within informal settlements would exacerbate the challenges faced in the epidemic response, but as will be discussed, many of these concerns were in fact addressed by the community-based epidemic response efforts.

This chapter begins with a brief historical overview of EVD outbreaks in the past, as well as a discussion about the nature of this disease and an account of its spread in West Africa. Next, we consider issues related to the disease ecology and viral traffic of EVD, which we subsequently situate within the context of colonialism in general, and particularly within the informal settlements of the postcolonial city. To illustrate the principles involved, we turn to the case of the West Point informal settlement in Monrovia, Liberia. We conclude by discussing how a successful EVD response was mounted in West Africa despite the formidable challenges faced due to severe resource and infrastructure limitations, particularly within informal settlements.

BACKGROUND

Ebola virus disease is difficult to study because of the character of the virus itself. Outbreaks of the disease are relatively rare, and when they do emerge, they generally occur in areas far from research hospitals and medical institutes that have the resources to quickly respond and study the disease (Quammen, 2014). Further adding to the challenges, the dynamics of EVD transmission are complex, involving a multiplicity of variables including seasonal factors, weather, the geographic patterns of outbreaks, and the circumstances that bring reservoir animals or their droppings into contact with apes or humans (Quammen, 2014). Prior to the West African epidemic, there were between twenty and thirty smaller EVD outbreaks in various countries within Central Africa including Gabon, Congo, South Sudan, and Uganda, with nine of these occurring in the Democratic Republic of the Congo (DRC) alone. The DRC was also the country in which the first known outbreak occurrence was documented in 1976, in the small rural village of Yambuku situated on the Ebola River (when the country was called Zaire). More recently, the DRC has experienced several outbreaks. In 2018, EVD outbreaks in the northeastern North Kivu province of that country led to 2,200 deaths and was the second-largest recorded outbreak of this disease (after the West African outbreaks). Fortunately, soon thereafter, the development of an Ebola vaccine, in conjunction with community-based interventions, helped to curtail the spread, and in June 2020 the WHO declared the outbreak over (CDC, n.d.). The EVD epidemic in West Africa remains the largest on record and claimed over 11,000 lives.

Originally, Ebola virus disease was commonly referred to as Ebola haemorrhagic fever because in some cases the disease was associated with internal bleeding in various places in the body. The proliferation of dramatic media images of patients bleeding out, or sensationalistic depictions in journalistic accounts, such as in *The Hot Zone* by Richard Preston (1994), falsely conveyed to the public the impression that the disease was a death sentence that wreaked havoc on the body by liquefying organs (Adeyanju, 2010; King, 2002). In reality, more than half the patients do not suffer from internal bleeding at all and die of other causes such as respiratory distress and the shutdown – not the dissolution – of internal organs (Quammen, 2014: 47). Thus, although in some cases internal bleeding does occur, it is not a prominent symptom of infection. Furthermore, early recognition of the disease coupled with treatment through appropriate hospital and medical measures, such as oral rehydration therapy and intravenous feeding (all of which are readily available in the Global North but not necessarily so in the Global South), means the likelihood of survival of those infected is reasonably high (Farmer, 2020). Acknowledgement of this understanding has prompted the use of the term Ebola virus disease instead of Ebola haemorrhagic fever. EVD spreads to people through direct contact with body fluids and tissues of infected people and animals. Notably, the disease is most contagious during the later stages of illness, including the period after death. Indeed, direct contact during funeral ceremonies with those who died of EVD proved be a key means through which the disease spread during the early period of the West African epidemic, before the adoption of what came to be known as safe and dignified burial practices – as we will discuss later, this was a critical intervention in controlling the epidemic.

The West African EVD situation was different from previous outbreaks in various ways. First, as mentioned above, the sheer magnitude of the numbers of those affected and of lives lost was much greater. Second, healthcare workers represented 3.9 per cent of all confirmed and probable cases in the three West African countries combined, with the majority (74 per cent) of transmission events involving family members (CDC, n.d.). In contrast, during the 1995 Kikwit outbreak (see below), 25 per cent of those infected were healthcare workers (ibid.). Third, as alluded to above, the West African epidemic involved disease spread through major urban centres and notably the capital cities of the three countries. This was in stark contrast to earlier EVD outbreaks in Central Africa that were largely limited to isolated and sparsely populated areas – which in turn limited the disease spread.

The initial zoonotic crossover incident is believed to have occurred in December 2013 in the town of Meliandou, located in southern Guinea in the Guéckédou district near the borders of Sierra Leone and Liberia (WHO, 2015). Meliandou is situated in a relatively remote location that is sparsely populated, with only thirty-one households. It requires a minimum of 12 hours' drive over rough roads to reach from the capitals of Guinea, Liberia, or Sierra Leone. It is suspected that the zoonotic spillover occurred at a particular site in the town where there was a large hollow tree that served as a roost for fruit bats. An 18-month-old boy was thought to have become infected with EVD from a bat while playing near that tree. The toddler succumbed to the disease on 28 December 2013. This led to a chain of infections involving members of the immediate and extended family, as well as several midwives, traditional healers and staff in the local hospital who took care of the increasing number of ill people. As the prevalence and incidence rates continued to increase, on 24 January 2014 the head of the Meliandou health post issued an alert and investigations were initiated by local and international health officials. By 23 March 2014, the Institut Pasteur in Lyon, France, had analysed samples and identified a filovirus as the causative agent of the disease later identified as the most lethal virus in the Ebola family, namely the Zaire strain. By this time there were forty-nine cases and twenty-nine officially recorded deaths (WHO, 2015).

MICROBIAL TRAFFIC AND EBOLA VIRUS DISEASE (EVD)

Almost all EVD outbreaks prior to the West African ones unfolded in human settlements in remote forested areas. One exception was the 1995 outbreak in the city of Kikwit, Zaire. This city had a population at the time of 200,000 and is located about 240 miles east of Kinshasa (Quammen, 2014: 26). Kikwit was, as Quammen observes, connected to the wider world in a way that other outbreak sites were not. Nevertheless, similar to other outbreak sites, Kikwit was surrounded by forest. Yet international spread did not occur, and of the 280 people who died of the disease and the 318 infected, about a quarter were healthcare workers employed in one of the city's four hospitals. Notably, the index case for the Kikwit outbreak was connected to the forested area surrounding the city. This individual was a farmer who made charcoal from the timber he cleared to plant corn and cassava. The plots of land the farmer worked on were located about five miles southeast of the city (Quammen, 2014). From a landscape political ecology perspective, the action of clearing the land represents an ecological disruption, and as we shall discuss now, ecological disruption is a key factor implicated in the microbial traffic of EVD.

Although the fruit bat may have a high probability of being the primary viral reservoir for EVD, research has not yet conclusively determined this – though the fruit bat is believed to be a top contender, based on polymerase chain reaction (PCR) and serologic evidence accumulated over the past decade (Bausch and Schwarz, 2014). The possibility nevertheless remains that the fruit bat may not necessarily be the only reservoir (Quammen, 2014). As was the case with SARS, the question is still open as to whether EVD transmission to humans occurs directly, for instance through eating bats, or through exposure to an intermediate host. It is known that there can be direct transmission from dead apes to humans, but not necessarily that there is direct transmission from bats to humans.

EVD outbreaks appear to arise in a sporadic fashion, with years sometimes passing between episodes. What these gaps imply is that zoonotic spillover from the viral reservoir to humans is a relatively rare occurrence (Quammen, 2014: 28–9). Questions then arise as to where the virus hides between outbreaks and under what circumstances it travels from that hidden reservoir into other animals such as apes and humans. The gaps in time between outbreaks suggest two possible clues to answering these questions. First, this may indicate that the viral reservoir itself involves a rare animal or an animal with which we as humans rarely come in contact. This makes the identification of the EVD reservoir challenging. A second important clue in helping to identify the viral reservoir is to look at situations of ecological disturbance. When biological diversity is high and the ecosystem is relatively undisturbed, it is easier for the virus to reside undetected within a reservoir host. The viral reservoir remains "under the human radar." However, the converse is also true: ecological disturbance causes diseases to emerge (Quammen, 2014: 4). This is because biodiversity acts as a sort of natural buffering system that reduces the chances of zoonotic spillover events that facilitate the transmission of viruses from the reservoir to humans. The possibilities of zoonoses are therefore amplified through human encroachment in nature, which may happen through a wide assortment of human activities that include, for example, the destruction of natural habitats and biodiversity that either compromises or displaces wildlife. In this light, one important human intervention in nature that is especially pertinent to disease outbreak emergence is deforestation.

A significant link has been documented between forest loss and fragmentation and EVD outbreaks (Bausch and Schwarz, 2014). Historically, infectious disease outbreaks have occurred in areas of heavy deforestation (Dorit, 2015), and for this reason, deforestation has been hypothesized to be a significant driver of emerging infectious disease. The level of deforestation needed to initiate zoonotic spillover and outbreak emergence varies. For instance, as mentioned above with respect to the 1995 Kikwit outbreak, the amount of forested area that was cleared by the one individual farmer to make charcoal was probably very modest. In contrast, monoculture plantation agriculture and mining may contribute to relatively greater removal of trees. Thus, for example, the Firestone Rubber Company's rubber plantation near Monrovia in Liberia and various mining operations for iron, bauxite, gold, diamonds, etc. throughout West Africa require forest clearance for the mining activities themselves, and in addition, the land is cleared to build housing for workers. Housing often consists of logging and mining camps that are essentially de facto villages, maintained through the supply of shelter, food, and fuel, which in turn also causes disturbances to the forest canopy and the wildlife that resides within it. Notably, mining settlements are well-documented sites for numerous outbreaks through central Africa, including earlier outbreaks in gold-mining camps deep in the rainforests of Gabon (Quammen, 2014).

Other than the increased potential for zoonotic spillover because of the ecological disruption caused by the presence of camps, the labour-intensive nature of mining and mineral extraction, coupled with predatory extractive capitalist practices, has meant that many people end up living in confined spaces with poor hygiene. According to well-known West African researcher Melissa Leach, mining in the Mano River Union countries has grown dramatically over the last couple of decades and presently represents a popular livelihood option for many (Leach, 2015). Consequently, more and more mines and mining camps have been constructed in forested areas. As Leach further notes, the proliferation of mining has served as an impetus for the immense movement of people throughout and between West African countries as people seasonally move in and out of mining areas. Such travel involves movement from rural to urban settings and back for temporary periods for reasons of work and visiting relatives (Onoma, 2016), and this can facilitate disease spread.

Large-scale agriculture and logging operations have an even greater environmental impact because of the scale of operations. In the case of Sierra Leone, for instance, logging, slash-and-burn agriculture, and chopping down trees have intensified to unprecedented levels because of an increased demand for firewood. Industrial logging is therefore a significant driving force in deforestation. The United Nations Environment Programme (UNEP) notes that total forest cover in Sierra Leone has now dropped to just 4 per cent, and warns that if deforestation were to continue at the current level, forest cover would disappear from that country altogether within the next few years (UNEP, 2010). Similarly, more than half of the forests in Liberia were sold off to industrial loggers during President Ellen Johnson Sirleaf's administration from 2006 to 2018 (Ford, 2012).

It has been argued that deforestation in Africa has accelerated because of climate change and that the impact this has on seasonal weather patterns has also influenced the potential for disease outbreaks. For instance, Johnson et al. (2013) found that West African countries are experiencing more "seasonal droughts, strong winds, thunderstorms, landslides, heatwaves, floods, and changed rainfall patterns." These changes in climatic conditions will alter the very nature of the forested areas. In this light, perhaps the most significant impact of climate change is the onset of drier conditions that can lead to fires that will ultimately result in the splitting up of forests – a phenomenon referred to as forest fragmentation (Laporta, 2014). The city of Guéckédou is itself situated in a fragmented forest landscape described as a somewhat urbanized location that contains forest patches (figure 4.1).

The edge density between anthropogenic urban environment and forest patches is ten to twelve times higher than in landscapes without fragmentation (Laporta, 2014). This change in landscape provides greater space between urbanized areas and forest habitats that can be settled by larger numbers of people. It is in this context that landscape fragmentation can play two roles in Ebola transmission dynamics. First, landscape fragmentation can serve as epidemiological corridors wherein pathogen-carrier reservoirs can maintain and spread zoonotic cycles. Second, landscape fragmentation can provide a frontier of contact between forest fringes and anthropogenic urban environments. The first development may contribute to increased variability of genetic pools of the pathogen within the zoonotic Ebola transmission cycle, thus leading to the possibility of mutant strains emerging. The second development may enhance the potential for contact between humans and the pathogen. These mechanisms together may have ultimately been linked to the Ebola virus that infected humans, thus playing a critical role in the onset of the West African epidemic (Laporta, 2014). On this basis, the question may be raised: will these types of mechanisms contribute to the development of Ebola outbreaks in the future?

Based on the best available evidence to date (although it is noted that such data may not be complete), Bausch and Schwarz (2014) argue that it is reasonable to hypothesize that drier conditions have influenced the number or proportion of Ebola-virus–infected bats and/or the frequency of human contact with them. This is because

Figure 4.1 Village in the city of Guéckédou situated in an area of fragmented forestation

Source: Wikimedia Commons

the loss of trees and the resultant fragmented forest configuration will displace bats from the places they normally roost, thereby increasing the likelihood they will try to find other places to live, especially amongst human populations that have settled close to what was previously the forested area.[1] These environmental changes in forest cover, coupled with settlement patterns, have resulted in an increasing number of West African villages that are surrounded by a topography based on forest and agriculture, resulting in a situation where bats have become much more commonplace in the living conditions of humans – thus increasing the potential for zoonotic crossover. It was just such a series of circumstances that could be observed with reference to Meliandou, the suspected "ground zero" of the West African EVD epidemic.

Even though the popular image of Ebola is that of a virus mysteriously and randomly emerging from the forest, Bausch and Schwarz (2014) note that the sites of attack are far from random. Rather, large haemorrhagic fever virus outbreaks almost invariably occur in areas in which the economy and public health system have been decimated from years of civil conflict or failed development. Consistent with the landscape political ecology of disease approach we are emphasizing in this book, Bausch and Schwarz's insight is in line with the idea that we need to take more seriously the role of the social, political, and economic factors in disease outbreaks more generally. An exclusive focus on the purely ecological dimensions of outbreaks runs the risk of what Robbins (2012: 14) refers to as "apolitical ecology." The adoption of an apolitical ecology stance leads to the neglect of the broader context and embedded issues and conflicts pertaining to issues of power and political dynamics. Consequently, apolitical ecological analysis tends to claim that when conflicts, crises, or processes arise, they are "natural," hence a static and a priori given that is situated outside of human influence and rendered politically objective and inert. Power and politics do play a role in disease outbreaks in many different ways.

In this connection, Bausch and Schwarz (2014) note, although ecological pressures may govern the dynamics of the virus in the forest, it is clearly the socio-political landscape that dictates where it goes from there: does the presence of the virus result in an isolated case or two, or does it lead to a large and sustained outbreak? To address this question, we turn now to a consideration of the West African socio-political landscape.

COLONIALISM AND THE DISEASE ECOLOGY OF EBOLA

The colonial nature of global health conditions has been subject to much scrutiny lately (Richardson, 2020). Owing to their colonial histories, the West African nations of Guinea, Liberia, and Sierra Leone have long been dependent on export-oriented, extractive economies based on minerals and cash crops (Abdullah and Rashid, 2017: 5). During the postcolonial period, the political economic trajectories of these three countries, like those of many African countries from the 1980s onwards, were strongly influenced by the imposition of harsh structural adjustment policies by the World Bank and the International Monetary Fund (IMF) (Howard, 2017). Restrictions were imposed on public spending so that funds could be redirected to service the national debt incurred through World Bank and IMF loans. Consequently, few to no funds were directed towards education and health systems. At the same time, predatory and military regimes drained the national treasuries of each of these nations (Howard, 2017: 19).

Despite some differences between the three countries, the influence of the structural conditions outlined above has meant all three have undergone a similar political economic trajectory based on common features. These include the political and economic domination of the nation state by multinational firms; deepening rural impoverishment; a dramatic increase in the youth demographic; the rapid growth of cities and slums (coupled with high incidences of urban unemployment); and falling prey to dictatorships, unbridled corruption, and recurrent military coups since the mid-1990s (Howard, 2017). These structural conditions had important implications for the nature of the EVD response that unfolded. For instance, these conditions resulted in an inadequate infrastructure, causing logistical and resource mobilization challenges faced during the response; they contributed to a low level of public trust in public health officials, and to the development of conspiracy theories and rumours, all of which together hindered the EVD response in significant ways. We will now turn our attention to how these postcolonial conditions, linked to the continued political disempowerment and economic dependency of West African nation states, are related to socio-ecological changes that have increased the potential for disease outbreaks in that region. In particular, economic dependency via structural adjustment policies, and the poverty that resulted, played an important role in enabling the conditions for the EVD outbreak to emerge in Guinea. We will return later to issues of public trust and conspiracy theories in our discussion of the West African EVD response in subsequent sections of this chapter, as they have particular relevance to issues of governance during an epidemic.

The stalled economy in Guinea led to mass poverty that forced people to expand the range of their livelihood activities in order to simply survive (Bausch and Schwarz, 2014). This meant that people were compelled to venture further into untouched natural environments, thus expanding their geographic range, and increasing thereby the likelihood of coming into contact with an expanded number of animal species in the wild. For example, individuals would go deeper into the forest to find wood to make charcoal, or for hunting game and to even increase their range of hunted species, while others went deeper into mines to extract minerals. These types of activities, as Bausch and Schwarz (2014) argue, enhanced people's risk of exposure to Ebola virus and other zoonotic pathogens as they ventured into more and more remote areas of natural ecosystems. It should be kept in mind that such changes in human activities that increased the potential for zoonotic transmission were linked to political economic machinations. In the case of Meliandou and the Guéckédou district of southern Guinea, the inhabitants of this area were comprised of small and isolated populations of diverse ethnic groups who held little power compared to the politically elite decision makers in the capital city of Conakry (Fairhead, 2016).

The views and concerns of the local people in the Guéckédou district were habitually neglected or ignored as decisions were made in the interests of foreign corporations such as those involved in logging. Consequently, the region was systematically plundered, with the forest area decimated by clear-cut logging despite local protest (Fairhead, 2016). This was a situation that was mirrored in Liberia, where the Americo-Liberian elites (i.e., a ruling class comprised of the descendants of freed American slaves who settled in what became the national capital city of Monrovia) tended to neglect the local Indigenous concerns of those in more rural villages, while surrendering these areas to foreign capital (mostly American interests) for natural resource extraction (Howard, 2017). It was these sorts of structural developments that, as discussed above, resulted in the forest fragmentation that was conducive to zoonotic spillover in Meliandou and the Guéckédou.

After the initial zoonotic spillover, human-to-human spread became the main mode of transmission during the outbreak. Proliferation through the human population was also influenced by the post-colonial social structure in various ways, particularly those in which the social structure impacted on the ability to respond to EVD because of the lack of available resources and inadequate infrastructures. For instance, the inability to invest in the public health and medical care systems due to the imposition of structural adjustment programmes, coupled with further decimation of such systems because of civil wars in West Africa, meant that EVD spread was facilitated by the fact that healthcare facilities did not have a sufficient supply of gloves, clean needles, and disinfectant. This left both patients and healthcare workers alike vulnerable to nosocomial transmission (Bausch and Schwarz, 2014). Chains of infection were initiated through hospital-acquired infection, as infected persons returned to their homes while incubating the virus. As Bausch and Schwarz (2014) note, this chain of transmission was the classic pattern that unfolded in Guinea, where early infection of a healthcare worker in Guéckédou triggered spread to surrounding prefectures and eventually to the capital, Conakry. Not only did postcolonial healthcare systems suffer from a lack of resources and inadequate infrastructure, but so too did informal (slum) settlement areas, raising fears that spread in these particularly vulnerable places was inevitable – though, as we shall discuss below, unmitigated disease spread could still be halted despite the significant structural challenges faced in these types of settlements.

INFECTIOUS DISEASE, SLUM SETTLEMENTS, AND THE POSTCOLONIAL CITY

The city played a critical and instrumental role in the building of empires by facilitating the economic and social restructuring of newly colonized regions. In this connection, colonial cities were an integral part of the overall transport, trade, and administrative systems that were developed and mobilized to maintain the continued exploitation of the colonized people and their natural resources. As such, in the nineteenth and early twentieth centuries, African colonial cities were recreated or restructured to meet the needs of the colonizers, while at the same time the needs of the Indigenous communities were woefully ignored by colonial authorities (Njoh, 2010). Not only was the provision of infrastructure, housing, and social welfare services severely limited for the colonized, but restrictive urban migration rules were consciously designed to limit the number of Indigenous people allowed to settle in urban centres. Furthermore, existing Indigenous populations were limited to those areas of the city that were already under-serviced. This type of spatial segregation was reinforced by colonial public health, infectious disease, and security/military policies of the day.

In an effort to isolate and "protect" European colonizers from the perceived health risks associated with Indigenous areas, a strategy referred to as the "sanitation syndrome" was adopted. Accordingly, in Francophone Africa, strict boundaries in the form of "cordons sanitaires" were enforced to maintain a spatial separation between the colonizer and the colonized. Similarly in early twentieth-century South Africa, the apartheid policy was adopted based on the preju-diced notion that areas in which there was a Black urban presence were associated with squalor, disease, and crime. In reference to this type of colonial segregation in the West African context, it is instructive to consider the case of malarial control measures historically adopted in Freetown, the capital city of Sierra Leone.

Based on his work in India, Dr Ronald Ross of the Liverpool School of Tropical Medicine discovered the parasite that causes malaria in humans in the gastrointestinal tract of mosquitoes. This proved that the disease was transmitted to humans via mosquitoes, though the specific species had not yet been identified (Spitzer, 1968). In subse-quent work carried out between 1899 and 1902 in Freetown, Sierra Leone, Ross identified the host species as the Anopheles mosquito, and this discovery laid the foundation for combatting the disease in that city. Unlike other mosquito species that can breed anywhere, the Anopheles breeds specifically in areas where stagnant water is found, for example, in rocks, ditches, tubs, pots, and containers. The malarial threat could therefore be dealt with in two ways (Spitzer, 1968). The first strategy involved the elimination of puddles of stagnant water where the mosquito larvae lived. However, attempts to do this in

EBOLA AND AFRICAN URBANIZATION

Freetown proved to be unsuccessful because drainage and sanitation infrastructures were essentially non-existent. The second strategy was based on health segregation. Segregation of this type was already carried out in India, as British military personnel and troops lived in areas that were separated from the locations where Indigenous people resided. In the case of Freetown, this was not the existing practice, although efforts were starting to be made to establish a colour bar against educated Africans in a wide range of social and economic sectors.

The strategy of segregation based on protecting the health of Europeans from exposure to "native diseases" served as a rationale that bolstered the impetus towards the colour bar as a policy (K'Akumu and Olima, 2007). This in turn ultimately contributed to the establishment of segregated living arrangements in this city. In Freetown, the city core is surrounded by hills, and it was soon recognized that those living in these hills would be protected against the risks of malarial infection because mosquitoes tended to thin out at higher altitudes. Based on this rationale, the British moved to these higher-lying areas and lived in two-storey colonial-style homes with spacious gardens and furnished with fans and mosquito nets, leaving behind the Indigenous Africans in the more malaria-prone and under-serviced zones of the city. Thus, it was not surprising to learn, for instance, that a light rail service was constructed to transport the British and other Europeans from their hilltop residences to the downtown, while the rest of the city did not have any form of public transit at all (Lynch et al., 2020).

As a result of such developments, colonial planning and policies created colonial cities with municipal administrations that were ill-prepared to address the challenges of the post-independence era, including the EVD threat. As mentioned in our first chapter, although the bacteriological city was largely successful in combating infectious disease spread in European cities, the success was uneven in colonial cities (Gandy, 2006). This was because certain areas of the colonial city and surrounding region simply did not benefit from the technological advancements associated with the bacteriological city in comparison to those areas where the Europeans and British resided. As such, the British as a colonizing power refused to finance basic services such as water and sanitation to reach the areas where most Africans lived, and instead, if any infrastructure was built, it was for purposes of supporting resource and commodities extraction, not to provide intra-city services or mobility for urban dwellers (Corburn and Karanja, 2016).

In the case of Freetown, for instance, about four fifths of the city population do not have waterborne sewerage, while half do not have access to piped water supplies, and some three quarters have no on-site access to fresh water – one of the lowest levels in Africa – forcing the majority of city dwellers to rely on water supplied by vendors (Lynch et al., 2020). Moreover, the racial segregation and the shunting of Indigenous people to the most marginal and risk-prone areas of the city are a continuing legacy of colonial-era planning and policy-making – the effects of which we see most vividly in the case of informal settlements (also referred to as slum settlements) in the postcolonial era of today (Corburn and Karanja, 2016).

The proliferation and expansion of slum settlements that followed in the wake of many African nations gaining independence may therefore be understood to be the net result of colonial policies. That is, colonial cities that were originally designed for European elites were rendered incapable of coping with rapid population growth (Lynch et al., 2020). These policies also led to a continued reliance on foreign planners and aid agencies who would sometimes import and implement Western management and planning approaches. These were not suited to the colonial setting because weak local development and planning capacities, in conjunction with fragile economic systems, meant that Western planning approaches were wholly incompatible with the reality of the situation on the ground. As Lynch et al. (2020)

thus observe in reference to Freetown, the scene was set for the start of significant challenges pertaining to post-independence growth in a city that lacked the infrastructure, capacity, and resources to effectively manage intensified urbanization.

Africa's population has grown substantially over the last decades and the current population of 1.1 billion people is expected to double by 2050, with 80 per cent of that increase occurring in cities, especially slums (Sanderson, 2020). Notably, the West African capital cities of Conakry, Freetown, and Monrovia tripled or quadrupled in size between 1960 and the 1990s (Howard, 2017). This trend was the result of a combination of relatively high birth rates, rural impoverishment, and insecurity, which drove people to cities where better-paid salaried jobs, wage work, and informal sector opportunities were ostensibly available. The reality may, however, drastically vary from the popular perceptions people have of the economic vitality of African colonial cities. Today, as numerous researchers have pointed out, low levels of actual formal employment opportunities, minimally low base wage rates, and the inabilities of cities to cope with growth have resulted in the "urbanisation of poverty," with the most visible manifestation of this seen in the dramatic proliferation and expansion of informal settlement areas (Davis, 2005).

Intensified urbanization in Africa is unfolding at a dramatic rate, with much of the resultant population increases occurring in informal settlement areas (Bloch et al., 2022). Displacement and the effects of a series of civil wars in Sierra Leone (1991–2001) and Liberia (1989–2003) further intensified the rapid and generally uncontrolled urban growth, with much of this taking place in slum areas or informal settlement communities. Slums have been defined in various ways, but there are certainly some common attributes. For instance, Wilkinson (2020) notes that slum communities have at least some of the following features: a lack of formal recognition on the part of local government of the settlement and its residents; the absence of secure tenure for residents – residents face long-standing threats of eviction; inadequacies in provision for infrastructure and services; overcrowded and substandard dwellings; and location on land less than suitable for occupation. In addition, the UN has included in their definition of a "slum" the following related factors pertaining to the lack of: durable housing of a permanent nature that protects against extreme climate conditions, sufficient living space (more than three people sharing a room), easy access to safe water in sufficient amounts at an affordable price, and access to adequate sanitation in the form of a private or public toilet shared by a reasonable number of people (Corburn and Karanja, 2016). In the case of slum areas in Sierra Leone, Liberia, and Guinea, frequently housing structures are often poorly constructed from corrugated-iron sheets or mud bricks.

The social and physical conditions of informal settlements, such as poor housing quality, limited basic services, poor sanitation, and very high densities – informal settlements may typically be ten times denser than neighbouring areas of the same city (Muggah and Florida, 2020a; 2020b) – have led some observers to conclude that "megacity slums are incubators of disease" (ibid.; see also Davis, 2005). As Wilkinson (2020) has noted, these conditions may foster circumstances favourable to infectious disease transmission – what is referred to as "transmission vulnerability." For example, transmission vulnerability may increase due to the challenges faced by those in informal settlements to physically isolate or maintain proper hand hygiene as part of an outbreak response. At the same time, the rapidly increased urban population coupled with an under-resourced health sector may put further pressure on an already stressed system. That is, there may not be sufficient health service capacity to manage an epidemic situation. For instance, during the EVD epidemic, Sierra Leone had only 13,000 community health workers – two health workers for every 10,000 people – and about two thirds of this number lacked training in Western medicine (Lahai, 2017: 18). Similarly, in Liberia, there were only 10,052 healthcare workers (mostly located in Monrovia), while many highly trained health staff such as doctors, nurses, and other health professionals fled the country for safety during the civil war period (Kieh, 2017), leaving the nation of 4.3 million people served by just fifty-one physicians (Boozary et al., 2014). Yet, despite all these significantly difficult challenges and concerns, successful outbreak responses were eventually mounted in West African urban centres in general, and in informal settlements in particular. To pursue these response strategies required an openness to innovative approaches to disease response, especially those that emphasized the care of those affected by the outbreak over simply controlling people for the sake of outbreak containment (Farmer, 2020).

EBOLA VIRUS DISEASE AND INFORMAL SETTLEMENTS: THE CASE OF WEST POINT, MONROVIA

Although the political economic history of Liberia was different from those of both Guinea and Sierra Leone, all three countries were subject to predatory capitalist practices based on the colonial extraction of natural resources and the predatory practices of capitalist agri-business (Wallace and Wallace, 2016). Even though Liberia was technically not a colonized country, because of the disproportionate historical influence of the United States in nation state formation, a de facto colonization of Liberia by the United States may be discerned. Liberia was founded by manumitted slaves, settlers who, over time, came to dominate the Indigenous population. This group of settlers, referred to as Americo-Liberians, tended to politically, economically, and culturally dominate the newly forming nation state through American-supported missions whose objectives were to "civilize and Christianize" the Indigenous population (Kieh, 2008; 2012).

The power held by Americo-Liberian elites became consolidated in the nation's capital of Monrovia and this led to further alienation and disenfranchisement of the Indigenous peoples, who remained relegated to rural areas outside the centre of political and economic power. Thus, like the people of the forest region of Guinea, those who were not Americo-Liberians were marginalized by the political and capitalist elites in the nation's capital. This led to a constellation of power in which the central government came to be largely staffed by Americo-Liberians who pursued a policy of internal colonization of the hinterland based on resource extraction. This contributed to the exclusive enrichment of the Americo-Liberian elite class over other groups in the country. In particular, this ruling class facilitated the process whereby the Liberian import/export sector came to be completely dominated by foreign firms, particularly American ones such as Firestone Rubber Company (Kieh, 2017). In 1926 this company entered into a lease agreement with the Liberian government that resulted in the leasing of a million acres of land for ninety-nine years at an incredibly low rate (Du Bois, 1933). Further, Firestone provided the Liberian government with a loan of $5 million at an exorbitant interest rate (Chalk, 1967). The terms of the loan agreement also gave Firestone complete authority over state revenues until the loan was repaid in 1952 (ibid.). The legacy of such predatory capitalist practices persists today, as do similarly skewed and exploitative concession agreements. For instance, in 2006, Mittal Steel, one of the world's largest steel companies, gained control over the mining of iron ore in Liberia through a one-sided deal (Pallister, 2006). This agreement overwhelmingly catered to the private interests of the company over the public interests of the country. The agreement with the Liberian state gave the foreign-owned steel company inequitable royalty rates; a five-year tax holiday (with an option for extension); a takeover of state assets, whereby the company would assume control of a segment of the railway to transfer iron ore; the erosion of sovereignty, as the company could pick and choose which new laws it would comply with; and a lack of mechanisms for transparency in a nation in which governance was already known to be weak and impaired by endemic corruption.

Based on this political economic trajectory, Liberia faced circumstances similar to those in Guinea and Sierra Leone, with respect to an economic reliance on export dependency and the impact of structural adjustment policies that compromised the ability of the nation state to build physical infrastructure and social welfare systems, including, most notably, publicly funded healthcare systems. As in the two other West African nation states, therefore, a climate of suspicion and distrust also took hold at the political and cultural level in Liberia; and both there and in Sierra Leone, such conditions were worsened by civil war. And again, these developments had implications for the disease response. Perhaps the most vivid example of how suspicion and distrust between government and citizens played out in Liberia during the pandemic was the case of the stand-off that occurred in the West Point informal settlement in Monrovia.

Following the ransacking of an Ebola treatment unit constructed in the West Point community, the government, without prior warning or announcement, imposed a twenty-one-day quarantine on the residents. On 20 August 2014, a military checkpoint was erected, and the informal settlement area was enclosed within barbed-wire fencing to prevent the entry and exit of people. The government insisted that the imposed quarantine was necessary to contain disease spread after that Ebola treatment unit incident. Sources who monitor the security sector, however, noted that the decision was really a politically motivated action intended to show that the government was in control of the situation (MacDougall, 2014). The residents of West Point noted that one of the reasons that served as a trigger for the ransacking of the treatment unit was a sense of betrayal felt by the people. Based on consultation and agreement with the community, the original intent of the treatment unit was to help the residents of West

Point. Suspicions arose, however, that those infected with Ebola from outside the community were being transported into the West Point facility secretly, thus increasing the potential for disease spread in the community. West Pointers felt that their settlement was being used as a sacrifice zone. Based on their unfair and marginalizing treatment by the government in the past, in the eyes of some West Point residents, there existed some grounds for their suspicion. A tense confrontation arose between police and military officials, who were keeping guard, and the residents, who increasingly felt that they were trapped in the locale while being unjustly deprived of their ability to earn a livelihood and obtain food. The stand-off intensified and eventually led to gunfire by officials that resulted in the tragic death of a small boy (Ali et al., 2022b).

As the West Point situation indicates, a lack of inclusion drove fear and insecurity in subtle ways, for example through the inciting of rumours and resistance. Rumours and resistance are, as Wilkinson and Leach (2015: 144) note in relation to the Liberian context more generally, the product of long-standing grievances with state and foreign actors who are often seen as oppressive and self-serving. For example, in the Liberian case, the political administration of President Ellen Johnson Sirleaf was repeatedly accused, and in some cases found guilty, of corruption. It was in such a political context that Ebola was viewed by some as a ruse to make money for the country's elites (ibid.).

Despite the formidable challenges faced in the West Point informal settlement, ranging from, among many other factors, overcrowding, poor infrastructure, and a climate of distrust, an effective EVD response was nevertheless mounted there. Indeed, the particular type of outbreak response pursued at West Point – known as the community-based approach – proved to be successful and the model was quickly emulated at sites across the nation. Ultimately, the adoption of the community-based approach reversed Liberia's steep epidemic trajectory several weeks before that of Guinea and Sierra Leone (Fallah et al., 2015).

Figure 4.2 The West Point informal settlement in Monrovia, Liberia
Source: S. Harris Ali

THE COMMUNITY-BASED RESPONSE TO EBOLA VIRUS DISEASE

During the earlier stages of the EVD epidemic, international and domestic responders recognized that the lack of a proper healthcare infrastructure, coupled with community resistance, meant that conventional outbreak responses based on top-down medical approaches would not be effective (Abramowitz et al., 2015). With the EVD cases continuing to rise exponentially, it was realized that new approaches needed to be considered. Community-centred strategies commonly deployed in humanitarian and development initiatives seemed to hold some promise (Abramowitz et al., 2017: 59–60). Already in certain parts of Liberia, communities themselves took the initiative to respond to the EVD threat.

After the August 2014 confrontation at the West Point informal settlement, feelings of animosity, distrust, and suspicion directed towards official government and non-governmental organization (NGO) responders were heightened and it was realized that on the basis of that experience, governments should not impose top-down directives upon residents of informal settlements (Coburn et al., 2020). With this understanding it was acknowledged by government officials that an alternative approach, such as one based on greater direct community involvement, might be warranted in West Point (Schrieber and Widner, 2017). Dr Mosoka Fallah, the head of disease surveillance in Montserrado County (where Monrovia is located), came to know of successful community-based responses in suburban locales close to Monrovia.

One successful self-initiated and self-organized community-based response was spearheaded by Jonathan Enders, a local elementary school principal, who helped organize a team of local community leaders in the suburban community of Soul Clinic in Paynesville, outside Monrovia (Schrieber and Widner, 2017). This team helped coordinate community efforts to identify actual and suspected cases of EVD and to provide food, water, and support to those quarantined. Through community monitoring and surveillance they also helped to ensure that people did not violate the quarantine orders by moving about. Fallah recruited the assistance of Enders to establish a similar community-based initiative in the West Point informal settlement. The first step was the holding of an initial round of open town-hall meetings with groups of West Point leaders on 17 September 2014. From here a division of labour was established and different activities related to the response were allocated to members of the West Point community. The response activities that were assigned to community members included those pertaining to active case investigation; contact tracing; day-to-day monitoring of the sick, deceased, and quarantined; and visiting individuals. Neighbourhood taskforces were constituted, and bylaws were implemented to restrict movement, with fines imposed on those who violated these restrictions, while local groups carried out "house-to-house" checks and surveillance to identify new cases and contacts.

The results of adopting these community-based measures in West Point were nothing short of astounding. Within a day, the team of community-based responders in West Point had identified forty-two people with Ebola-like symptoms and arranged transport for them to treatment units, while uncovering thirty-four suspected Ebola deaths and a number of secret burials that had not been reported to the authorities through the existing government-led contact-tracing system (Fallah et al., 2015).[2] One of the keys to the success of the community-based response was that it addressed issues related to both control and care. The control dimension refers to community surveillance and monitoring efforts (including active case investigation and contact tracing), while the care dimension pertains to the establishment of a community infrastructure to provide food, water, and information for those quarantined. Variations on the Liberian

Figure 4.3 Certificate awarded to a member of an informal settlement community for his participation in the community-based response near Freetown, Sierra Leone
Source: S. Harris Ali

community-based response model were independently adopted in Guinea and Sierra Leone, but the core aspects of the response with respect to community engagement remained the same.

CONCLUSION

The case of EVD spread in West Africa reveals how changes in the natural environment that stem from (post)colonial and predatory capitalist practices have contributed to disease emergence in regions subjected to processes of extended urbanization, such as the development of forest edge areas and the proliferation and expansion of informal settlements in urban peripheries. Thus we see, for example, the amplification of the potential spread of zoonoses from animals to humans through increasing human encroachment on nature, resulting from the destruction of natural habitats and biodiversity. In this light, the landscape political ecology framework introduced in chapter 2 is useful for illustrating the landscape transformations and socio-ecological changes that can result in heightened vulnerability to infectious disease outbreaks.

The EVD case discussed here also reveals how the response to infectious disease may be hindered by the lack of effective governance and trust found in West Africa. Notably, this includes the emergence of unstable and ineffectual governments and a public health system decimated by structural adjustment policies that have contributed to a setting where suspicion and distrust prevailed. Further, the historical legacy of the postcolonial city has rendered a setting in which there was little to no investment in networked infrastructure for such essential services as sewage treatment, water provision, and electricity, which further exacerbated the challenges faced in the response within informal settlement areas in particular. Despite the formidable challenges, however, an effective EVD response was mounted in West Africa based on the mobilization of community members.

If SARS was an initial illustration of how quickly disease spread in the urban age could occur in some of the most technically advanced and wealthiest cities in the world, the spread of EVD in West Africa reveals how infectious disease spread was equally swift in some of the world's poorest cities. The next chapter will now turn to the COVID-19 pandemic, where the rapid spread of disease occurred in both the wealthiest and the poorest cities of the world. The chapter will reveal how the very socio-ecological changes brought on by urbanization resulted in the potential for the virus to spread well beyond the range of places affected by Ebola.

5 | COVID-19 and Extended Urbanization

Following our theoretical proposition in chapter 2, in this chapter we examine how the changing nature of urbanization has influenced the way the COVID-19 pandemic unfolded throughout the world. In previous chapters we have shown how both the SARS and Ebola outbreaks highlighted new aspects of global urbanization patterns manifesting at regional levels. SARS cast a light on the new connectivity of global financial centres that came to prominence in the final decades of the twentieth century, while the 2014/15 epidemic of Ebola virus disease in West Africa could be linked to the rapid and comprehensive urbanization trends observed on that continent. In this chapter, we pursue the idea that COVID-19 marked the emergence of a completely urbanized planet. We also note that to a large degree, COVID-19 was a disease of extended urbanization. Following Biglieri et al. (2022: 1), we put forward the idea that "where the virus is concentrated, you find the peripheral, in the city and in society."

We focus particularly on Toronto and its suburbs as illustrative cases, with the understanding that the experiences here will be somewhat generalizable to other metropolitan centres and their associated peripheries. In this sense, COVID-19 is an interrupted sequel to the story of SARS, which, as we have argued in chapter 3, was a suburban disease situated within a global city network. At the same time, the much larger scale and impact of the COVID-19 pandemic revealed other more notable aspects of how governance, socio-demographics, and infrastructure influenced disease spread – in ways that were not as apparent during the SARS experience. Notably, the COVID-19 experience in Toronto revealed how intertwined these three sets of factors actually are, and how their combined influence significantly impacted the microbial traffic of SARS-CoV-2 (SARS corona virus 2) – the virus that causes COVID-19. Thus, for instance, in this chapter we will explore how urban public health governance of COVID-19, exercised through the adoption and implementation of outbreak control measures, was unevenly applied across the city, and how this led to particular challenges for certain groups due to differential risks in viral exposure as well as access to appropriate levels of care. In this light, we will also consider how the uneven consequences of COVID-19 spread were exacerbated by existing inequalities based on socio-demographic factors such as race/ethnicity, the social class standing of certain neighbourhoods, and the infrastructure features associated with these. In reference to infrastructure considerations, this includes, for instance, the state of the housing stock (for example, differences between well-maintained condominium towers, dilapidated apartment complexes, and large multigenerational houses) and the location and types of industry present (for example, the presence of large warehouse and distribution centres supported by multi-lane highways, a well-developed trucking industry, and an international airport).

Our discussion begins with a brief overview of the unfolding COVID-19 pandemic to date. We then move to a discussion of certain aspects of the microbial traffic of SARS-CoV-2, including a consideration of the landscape political ecologies that influenced the path of this virus as it traversed the globe. Next, we consider the important role that inequality played in shaping how COVID-19 spread in cities. In particular, we focus first on how racialized minorities, and especially members of the Black community, living in the suburbs situated *within* the borders of Toronto but *outside* the gentrified city core, were impacted far differently from those residing in the neighbourhoods closer to the city centre. We then extend the analysis to consider how those living in the suburban cities just *west of the borders of Toronto* experienced an even greater COVID-19 burden. We conclude by noting how the changing nature of urbanization and the socio-spatial effects generated by these changes have influenced the manner in which the pandemic unfolded in cities.

BACKGROUND: THE COVID-19 PANDEMIC

The earliest identified cases of infection from SARS-CoV-2 occurred in late December 2019 in Wuhan, China, a city of more than 11 million people. Within the next month, thousands of new cases were reported in China, prompting the WHO to issue an official declaration of a "public health emergency of international concern" on 30 January 2021 (Taylor, 2021). By the third week of February, significant surges of COVID-19 were experienced in Italy and Iran, and within the subsequent month, COVID-19 spread to nearly all the countries of the world. Over March 2020, the gravity of the situation was being shockingly realized in the United States, which by this time led the world with 81,321 confirmed infections and more than 1,000 deaths. During this month, nations across the globe introduced various travel bans, limitations to social gatherings, complete lockdowns, and curfews (Taylor, 2021).

After the pandemic had first struck in the peripheries of larger urban centres, for example in the Lombardy region around Italy's financial centre of Milan, by May 2020 it was apparent that the greatest surge of COVID-19 cases appeared to be occurring in the densely populated areas of relatively affluent countries located in regions of temperate climate (Van Damme et al., 2020). Several world leaders, including those of Britain, the United States, Brazil, and Poland, became infected. Cases continued to escalate and by August 2020, global virus deaths surpassed 800,000. By September, large numbers of cases arose in India and Brazil, with each of these nations recording more than 4 million, second only to the United States, and pushing the global death rate to 1 million – only ten months from the start of the pandemic (Taylor, 2021). In November 2020 a ray of hope emerged as several promising vaccines were in the stages of final development, with the UK government giving emergency authorization for the Pfizer COVID-19 vaccine to be administered to the British public within the first week of December. Mass inoculations of Pfizer and other vaccines began in North America soon thereafter. The number of COVID deaths continued to climb, however, and by 17 April 2021, it surpassed 3.1 million worldwide (CNN Editorial Research Team, 2022).

Although COVID-19 is from the same coronavirus family as SARS, the two diseases diverge in their biological and clinical characteristics, which helps account for the differences in their respective patterns of spread. As we have seen, the promulgation of SARS through the global city networks occurred mostly through nosocomial transmission with some community spread, while COVID-19 has spread to all areas of the world with significant transmission through both healthcare and institutional settings as well as the community. Another key difference is that a significant proportion of COVID-19 transmission may have involved people with mild or no symptoms who nevertheless were able to inadvertently shed the virus to others (MacIntyre, 2020). By the time people developed symptoms that become severe enough to require medical attention, up to five days might have elapsed from the time they were infected. The clinical implication was that health authorities were not able to observe the presentation of symptoms to identify newly active cases, thus increasing the chance of undetected community transmission (ibid.). Further contributing to enhanced community transmission was the possibility of silent transmission through children, who were more likely be asymptomatic, as well as weak health systems and poor diagnostic capabilities within certain countries (ibid.).

From the beginning of the pandemic, almost all jurisdictions around the world issued public health intervention directives to properly wash hands, physically distance, and – after much confusion and controversy – wear masks, in conjunction with the deployment of large-scale testing and quarantine measures. Collectively, these measures were meant to slow down the rate of COVID-19 spread over time, or to "flatten the curve." That is, in aiming to reduce overall infections through these measures, the objective was to keep the number of COVID-19 cases below the threshold number that the healthcare system could manage.

During SARS in 2003, most attention was focused on international borders including airports as possible sites of infection from abroad, and on spread through international travellers and their contacts at hospitals due to the high number of nosocomial infections. It was significant that measures to curb the spread of COVID-19 were almost entirely focused on the management of urban public space: stay-at-home orders, curfews, lockdowns, quarantines, limiting the number of patrons in stores and restaurants, and social distancing. These measures dramatically and swiftly changed the face and rhythm of most cities around the world. The city itself became the arena in which the outbreak was meant to be managed. Still, although the strategy of "flattening-the-curve" was in theory effective, it glossed over the fact that the ability of specific locations to adopt practices that would help "flatten the curve" varied. While the multifarious nature of urban life was recognized as the potential heart of the pandemic spread, the creative variety of this nature was rarely enlisted to battle the virus in the community. Instead, universalist strategies of urban COVID-19 responses carried the day in the first few weeks, as people around the world learned to provision their locked-down households with food and other necessities and dealt with the simultaneous challenges of schooling children and working from home (where possible), while avoiding contact with other people, even close friends and family. As we shall discuss, the ability to "flatten the curve" varied not only between nations or cities, but between different communities or neighbourhoods within cities: the particular constellation of work and family-related structural circumstances faced by those residing and working in certain neighbourhoods is an important yet neglected consideration in pandemic response. Notably, these circumstances profoundly affected people's ability to physically and socially distance, or undergo quarantine. As a result, a close association could be found between exposure to COVID-19 and the neighbourhood in which one resided and/or worked.

A PANDEMIC TAKES ITS COURSE

In February 2020, due to strict enforcement of public health measures in China, the disease spread seemed to be under control in that country, but disease spread to different sites across the world continued uninterrupted. Evidence of such spread could be seen in outbreaks arising on cruise ships docked in Japan, Korea, Italy, and Iran as well as in closed settings such as long-term care facilities, prisons, and hospitals. Taken together, this was indicative of the global reach of the virus (MacIntyre, 2020). Van Damme et al. (2020: 3) contend that the global spread of COVID-19 was largely the result of international travellers seeding outbreaks first in large urban centres. Further, it was found that, oftentimes, it was the more affluent groups in urban centres that were first afflicted, and from there the virus spread at variable speeds to other population groups. For instance, some of the earliest identified COVID-19 cases occurred in northern Italy in places such as Codogno in the Lombardy region (one of the most prosperous and densest regions in Europe) and the cosmopolitan city of Milan (Goumenou et al., 2020). Italy has the population with the highest average age in Europe and this may have been reflected in the COVID-19 infection rate, as the highest proportion of those affected were the frail elderly in hospitals and retirement homes where adequate capacity to deal with a surge of illnesses was lacking due to underfunding (Rudan, 2020). Indeed, in the crosshairs of "long-term trends and short-term failures," the healthcare system in the Milan region, for instance, was subject to the devolution of responsibilities while simultaneously facing cuts in funding (Biglieri et al., 2022). Perhaps further intensifying the disease spread was the possibility that younger infected individuals from the region may have inadvertently spread the disease to France, Switzerland, and Austria through travel to European ski resorts. Such resorts were in fact later identified as superspreader venues in late February and early March 2020 (ibid.). In considering the Italian disease response, Rudan (2020) notes that the exclusive focus of government surveillance was on those arriving in Italy from Asia, rather than on the monitoring of those Italian nationals returning from ski trips in other European countries. It would, however, be mistaken to think of COVID-19 as an exclusive disease of the affluent that was restricted to international jet-setters, cruise-ship passengers, and alpine skiers (Gebrekidan et al., 2020).

Nevertheless, similar to the 2003 spread of SARS among the relatively affluent via travel through the global cities network, the initial "seed" for the spread of COVID-19 may have occurred through international travellers. Yet the geopolitical tectonic shifts during the first two decades of the twenty-first century were dramatic and reflected a changing planetary urban geography characterized by intense processes of urban concentration and extension, fuelled by dramatic demographic shifts, infrastructural change, and the restructuring of governance and politics at different scales. We could argue, for example, that the 2003 SARS outbreak which affected eastern Asia and Canada exposed the *exoskeleton* of the globalized economy predicated upon the global city system through which the disease spread. As discussed in chapter 3, the international control centres of Hong Kong, Singapore, and Toronto stood out as hubs in the network of that disease spread. At the time, the diffusion of the disease in this manner sent a poignant warning signal around the world that there could unfold a swift and devastating epidemic event that could threaten urban life across several continents in quick succession. Globalization as an economic and cultural phenomenon at the time of SARS was still a spectre that loomed but not an experienced reality.

Things changed dramatically in only fifteen years. As mentioned above, SARS-CoV-2 raced around the world in early 2020 and had claimed 5 million lives at the time of this writing, despite unprecedented global health measures based on lockdowns, mobility restrictions, and social distancing, as well as the unprecedented massive vaccination campaigns (at least in the Global North) that began less than a year after the World Health Organization had declared the disease a pandemic. COVID-19 exposed the *flesh and bones* of a global capitalist system that was now a more intensively and extensively developed form of globalized capitalism than that which existed when SARS traversed the world a little more than a decade before. Everything was now an "innerland" of capitalism, not just a "hinterland." This was perhaps most obvious in China itself, as became apparent in this observation by a journalist early in the pandemic: "Wuhan [the outbreak's original epicentre] is one of the 'newly discovered' *innerlands* of the global production chain as the Chinese coasts have become more expensive" (Zairong, 2020, emphasis added). The expansion of capitalist reach in urban space today was also accompanied by the continued annihilation of space through time due to rapidly accelerated mobility patterns. Today, our means of transportation have gathered speed, and the routes of connectivity have been shortened. At the time of SARS in 2003 the global airline industry transported just under 2 billion annual passengers. When SARS-COV-2 began its spread, that number had risen to 4.7 billion.[1]

Although these structural changes in global capitalism occurred at the planetary level, they had significant ramifications at the level of the urban region. Thus, for instance, in relation to disease spread, once the virus entered a city, it was able to spread through its capillary systems from the most mobile and often wealthy demographic groups to affect anyone – particularly, as we will discuss later, the most socially marginalized. The interconnection between disease spread and the level of affluence associated with place can perhaps be most vividly illustrated by considering the direction of disease spread of two very different diseases within the same geographic areas at different moments in time, namely Ebola and COVID-19 in West Africa. Ebola virus disease (EVD) initially spread from rural outer-lying regions and villages into informal settlements in urban centres, as people moved from the rural to urban sites to visit and stay with relatives for social and familial reasons (including for funerals and healthcare purposes), or relocated temporarily or permanently for the purposes of finding seasonal employment. From here, EVD spread amongst residents of informal settlements, some of whom worked as drivers, domestics, nannies, cooks, gardeners, and security personnel for those residing in the more affluent areas of the cities (Fallah et al., 2022: 15). Consequently, EVD spread to those in the more affluent neighbour-hoods as employers of residents from the informal settlements became infected. In contrast, the spread of COVID-19 in Monrovia took place in the reverse direction. Affluent international travellers from West Africa would travel for purposes of business, conferences, education, etc. and bring COVID-19 back with them, thereby infecting not only other family members, but also those employed in their house-holds. These workers would then bring the virus back to overcrowded quarters in informal settlements. In many cases, a contributing factor to disease spread in this manner involved the fact that some workers served as de facto caregivers for their stricken employers and their family members. From the informal settlements in Africa and the Indian subcontinent, COVID-19 spread to the more rural locations at a slower and less intense pace, contributing to a time lag before these areas of the world experienced an exponential rise in cases (Van Damme et al., 2020).

COVID-19 AND URBAN INEQUALITY

The various urban geographies and regional socio-economic aspects of the COVID-19 pandemic have been subject to numerous scholarly and policy publications (Andrews et al., 2021; Doucet et al., 2021; Shin et al., 2022). The differential impact of COVID-19 reflects the pre-pandemic patterns of urban social inequality, and as such, we can analyse the impact through the lens of conventional sociological and demographic variables that inform marginalization within and between societies. These include variables such as social class and income, race/ethnicity, neighbourhood profile, and gender. These demographic variables, in turn, are reflected in infrastructural mobility patterns (Adey et al., 2021; Sheller, 2018) and differential access to governance and decision-making powers (Allahwala and Keil, 2021). The effect of these variables on vulnerability to COVID-19 infection, the ability to recover once inflicted, and their relationship to mobility and power is the subject of this section. In particular, we focus on how certain racialized and economically impoverished groups that have long been subject to neglect and inaction were at an elevated risk of COVID-19 infections. For example, a study conducted early on in the pandemic by the local public health agency in Toronto found that lower-income people and newcomers were at higher risk of COVID-19 infections.

Peripheries and margins

COVID-19 has to be analytically and, as argued previously, "heuristically" repositioned at the social, institutional, and spatial periphery of urban society (Keil et al., 2022). Often, the spatial periphery has been the location where one finds the "urban margins," meaning "groups forced to the economic, cultural, and political edges of urban society, located there because of the inequalities of the urban world they live in, not because of their own actions" (Lancione and McFarlane, 2016: 2405). For example, "[t]here have been decades of underinvestment in social, health, housing and transportation infrastructures in the peripheries of Canadian cities like Toronto, and the peripheries are experiencing exponential growth, as well as being more hyper-diverse and disadvantaged than ever before" (Biglieri et al., 2020: 2). But the periphery is not just an analytical category, it is also where the most vulnerable people often live and work. When COVID-19 arrived in urban regions around the world, it mattered where in the city you lived. Intersectionalities of racialization, poverty, and other forms of marginalization within certain parts of the urban region created a mix of heightened risk and vulnerability. That mix is especially observable in Toronto's "inner suburban" northwest. It is home to large numbers of racialized communities, and a place of socio-economic distress.

The question of intra-urban differentiation is also linked to the governance of real and imagined differences between the city and the countryside. After the first and second waves of COVID-19 in 2020, municipal and regional jurisdictions in Ontario, Canada, experienced "reopening" in rather different ways, with rural communities opening up first, while the three most urbanized regions – Ottawa, Peel, and Toronto – had to wait the longest to have their bars, restaurants, and fitness studios reopened. The notable exceptions here were those agricultural areas in Canada where foreign migrant labourers, working and housed in criminally unsanitary conditions, fell ill and died from COVID-19.

Relational and comparative aspects of different places also matter when discussing urban peripheries. Patrick Brown, mayor of Brampton, a suburban city of 600,000 northwest of Toronto, bemoaned the way "a pandemic like this lays bare the socioeconomic inequalities" across locales. Brown noted that the city received significantly less healthcare funding and support than comparable cities: fewer hospital beds, fewer testing centres, fewer tests, and longer waiting times are some of the metrics of inequities the city suffered (CBC, 2020). The mayor further noted, on a regional morning radio show on 14 September 2020, that Brampton was vulnerable due to a number of factors, such as the dependence of many residents on jobs at the nearby international airport, the particular exposure of workers in the city's large resident trucking industry, the fact that its large immigrant population was connected through international flights to places far away, and the preponderance of multigenerational households in immigrant communities. Moreover, outbreaks at workplaces in that year – a chicken processing plant in Brampton in May, and an undisclosed factory in the neighbouring city of Mississauga in September – demonstrated another aspect of vulnerability that the suburban community had been experiencing (Cribb, 2020). Representatives of affected communities in Brampton, however, rejected the focus on alleged cultural characteristics such as multigenerational living and diaspora travel as misguiding, distracting, and racist. As such, they urged policy-makers to instead consider and emphasize how the conditions under which members of their communities lived and worked were impacted by structural underfunding and the lack of necessary services (Nasser, 2020a).

COVID-19 and race/ethnicity in the city

Who was affected by COVID-19, who was counted, and how the counted were governed all exposed areas of dramatic disconnect in the pandemic response in many cities. In a news report by the Canadian Broadcasting Corporation (CBC) at the outset of the pandemic, journalist Shanifa Nasser noted that even though Black residents constituted 30 per cent of the population of Chicago, from the beginning of the pandemic to April 2020 they made up more than 70 per cent of the COVID-19 deaths. In the same report, a Toronto-based paediatric infectious disease specialist noted that during the

H1N1 (swine flu) pandemic in 2009, Indigenous people in Canada were six-and-a-half times more likely to require intensive care (Nasser, 2020b). As the pandemic unfolded in Toronto, it was becoming increasingly evident that health inequities were leading to greater COVID-19 illnesses and deaths among people of colour. With this awareness, lobbying efforts were made by local public health officials to officially adopt strategies to track racial data related to COVID-19 infections. These recommendations by Toronto Public Health were, however, met with resistance at the provincial and federal levels. Thus, in responding to the request by Toronto Public Health, the province's chief medical officer of health replied that the groups identified as most at risk of COVID-19 infection were the elderly, people with underlying conditions, and those with compromised immune systems, and for those reasons race or ethnic background would not factor into provincial considerations regarding disease tracking (Nasser, 2020b). At the same time, at the federal level, the Public Health Agency of Canada noted that they were not planning to consider more social determinants of health factors – such as education and income – as risk factors for COVID-19 data collection. Healthcare advocates and professionals were dismayed by this response by higher levels of government because it did not acknowledge the reality of existing health disparities. According to these critics, the absence of such considerations meant that it was not possible to fully understand the impacts of COVID-19 in vulnerable communities, which in turn meant more effective strategies to support such communities could not be developed in a focused way.

It was recognized by Toronto Public Health (n.d.) that racialized and low-income groups were more susceptible to COVID-19 infection for a host of reasons related to pre-existing health, social, and economic disparities. These disparities were deepened by the pandemic and included systemic racism and other discrimination that created unfair barriers to opportunity, health and well-being, safety, fair treatment, and resources for some groups of people. Such factors resulted in inequitable access to healthcare and social services, as well as in living and working conditions that put some people at higher risk of COVID-19 exposure. These influences were particularly evident in relation to essential workers, many of whom were not able to work from home, had little to no job security, had few or no paid sick days, were dependent upon commuting on crowded public transportation, and had no option except to live in conditions of crowded housing. Based on the first-hand awareness of the impacts of these factors on COVID-19 spread, and despite a lack of buy-in from other levels of government, Toronto Public Health developed their own system for collecting race- and income-based data. Toronto became the first major Canadian city to release data on COVID-19 infection rates and per capita testing rates by neighbourhood (which served as a proxy for socio-demographic differentiation). A report of their findings covering the period from 20 May to 16 July 2020 was released on 30 July 2020 (Toronto Public Health, 2020) and confirmed that:

- 83 per cent of people with reported COVID-19 infection identified with a racialized group,
- 51 per cent of reported cases in Toronto were living in households that could be considered lower-income, and
- 27 per cent of COVID-19 cases were among individuals who live in households with five or more people.

Acting on these findings, the City of Toronto conducted a series of consultations with affected community groups and implemented targeted programmes designed to help reduce virus spread and prevent further transmission. This included health promotion messages geared to specific groups, and the introduction of enhanced testing facilities such as pop-up and mobile clinics in those locales vulnerable to disease spread – first for COVID-19 testing, then later to administer vaccines.

The study initiated by Toronto Public Health also led to other strategies and follow-up studies to address health inequities amongst the Black community during the pandemic. For instance, data collected in late 2020 revealed that Black people of African and Caribbean descent represented 26 per cent of COVID-19 cases in Toronto, despite the fact that this group comprised only 9 per cent of the city's population (Wilson, 2021). At the same time, about one third of Canadians who expressed COVID-19 vaccine hesitancy – a delay in acceptance or refusal to take a vaccine despite access and availability – were Black. In the face of mounting evidence from Toronto Public Health, the Public Health Agency of Canada (PHAC) could no longer neglect the issue of the disproportionate impact of COVID-19 on racialized communities, and released its own findings based on data collected from across the nation (PHAC, 2021). These findings generally corroborated what was found by Toronto Public Health. For instance, based on surveillance data from Toronto and Ottawa, PHAC found that COVID-19 cases were 1.5 to 5 times higher among racialized populations than non-racialized populations in these two cities. Further, data from First Nations people living on reserves found infection there to be 69 per cent higher than that found in the general population. PHAC noted that these trends were not unique to Canada, as evidence from other high-income countries such as the UK and the US revealed similar trends amongst racialized communities. As the evidence mounted, the mayor of Toronto announced the development of a Black Community COVID-19 Response Plan that was to be supported by a fund of $6.8 million. The objectives of the plan were to support community health agencies in predominantly Black communities in various ways, such as developing methods of community outreach to address distrust and combat social media misinformation and vaccine hesitancy, and later enhancing vaccine rollout in racialized communities (Kennedy, 2021).

COVID-19 AND SOCIO-SPATIAL EFFECTS

As we saw with the spread of SARS in 2003 in Toronto, the virus impacted different neighbourhoods in different ways. With reference to COVID-19 spread, this was true not only with respect to inner suburban neighbourhoods but also in relation to the higher infection rates evident in the outer suburbs. Although much of our focus in this section is on the City of Toronto, in some significant ways Toronto represents a microcosm of what was happening in cities around the world: what was common to all cities (within both the Global North and South) was that marginalization of groups within the urban population was associated with differential vulnerability to COVID-19 (Bader et al., 2021; Mariette and Pitti, 2021; Mullis, 2021).

Indications from around the world of the differential vulnerability to COVID-19 infection for the marginalized were already apparent during the early stages of the pandemic, and revealed the intricate relationship of demography and mobility. For instance, of the five boroughs of New York City, the highest rates of COVID-19 hospitalizations and deaths occurred in the poorest, the Bronx, which was also home to the highest proportion of racialized minorities (Wadhera et al., 2020). Another indication was found during the early days of the pandemic in London. During this period, although the number of bus passengers fell dramatically, the ridership decline on the Tube (subway) was almost twice as great (BBC, 2020). Since those who use the Tube tend to be typically wealthier, suburban commuters, their comparative absence from the Tube system relative to the bus system indicated that they were in a better position to reduce their risk and vulnerability to COVID-19 exposure by either working from their suburban homes or walking or cycling to work from their gentrified downtown locations. Thus, as Reuschke and Felstead (2020) observe, those in inner-city neighbourhoods with high proportions of professional workers, as well as in suburban areas with large properties and high proportions of homeowners, have a privileged pre-pandemic socio-economic profile (Moos and Skaburskis, 2007). This differential pattern in relation to the risk of COVID-19 exposure between the non-marginalized and the marginalized was quite evident in the case of Toronto.

If one compares the map of COVID-19 infection rates within Toronto with an income map of the city, it is impossible not to notice how closely the two align. Those neighbourhoods most affected by COVID-19 generally tended to cluster in the northwest and northeast shoulders of the city, whereas the neighbourhoods closer to the downtown core were the least affected. The most affected areas were home to higher proportions of low-income "essential" workers living in crowded multi-unit residential complexes, whereas the most prosperous neighbourhoods of the city were the least impacted by COVID-19 infections (Gee, 2020; Seoni, 2020). Highlighting again the imbrications of demographic and mobility dimensions, the hardest-hit neighbourhoods were also the ones with the busiest public transit use; thus, for instance, one of the neighbourhoods with the highest COVID-19 rates – the northwest outskirts community of Weston-Mount Dennis – was host to an area with one of Toronto's busiest bus lines, as many relied on buses to travel for their work in factories, grocery stores, and nursing homes.

In discussions of the relationship between neighbourhood type and COVID-19 spread, density is often proffered as an important explanatory variable. Although it does play a role in the differential spread of COVID-19, it is not density in and of itself that explains the difference. Rather, explanations must take into consideration the social and economic context to get a true account. The question of density and crowding cannot be separated from issues of access and availability of institutions and the more or less reasonable existence of territorial boundaries in an allegedly boundaryless world. The oscillation between hope and panic related to urban densities has been erratic and intense during the COVID-19 pandemic (Keil, 2020b; Boterman, 2020; 2022;

Moos et al., 2020). One comprehensive report concluded in October 2020 that the public health emergency did not produce, but rather "amplified," two density-related urban problems: "First, higher density urban environments function best if they are connected with appropriate open space, which includes things like courtyards, balconies, rooftop gardens, as well as surrounding public green spaces such as parks. Second, higher density built form is prone to overcrowding when housing affordability is an issue" (Moos et al., 2020: 11). For instance, two neighbourhoods may have equally high density, which according to a mathematically defined, narrow, and decontextualized view would put both at equal risk of infection. This is because an equally high number of people per unit area in both neighbourhoods increases the chance of exposure in both equally. However, when one considers other more context-sensitive factors, a different picture emerges. For instance, the Thorncliffe Park and Yonge/Eglington neighbourhoods in Toronto both host complexes of apartment building towers and have similar densities of close to 7,000 people per square kilometre.[2] Yet, despite the similarities in density, the neighbourhood characteristics are quite different in terms of income, with the median household income in Thorncliffe Park being $46,595, in contrast to Yonge/Eglington with a median household income of $80,896. The race/ethnicity composition of the two communities is also markedly different. Thorncliffe Park consists of 67 per cent newcomers, including 19 per cent recent newcomers and a visible minority component of 71 per cent, whereas Yonge/Eglington consists of 27 per cent newcomers, including 5 per cent recent newcomers and a visible minority component of 26 per cent. And more dramatically and to the point, as of 2 February 2022, the COVID-19 infection rates were strikingly different, with a rate of 13,331 per 100,000 people in Thorncliffe Park compared to 5,890 per 100,000 people in Yonge/Eglington.[3]

It should be noted that in the case of Thorncliffe Park, which has a much higher proportion of newcomers, many of these are employed as "essential workers." Many of the ageing apartment buildings in which Thorncliffe Park residents live have fifteen to twenty-five floors, but usually only two working elevators. Consequently, while in more middle-class communities, work was done from home, 2,000 to 3,000 people used the elevators during peak periods in this working-class community as essential workers continued to travel to their workplaces daily – thereby increasing their risk of COVID-19 exposure. It is not surprising to find, therefore, that this neighbourhood was one of the hardest-hit areas during the pandemic (see figure 5.1).

The relationship between race and COVID-19 mirrors the association between income and the disease. For example, two areas that

Figure 5.1 Thorncliffe Park neighbourhood in Toronto
Source: S. Harris Ali

have higher proportions of Black residents, namely Weston (33 per cent) and Mount Dennis (32 per cent), as of 30 May 2020 had COVID-19 rates of 1,729 and 1,530 per 100,000 respectively. This stands in stark contrast to those areas that have the lowest percentage of Black residents, such as The Beaches (2 per cent) and Lawrence Park North (1 per cent), which have COVID-19 infection rates of 74 and 116 per 100,000 respectively. A vast differential in COVID-19 infections clearly exists and is even more pronounced when one takes into account visible minority status instead of Black status exclusively. Thus we see, for instance, that York University Heights, an area where 69 per cent of residents identify as belonging to a visible minority, has twenty times the rate of infection found in The Beaches neighbourhood (Amin and Bond, 2020).

The unequally patterned distribution of COVID-19 impacts is not only demonstrated in relation to differential infection rates but also – unsurprisingly – found in relation to differential vaccination rates. Studies in the US have noted that those in under-served neighbourhoods face numerous obstacles in accessing vaccines, such as taking hours to navigate registration phone lines and websites (if they even have access to the Internet), the lack of transportation or the ability to take time away from work to get to appointments, and the prevalence of vaccine hesitancy amongst some groups. The effects of these barriers were evident in cities throughout North America. For example, during the first weeks of the vaccine rollout in Philadelphia – a city whose population is 44 per cent Black – only 12 per cent of those vaccinated were Black (Goodnough and Hoffman, 2021). In relation to receiving vaccination, another manifestation of the divide between the marginalized and the non-marginalized has also become apparent. Health officials in numerous cities have reported that people from wealthier, largely white neighbourhoods have been flooding the computerized vaccine appointment systems and monopolizing a disproportionate share of the limited vaccine supply – a practice that reflects the hoarding of vaccines by the Global North to the detriment of the Global South (Fallah and Ali, 2022). Local public health units, including Toronto Public Health, made efforts to address these developments by setting up mobile units in under-serviced areas of Toronto (Grant, 2020), while in Baltimore, local public health officials went door to door in housing complexes in which the elderly resided to offer the vaccine (Goodnough and Hoffman, 2021). Turning our attention now to the suburban municipalities that are just adjacent to Toronto, we see an even more pronounced pattern of differential impacts.

COVID IN THE OUTER SUBURBS

As of September 2020, the region of Peel, located to the west of the City of Toronto (see figure 5.3), had the highest rate of COVID-19 infections in the province of Ontario, surpassing both Toronto and Ottawa. The three together were the hardest-hit areas in the province (Nasser,

Figure 5.2 COVID-19 mobile vaccination clinic stationed at a strip mall parking lot in Mississauga (Peel Region)
Source: S. Harris Ali

2020a). Peel Region consists of the three suburban municipalities of Caledon, Brampton, and Mississauga. These three municipalities make up less than 10 per cent of the province's population but accounted for 22 per cent of all cases in the province at the time (ibid.). Over the last few decades, the three municipalities of Peel have experienced rapid growth in manufacturing, warehousing, and shipping operations. During the same period, Peel Region (figure 5.3) became home to a sizeable minority of Canadians from South Asian backgrounds who found employment in such facilities. Notably, during the COVID-19 pandemic it was this group that was disproportionately impacted, as 45 per cent of cases in Peel were recorded in the South Asian Canadian community, even though they comprised only 32 per cent of Peel's population (Grant, K., 2020). In particular, in November 2020, one community situated in the northeast corner of Brampton, referred to by its postal code designation of L6P, had a COVID-19 test positivity rate of 19 per cent – a rate that exceeded those of all neighbourhoods in the Greater Toronto area and vicinity (Grant, K., 2020).

According to census data, 89 per cent of the residents in L6P are racialized, with 66 per cent of these identifying as South Asian (Bascaramurty and Bhatt, 2021). The median household income of $102,070 is 45 per cent higher than the national average, but this was because the figure represented the combined income of several family members. If this figure is disaggregated, the individual income is just $26,139. As indicated by the household income figure, many households in this area consisted of individuals from multiple generations living within the same house. Census data confirmed this, indicating that 49 per cent of homes were occupied by five or more people, a housing density that is greater than that of cities like Toronto and Ottawa (Grant, K., 2020). Further, the type of household arrangement found in Peel accounted for over 40 per cent of the COVID-19 cases during the first two weeks of November 2020. Again, though, it is not density alone that accounted for the high case count. Rather, it

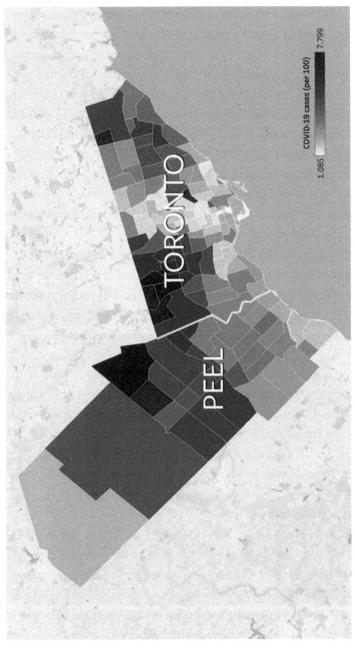

Figure 5.3 Cumulative COVID cases per 100 individuals in Toronto and the Region of Peel (up to 12 April 2021)

Source: The Local (https://thelocal.to/you-cant-stop-the-spread-of-the-virus-if-you-dont-stop-it-in-peel/)

was the relationship between the type of work pursued by family members that was critical to consider, especially in terms of people not having the means to self-isolate while at the same time working in certain types of jobs where the risk of exposure to the virus was higher. Specifically, these circumstances increased the opportunistic chance for COVID-19 spread because many of those in Peel were essential workers who needed to continue their work, often in warehouse and retail settings where operations were run in ways that increased the chance of exposure. Once exposed, essential workers inadvertently brought the virus back to their household, where other family members could become infected. In going to their own jobs, these other infected family members could then spread the virus to their respective workplaces (again, often in warehouse settings).[4]

As Bascaramurty and Bhatt (2021) observe, those in the L6P area of Brampton did not live in the kind of clustered, ageing high-rises that dominated many other neighbourhoods inhabited by essential workers (such as Thorncliffe Park). Rather, the housing in the L6P area consisted of a suburban patchwork of brick-clad townhouses, single-family dwellings with double garages, and large mansions on two-acre plots (see figure 5.4).

This census tract is in fact one of the fastest-growing parts of the country and is a prime case of the "suburban financial nexus" that has now become the economic core of the Canadian urban model (Keil and Üçoğlu, 2021: 110). Census data for L6P reveals a dense population of essential workers, with 22 per cent working in manufacturing and 16 per cent in retail (Grant, K., 2020). The area also consists of residents with some of the lowest education levels, as 60 per cent of the residents did not attend post-secondary colleges or universities. During the early stages of the pandemic, residents of Peel in general, and the L6P region in particular, were impacted by a number of large outbreaks in workplaces in the region. According to Peel Public Health, of the 137 workplace outbreaks that had

Figure 5.4 The L6P postal code area in Brampton, outside Toronto
Source: S. Harris Ali

unfolded in Peel Region by November 2020, one third occurred in warehouse settings, 14 per cent in retail settings, and 11 per cent in food processing facilities (Thompson, 2020). Peel Region over the last two decades has experienced strong growth in the number of manufacturing, warehousing, and goods-movement-related businesses that located there (Saiyed et al., 2012). This occurred for a number of reasons, including proximity to multimodal transportation networks required for the movement of goods. Thus, Peel Region is host to a dense network of multi-lane ("400 series") highways connected to the Greater Toronto Area (GTA); Canada's largest airport; and mainline tracks for Canada's two major railroads. Together, these serve to connect Peel Region to major North American and world markets in such a way that only a few days' travel time is needed to make these connections (Keil and Üçoğlu, 2021: 107). As a result of this infrastructure, freight transport and warehousing account for 11 per cent of Peel's employment (about twice the share of other regions in the GTA), and when this is combined with manufacturing, these sectors account for 27 per cent of Peel's employment (Saiyed et al., 2012). Notably, Peel is home to Canada's largest concentration of distribution centres for major companies (Inside Logistics Online Staff, 2021). The importance of these types of facilities for the Canadian economy has recently increased even more with the rise of big-box stores, just-in-time delivery systems, e-commerce, and logistics operations (Saiyed et al., 2012). Thus, from 2002 to 2012, the number of logistics-related firms increased in Peel Region by 80 per cent and Amazon alone opened three new "fulfilment centres." Currently, Peel hosts 80 per cent of all companies in the Greater Toronto Area and the majority of Amazon fulfilment centres, and processes 40 per cent of all packages that come to Canada (Inside Logistics Online Staff, 2021). Notably, it was exactly in these types of settings that COVID-19 outbreaks emerged in the suburban municipalities of Brampton, Mississauga, and the Town of Caledon.

As the pandemic unfolded, numerous warehousing, manufacturing, and distribution centres were ordered to fully or partially close by Peel Public Health for the 14-day quarantine period (Inside Logistics Online Staff, 2021). It is worth noting that these types of centres were not the only facilities impacted by the pandemic; other associated transportation-related services were similarly affected. And after reopening, workers' safety was still called into question (Cabana, 2021). Peel Region also hosts a significant trucking sector. In fact, one of the highest levels of truck traffic on the continent takes place on the highways running through Peel, with trucks transporting not only loads from Toronto's Pearson International Airport (located in Mississauga) but also billions of dollars' worth of goods weekly to and from the United States (Bascaramurty and Bhatt, 2021). Brampton's strategic location as a hub of national logistics has now been recognized in post-pandemic planning for the community (Keil and Üçoğlu, 2021).

It is likely that pre-pandemic working conditions that existed within warehousing centres were conducive to COVID-19 spread. For instance, a US legal proceeding revealed that Amazon warehouse workers were monitored through electronic scanners. Employees would be penalized if too much time was spent outside their work areas during successive scans (Yusuf, 2021). During the pandemic, these types of surveillance measures would effectively prioritize high production rates, and would not take into account the additional time required to conform to physical distancing requirements and the adoption of other health and safety precautions. In a work setting where employees are chastised for minor slip-ups or being late by a few minutes, it was the case that sometimes COVID-19 safety protocols were overlooked or forgotten, thus setting the stage for disease spread.

The living, commuting, and working conditions faced by those in Peel Region certainly contributed to an increased vulnerability to COVID-19. This vulnerability did not translate into increased attention or care from the government. Evidence of this can be seen on several fronts. Brampton receives nearly a thousand dollars less in healthcare funding per capita than elsewhere in Ontario (Nasser, 2020a). The monthly $1,800 government assistance payment during the pandemic did not come close to covering the monthly costs of many workers in Peel, forcing them to take out second mortgages or lines of credit to feed their families (Bascaramurty and Bhatt, 2021). Fearing the possibility of losing income or their jobs, some workers were reluctant to get tested for COVID-19, a situation which the head of Peel Health noted could be addressed through paid sick leave for a period longer than the three days covered by the provincial government's existing pandemic benefits plan. Those in Brampton were also neglected in terms of the vaccine rollout (Bascaramurty and Bhatt, 2021). The vaccine doses the city received fell short of the per-capita allotment they were promised, which meant that of the 325 pharmacies that began offering vaccines in early March, none was initially in Brampton. Furthermore, when pop-up clinics were opening in identified hotspot areas in Toronto, it was only several weeks thereafter that Brampton received approval to do the same, despite having far higher COVID-19 rates. Lastly, despite the extremely high case count, especially in comparison to other districts, the hospitals in Brampton received little in terms of resource support for increasing surge capacity. From March to April 2021, this resulted in a weekly average of 116 patients being transferred out of Brampton to other hospitals in Ontario, sometimes located quite a distance away (Bascaramurty and Bhatt, 2021).

Despite the challenges faced, it should be noted that as the COVID-19 pandemic wore on, Brampton and Peel Region went through a shift in what was happening on the ground and how the area was perceived. Due to an unprecedented effort by the community, the region shed its reputation as a helpless victim of transmission and became an exemplary case of resurgence and resilience. Vaccination rates, once far below regional levels, were brought to higher percentages as public health and community actors collaborated to turn things around. As the Delta variant raged through communities everywhere, Brampton found new life: "Once the forgotten and ill-understood suburb, rich in mobility infrastructures, logistics and manufacturing, Brampton became recast as the 'vanguard' of the vaccination strategy in the race against challenges brought on by the new variant" (Biglieri and Keil, forthcoming). With this, the extended urban periphery becomes a place of active transformation, rather than a mere canvas for the ravages of globalization.

CONCLUSION

The COVID-19 pandemic exposed how the spread of disease reflected existing patterns of social inequality. This was perhaps not surprising given that vulnerability to all sorts of threats has tended to fall to the marginalized in society throughout history. What was surprising, however, was not the extent to which the spread of COVID-19 affected those marginalized, but the different ways in which this happened. Thus, as we have discussed, at first the disease spread from the more affluent to the less affluent, but once the virus entered the latter sections of society, it swiftly took hold, affecting much more dramatically those with minority status and low incomes. Notably, COVID-19 had greater impacts on the suburbs – both those suburban neighbourhoods just outside the city core and suburban satellite cities located outside the central city itself.

In the case of Toronto, although both of these types of suburbs had the highest COVID-19 case counts in the region, and both types of areas were home to a high number of "essential workers," specific neighbourhoods in each of these areas were quite different. Thus, those suburban neighbourhoods located within Toronto consisted of ageing apartment towers where the Black community was disproportionately affected. In contrast, in the suburban neighbourhoods outside Toronto, relatively newly constructed, detached and semi-detached housing dominated the landscape, with those most affected by COVID-19 from the South Asian Canadian community. Notably, this led to different types of transmission dynamics, especially in relation to routes of exposure. Thus, for instance, increased risk of exposure could occur through crowded elevators in the Toronto neighbourhoods, while exposure through workplace and family members was the more likely route in the satellite suburban communities.

What the case of the Toronto region has demonstrated is the role that spaces of extended urbanization have as places of origin and sites of infection. The case also highlights the importance that suburbs now play in sustaining inequality and illustrates the devastating effects inequality had during the pandemic. Such an unequal pattern in the distribution of COVID-19 can undoubtedly be found, to varying degrees, in other cities.

Health Governance on a Planet of Cities

In this chapter we look at pandemic governance in and by cities. Given the theoretical and conceptual focus for this book, this will be a discussion not simply of local or municipal politics, but rather of the role of governance in a globalized urban society. Following the concepts of urban and landscape political ecology discussed in chapters 1 and 2, we now focus more explicitly on the notion of urban political pathology (UPP), taking our cues from the work of David Fidler (2004a; 2004b), who put forward this notion with respect to the SARS epidemic in 2003 (see chapter 3). Fidler argued that SARS, referred to as "the first severe infectious disease to emerge in the 21st century" by the World Health Organization, was "the first post-Westphalian pathogen" and also the harbinger of a changing global landscape of health governance (2004c). While Fidler's attention was on the international system, we use the qualifier "urban" with "political pathology" to highlight both the role cities play in the overall architecture of global healthcare governance and how cities have responded to the COVID-19 pandemic. In both instances, we do not just think of cities as municipalities or local government, but also take into account the role of urban civil society and grassroots initiatives. If we assume that urbanization has now changed in dynamics and form, allowing for both more massive and more informal modes of urban expansion which we discussed in terms of extended urbanization in chapter 2, disease response mechanisms and other forms of governance will need to be equally reassessed in this light. Not only has urbanization led to the proliferation of disease *threats* and the multiplication of *vulnerabilities* to emerging plagues, but it has also contributed to the propagation of disease *responses* by states and citizens (which, one must add, at times contributed to the emphasis on increased securitization under conditions of "the new normal" and heightened characteristics associated with surveillance society more generally – see, for example, Hooker and Ali, 2009). While this expansion and amelioration of responses has taken place, it has not occurred evenly across all urban areas or areas of any city-region. As such, continued privilege is maintained in the centre, while at the same time deficits of service continue to be faced in places of higher vulnerabilities in urban society's peripheral domains – thus leaving those already marginalized more vulnerable to disease outbreaks and their effects (Keil et al., 2022).

In this context, writing from a structural perspective, Kaup (2018), for instance, has drawn attention to neoliberalization and privatization – or rolling back of government services – as a factor influencing disease outbreaks, particularly in ex-urban areas. As he notes, this results in a decreased state ability to respond to outbreaks when they do occur, while at the same time making it difficult for governments to take preventive or proactive action in terms of creating the conditions in which outbreaks are less likely. Corroborating this finding, in his study of how neoliberalization contributed to a deadly *E. coli* outbreak in Walkerton, Ontario, in 2000, Ali (2004) also found increased and greater vulnerability arose due to the decreased capacity of the state to respond to outbreaks (Ali, 2004; see also Keil and Ali, 2007, with respect to SARS 2003). During the COVID-19 pandemic we also arguably saw an unprecedented elevation of science as a direct contributor to and legitimizing influence on government policy and governance (Alwan et al., 2020; Horton, 2020a; 2020b), while "COVID sceptics" remained adamantly critical of the influence of what they believed were organized attempts at manipulation and influence by corporate actors (Bill Gates and the pharmaceutical industry, for example), reaching into conspiracy narratives with often racist and xenophobic subtexts.

URBAN POLITICAL PATHOLOGY

There is no doubt that epidemics have always been predominantly an urban phenomenon, and responses to infectious disease have been one of the prime areas of responsibilities for governmental agencies in the local state. The means employed by cities before the modern period were meant to be protective of local populations and typically restrictive of access and mobility, such as using existing defensive built environments (walls, bridges, gates) to keep outsiders from entering the city. The logic of quarantine stems from this period of the fortified city. During the twentieth century, public health became one of the chief concerns of modern urban government. In the long historical perspective, the nation state and supranational organizations have only recently been in the foreground of pandemic response and preparedness, while cities have been involved in pandemic governance since the inception of urban living. This is, of course, not surprising because cities as a form of social and political organization are older than the modern state. The nation state and the international system of nation states that is commonly called "Westphalian" are historically only present after the Thirty Years War and the Peace of Westphalia (1648), after which the system is named (Fidler, 2004c). At the same time, urban populations remained a minority in mostly rural and agricultural societies.

TOWARDS URBAN HEALTH GOVERNANCE

Today, the world could not be more different: the majority of the world's population lives in cities and most, even non-city dwellers in the strict sense, live urban lives. While urban life has proliferated and is now a majority experience, governance of infectious disease has increasingly become a matter of regional or nation state government. At the start of the twenty-first century – "the urban century" by many accounts – the response to and preparedness for pandemic disease were assumed to become more of a responsibility of municipal government. Yet, in contrast to such practice during the "bacteriological" twentieth century, cities would not just be responsible for their own population by providing public health measures in situ (Gandy, 2006). Cities were also assumed to play a bigger part in the governance of global health overall (Bollyky, 2019).

The term "governance" refers to how societies structure responses to challenges they face. As Fidler (2004b: 7) writes, "Governance clearly involves government as part of the structuring process, but governance and government are not synonymous." Looking at SARS in 2003, Fidler (2004c) saw the Westphalian system of health governance ending. Fidler at the time was more concerned with the supranational dynamics that challenged the national sovereignty of countries. He argued that "SARS is the first post Westphalian pathogen because its nonrecognition of borders transpired in a public health governance environment radically different from what previous border hopping bugs encountered" (Fidler, 2004c). Importantly, governance now had to recognize that the classical approach to global health, centred on the nation state, had to adapt to changing realities in a world that became both more transnational and more localized. The debate on global health security has since been constantly in the foreground of governance on a rapidly changing planet, especially after recent Ebola outbreaks in West Africa and the DRC (Halabi et al., 2017). The tensions embedded in this global health security debate, for instance, became most evident in the political controversies that arose over the timing and perceived necessity for the WHO to officially declare a "Public Health Emergency of International Concern" during both the Ebola epidemic and the COVID-19 pandemic (see also chapters 4 and 5). Such declarations often drew criticism not only from nation states but from cities themselves: both were concerned with the political and economic consequences affecting trade and travel to their respective jurisdictions. But we can also argue that in a world where (large) cities became politically more powerful inside the Westphalian system, they began to claim responsibility for governance, including, as they had before the formation of the nation state, the response to and preparedness for pandemic disease. The World Health Organization accepted and reacted to this incursion of urban power into the traditional Westphalian domain by thinking actively about how they could harness the power of municipal governance for global health concerns (WHO, 2009) and how health was figuring on a broader urban agenda (WHO, 2016). A Global Parliament of Mayors (2021: 1–2) noted that "[p]owered in large part by transnational city initiatives, cities have strengthened their multilateral governance processes," and added that "COVID-19 has demonstrated that mayors have unique expertise in developing and implementing local solutions with diverse stakeholders, as well as articulating the needs of their communities at national, regional, and international levels."

Politics in municipalities, between cities and other jurisdictions, and between municipalities and civil society actors and local communities has been crucial in our understanding of the role that urban health governance plays in an increasingly urbanized and globalized society (Acuto, 2020). In this context, municipalism is often cited as a seedbed of procedural and substantial democracy in general and the home of healthy and sustainable policy in particular. Traditionally, municipalism was associated with the power of local government; in its "newer" incarnations in various European and Latin American cities, it is more closely linked with the self-organizing and self-governing capacities of urban society and with "occupying and supplanting the state" (Beveridge and Koch, 2022: 123). As David Madden (2021) notes, in a review of Owen Hatherley's book *Red Metropolis*, municipalism is "a political stance as well as an approach to shaping the built environment. It represents a commitment to the provision of housing, infrastructure, and public space for all, using democratically responsive and resolutely public means. But municipalism is not just a byword for the urban welfare state. In its socialist versions, municipalism consists of concrete efforts at non-reformist urban reform," meaning efforts that lead to more fundamental changes towards permanent redistribution and lasting justice.

While municipalists are keenly aware of power relationships in urban governance, more mainstream urbanist voices often celebrate cities, historically derided as unsafe and unhealthy, as healthier than their country cousins and as strongholds of democratic virtue and life (Krugman, 2021). As Fudge and his co-authors (Fudge et al., 2020: 136) write:

> Urbanism will be a dominant concern of governments, policy-makers, planners, investors, businesses, and communities across the globe in the coming decades. It is projected that by 2050, up to 70% of the global population will live in urban areas. Cities and urban governance are being pushed to the forefront of both human and planetary health. However, whether health and equity will be prioritized as a basis for decision-making is open to doubt.

In an urban world, nation states have still been shown to have a firm grip on global health governance. Realist international diplomacy and the role of the United Nations organizations, especially the World Health Organization, to deal only or mostly with national governments are behind this. That makes sense to some degree, as the sovereignty of nation states still reigns supreme at the international scale. But the role of cities has, clearly, grown nonetheless. This is true inside countries, as we could see from the self-confident politics of mayors in the United States, for example, vis-à-vis a federal government that had largely abdicated its responsibility throughout much of the COVID-19 pandemic; and it is true globally, as organizations such as the C40 Cities global network of mayors have rallied to join forces in their fight against the impact of the pandemic on their cities.

As global public health superseded the formerly Westphalian health governance system, a new framing of global health issues started to emerge, at the urban scale (McInnes et al., 2012). When SARS-CoV-2 emerged in early 2020, a renewed re-evaluation occurred and, between the WHO and other superpowers (e.g., the US and China), a reaffirmation of the Westphalian system of the past three centuries appeared to be taking place (Bollyky and Fidler, 2020). On the other hand, with the predominantly urban nature of the crisis undeniably becoming clear, as it had during the SARS and Ebola outbreaks during the past two decades, the societal consequences of community-based containment measures manifested most acutely at the local level (e.g., unemployment, housing precarity, and reduction of social services, especially for the vulnerable, racialized, and poor). Furthermore, the strategic "front-line" role of local government in mitigating these consequences, and the value added of local governance responses, innovation, and leadership, came to the fore. The renewed focus on national strategies in the COVID-19 pandemic, and the simultaneous persistence of subnational public health governance institutions and practices, became a widely observed phenomenon (Bréville, 2020; Fidler, 2020; Flynn, 2020; Ren, 2020a; Davis, 2022).

During the early months of the COVID-19 pandemic, significant incompatibilities and limited policy coordination were obvious among different levels of government, which confounded outbreak efforts and impeded appropriate resource distribution (especially for those in vulnerable populations such as First Nations, the homeless, the elderly, the institutionalized, etc.). This laid bare a lack of collaboration among institutional structures, intergovernmental resource allocation, and inter-cultural agencies which severely hindered municipal policy responsiveness and planning capacity. At the same time, the specific role of urban governance in the overall architecture of global health governance during the COVID-19 pandemic emerged. This included the importance of municipal response strategies in the context of intercity networks, national and regional state hierarchies, international relations, global coordination, response systems, and crisis management in an urban world. Changing urban global health governance is the connecting theme in these developments (Acuto et al., 2020; Acuto and Steele, 2013; Ali and Keil, 2008; Crowley et al., 2017; Gill and Benatar, 2020; Gottschalk, 2016; Heymann, 2017; Rushton and Youde, 2014).

In wave after wave of the pandemic and in the waxing and waning responses by all levels of government that affected urban life, urban residents realized that "responses to pathogenic microbes are deeply political" (Bollyky and Fidler, 2020; see also Fidler, 2004a; 2004b; 2004c; Gostin and Friedman, 2014; Keil and Ali, 2007; Kock et al., 2020; WHO, 2009) and that pandemic governance included more than formal government. Indeed, the "local state" was shown to involve multiple actors at the municipal level (Acuto et al., 2020; Kirby, 1993; 2019; Magnusson, 2011), highlighting the political process, comprised of "governing institutions, and 'informal' or street-level politics, as well as the transnational connections that affect them" (Boudreau, 2017: 13).

THE LOCAL GOVERNANCE OF HEALTH EMERGENCIES IN THE EXTENDED CITY

In the history of public health, especially during the sanitary and Pasteurian movements of the bacteriological city at the turn of the twentieth century, those in charge of responding to infectious disease outbreaks were usually local agencies, including, for example, the first public health boards, like that of New York City (Colgrove,

2011). Outbreak response has tended to be downloaded or devolved historically to local (municipal or regional) level, and we have shown some of the dimensions of this in our chapters on SARS, Ebola, and COVID-19, especially when the downloading of responsibility to the local level coincided with depriving the local actors of resources via neoliberal policies, obstructing the ability of the local entities to effectively respond to disease outbreaks. Differences in local health governance have often decided life and death. Differences in response in historical health emergency events such as the smallpox outbreaks in Milwaukee (1894) and New York City (1947) (Leavitt, 2003), or the 1918 Spanish Flu pandemic in Philadelphia and St Louis, led to vastly different outcomes (Asmelash, 2020) and demonstrated the relevance and significance of *local* and *municipal* agency. The cholera outbreak in Hamburg in 1893 at once showed the flawed trial-and-error process of municipal public health measures and laid the groundwork for extensive sanitation reforms with effects way beyond the German port city (Evans, 2005). More recently, we have seen similar differentiation in cities during the 2003 SARS crisis and in the vastly different approaches to COVID-19 from Wuhan to Detroit, from Milan to Toronto, and from Belo Horizonte to Johannesburg (Biglieri et al., 2020; Harrison, 2020). In addition, community-based strategies in the West African cities affected by the 2014/15 Ebola outbreak were an important pillar of the overall response to that disease, as shown in chapter 4 (Richards, 2016).

While the governance of disease control and prevention has often taken place at a municipal scale, the increasing porosity between urban, suburban, and peri-urban places requires a new approach (see Houston and Ruming, 2014). Cities are thus reconceptualized "as unbounded and polyrhythmic spaces, no longer understood in terms of fixed locations in abstract space, but rather in terms of a continuously shifting skein of networks, with their own spatiality and temporality" (Ali and Keil, 2007: 1217). Thus, the growth of suburban

Figure 6.1 Social distancing campaign in municipal transit system, Toronto, 2021

Source: Roger Keil

regions and municipalities raises the critical question of who has the mandate to control outbreaks in such areas (see Keil and Ali, 2007). This issue of jurisdictional authority is particularly noteworthy in the context of public health and its connection to the unique type of governance relationships that may exist between urban and suburban centres. Experiences in one urban epidemic response are thought to allow policy-makers to identify areas for improvement in urban health governance, which will assist in preventing future outbreaks.

As the recent experience with urban health governance under COVID-19 shows, such lessons may not be clear and easy to learn.

Often people who live through events like the coronavirus pandemic of the early 2020s find themselves petrified and unable to act in the face of the threats to their life and health (Schaible, 2021). Such insecurity has been associated with what Bianca Wylie has called "a politics of salvage," by which she means:

> It starts with a baseline admission that things are broken and destroyed and in trouble, whether by design, negligence, malice or any other number of causes. … A politics of salvage offers a starting point of acknowledgement of this wreckage as shorthand, not only to describe it but to be instructive about what to do. To find what can be salvaged and reorganize it to our needs. Actively. As praxis. (Wylie, 2021)

The appeal here for a democratic praxis is different from the vacuous gesture that is often associated with ritualistic recitals of democratic values associated with liberal democratic states; instead, this appeal deals with urban life at its core. We find here reverberations of the politics proffered by Southern urbanists who claim that the pandemic needs to teach us that urban politics is about collective life: "Reading the pandemic through collective life means looking beyond formal actors and institutions, legible landscapes, neatly tabulated data, and linear economic rationalities" (Bhan et al., 2020). Such reading includes taking in the manifold relationalities of urban entanglements:

> Reading the pandemic with these forms in mind is to ask what the pandemic has done to these relationalities, these arrangements, and to discover which have survived and which have been unable any longer to hold vulnerabilities or make new outcomes possible amid deep and abiding constraints. It is to ask what new forms, practices and agencies have emerged as rearrangements and what they may teach us about what is happening in and to our cities. (ibid.)

In reality, of course, the pandemic unleashed a broad spectrum of urban politics and governance, diverse in both scale and substance. Appeals for democratization and organic solidarity in urban society – a certain "COVID collectivism" (Schneider, 2022), not to be confused with "pandemic populism" (Dodds et al., 2020: 292) – were countered by the restriction of freedom in consecutive lockdowns and the theatre of pandemic controls that were often administered primarily through agents of the local state (Meth and Charlton, 2020). While there was widespread paralysis throughout the pandemic as a consequence of political dithering and lack of leadership on the side of (local) authorities (Schaible, 2021), some saw a return to the care, reciprocity, mutual aid, and solidarity of prior human societies now corrupted through capitalist urbanization in general and austerity regimes in particular (Davies et al., 2022; Shabi, 2021; Springer, 2020; Standring and Davies, 2020). Others noted the possible creation of "spaces of solidarity for new democratic demands and challenges to the status quo" as the basis for renewed modalities of how urban residents governed themselves in and beyond the health crisis (Allahwala and Keil, 2021: 242). Urban pandemic governance also needs to constantly reassess the boundaries of its jurisdiction as it is challenged by dynamics as diverse as geopolitics and human–more-than-human relations (Perng, 2020).

A PANDEMIC FOR EVERY (URBAN) WORLD

Of course, pandemics always occur on the same physical planet, but they are experienced in vastly different imagined worlds, embedded in equally diverse political pathologies, and governed through disparate modes of pandemic governance. This is no different with COVID-19, caused by the novel coronavirus SARS-CoV-2, which brought the urban world in 2020 to a planetary standstill. The crisis of the early 2020s shows us the perimeters and the parameters of the world we

Figure 6.2 "No lockdowns no masks!" graffiti, Toronto, 2021
Source: Roger Keil

inhabit. Just seventeen years earlier, during the SARS outbreak caused by another coronavirus, the tenuous relationships of a globalized world economy run by neoliberal governments were fraying in that world's decision-making centres, such as Hong Kong, Singapore, and Toronto. Those "global cities" were exposed not just through their relationships in the capitalist commodity chain but also through their migrating diaspora populations. Today, the geography of the Belt and Road Initiative begins to display its reach, the world's two remaining superpowers square off (with one ostensibly rising, the other one descending), and the nature of human life has become vastly extended in extensive and massive forms of global urbanization.

Both SARS and COVID-19 had their origins in "complex and structural entanglements of state-making, science and technology and global capitalism" (Zhang, 2021: 3). Leaving aside China's complicated relationship with the WHO, the country has been extraordinarily successful, at great cost to urban communities caught in series of lockdowns, in suppressing a pandemic outbreak that, as far as we know, originated in its dynamic urban region of Wuhan. Isolating the urban story from this narrative leads us to argue that the success of the Chinese pandemic response is largely based on the country's rapid and unprecedented rate and type of urbanization and the quick and ruthless urban-based measures that were put in place by local, regional, and central governments (Yang, 2022). Such drastic measures in pandemic governance have come under scrutiny for their rather conventional approach – "mass mobilization for isolation and quarantine, handwashing and masking" (Zhang, 2021: 136) – combined with the most drastic limitations in mobility anywhere on the planet. This authoritarian approach was widely criticized as restrictive and full of negative consequences for the country's urban population and the global economy (Roth, 2022). Yet it has also figured as a point of contrast and projection screen for the many failures of Western governance models at all scales (Wallace-Wells, 2021).

Xuefei Ren's ongoing work on lockdowns in different urban territories and jurisdictions has revealed nuance in how this particularly heavy-handed mode of pandemic response differs in intensity and reach depending on the political system where it is applied (2020a; 2020b; 2022). In this work, Ren proceeds close to the ground, reportage-style, but ties such observations on rapidly changing real-world events sequentially and recursively to more structural thinking around state capacity in various national, regional, and urban contexts. With this method, Ren engages "ostensibly incomparable" cases in a "sequential, recursive format" and "produces emergent concepts" in such a way as to make the lockdown the key to the comparison, not the territories she engages (Teo, 2021: 6). These emergent concepts are generative, as they allow us to look at the subject matter of outbreak response through a dynamic lens in which the territorial responses are not locked in but themselves evolving.

One of the lessons from Ren's work is the insight that while there were endogenous governance approaches in different places during the onset of the pandemic in 2020, a centrally mandated format of responses has since taken hold as cities attempt to conform to the expectations of the central political powers (Ni et al., 2021; Ren, 2022). The attempt to comply with the central government's zero-COVID strategy, which allows for little leeway in responding to outbreaks, has led to grotesque examples of zealotry and symbolic over-reaction by some local officials. In December 2021, for example, in the city of Jingxi at the Vietnamese border, four persons who had contracted the coronavirus were publicly put in the pillory (Sander, 2021). In the end, it appeared to quite a few observers that while the benefits of the particular governance mechanisms that urban China had in store for the world were debatable, it was uncontested that the country's entanglements with the capitalist world economy and, as Zhang (2021: 9) noted, "its political responses to the current crisis reinforce the conditions for infectious disease with pandemic potential to emerge again and again, and yet this is not about China itself, but about the conditions of global capitalism in which China is embedded."

While the virus overran Western countries and cities from Milan to Madrid, Montreal, Melbourne, Manaus, Mexico City, New York, and London with lingering restrictions and lockdowns, Wuhan appeared to return to what resembled normal pre-pandemic life within the year. Early in the outbreak, before there was news about a small town in Lombardy called Codogno and before English and German skiers returned home from an Austrian ski resort called Ischgl (Armillei et al., 2021; Carey and Glanz, 2020), Wuhan and Hubei province imposed a strict lockdown on their residents that Western observers thought of as unimaginable in liberal democracies in Europe, North

America, and Australia, and as unpalatable to their democratically sensitized populations (Ren, 2020a).

Whereas the technological aspect of pandemic planning and response was shown to the world in real time as hospitals in Wuhan were built overnight, as streets were disinfected by fleets of military-style trucks, and as surveillance came to the fore throughout all Chinese jurisdictions, the particular social organization of Chinese urban neighbourhoods and workplaces was enlisted in the fight against the coronavirus. As Ren reported on Wuhan, the city's draconian lockdown measures in January 2020 relied on "a thick network of territorial institutions and authorities, such as resident committees (neighborhood-level government bureaucracy), *wuye* (property management companies), and government agencies of various sorts" (Ren, 2020a: 5). Concretely this meant that "[a]t the community level, community workers, property managers, public servants, and volunteers [had] been assigned to daily epidemic control and livelihood support" (Xu and Ding, 2021: 6).

As the pandemic progressed, as the West failed in combatting the spread of the virus in the cities that had been planned ostensibly to be healthy and safe, and as planning processes and emergency procedures designed to protect urban populations did not fully succeed, a partial re-evaluation of what Wuhan had accomplished came into play. A recent British report, for instance, poses the question "how best to reconcile stringent public restrictions and to ensure public compliance whilst protecting and valorising liberal democratic values" and the authors propose a "pandemic social contract and set of governance mechanisms and policy practices" meant to allow for drastic intervention and restrictions (Xu and Ding, 2021: 1). They build the thinking of this model on the Chinese experience in so far as the alleged early success of the lockdown in Wuhan, a city of 11 million people, serves as a reference (at the time of this writing, though, the city had experienced more than 50,000 cases, of which 3,800 were fatal). They further take from that experience three important aspects of pandemic response that might find entry into Western urban planning practice despite the systemic differences in which they were developed: "rapid production and circulation of intelligence and data on the uneven impacts of COVID-19 on places, sectors and social groups," the trigger of "a technological jolt," and "the concept of high-quality growth" (Xu and Ding, 2021: 2). Importantly, in terms of urban governance and future directions in socio-spatial organization, the Chinese pandemic strategy of 2020 did not stop at the draconian territorial emergency measures that were introduced, but led to immediate long-term planning initiatives in digital infrastructures and in economic and monetary reforms that will rather drastically alter urban life, and that have the potential to set the pace for the structuration of urban space (including its digital dimension) elsewhere (Xu and Ding, 2021; for similar experiences in India, see Datta, 2020).

Another storyline that added to the complex picture of urban governance and planning and the pandemic was the experience in what is commonly referred to as the Global South, which is often a stand-in for informal urbanization. This type of urbanization is commonly considered particularly vulnerable to outbreaks and helpless in fighting them effectively. The assumption is not entirely unfounded. As alluded to in chapter 4, the 2014/15 outbreak of Ebola virus disease in West Africa showed there was reason to believe that we have entered an era where diseases previously considered rural and limited to isolated outbreak events have now become urban. As a result, overcrowded and under-resourced places like the West Point informal settlement of 70,000 in Monrovia, Liberia, became sites of disease spread and subject to disease control efforts (Ali et al., 2016; 2022b; see chapter 4 above). Yet, while many African and Indian cities, for example, suffered from COVID-19 eruptions in 2020, they tended to do much better than their counterparts in the North, despite the obvious issue related to overcrowding that made difficult any measures based on social and physical distancing, home quarantine, and hygiene models built on the availability of networked infrastructures. Some have seen strong planning and preparation and swift, community-based reaction as responsible for this rather unexpected turn of events.

There certainly have been instances where COVID-19 responses reverted to the segregationist policies of the Southern cities' colonial past, leading to an expulsion of unwanted populations from cities or a "pathologization of structural poverty" (Finn and Kobayashi, 2020: 219). In some cases, governance meant that the full force of the state was brought to bear on politically and socially vulnerable neighbourhoods, as had been the case in the West Point incident reviewed in chapter 4. Yet, while recognizing the systemic inequalities that weaken the defences of informal settlements, and the large-scale biopolitical confinement (South Africa) or displacement (India) measures against the poor and migrants, it is also now being accepted that the sweeping uniformity of conventional international aid and top-down planning is less effective on the ground, and that "locally led and adapted responses that take into account the diversity and complexity of urban settings are key to effectiveness and reduction of harm" (Wilkinson, 2020: 9).

GOVERNANCE IN AN URBAN WORLD

The importance of cities as sites of global health governance seemed to have grown after the SARS epidemic and put large urban regions and their interconnectedness on the map. Yet, during COVID-19, most prominently, China and the United States (among others) battled over the dominance in the discourse (and the blame game) about the origin and spread of COVID-19 and the response to it. Behind the strategic facade and the (non-)diplomatic bluster, Beijing and Washington have had to deal with a host of issues internally that are reflective of the urban nature of the crisis. In China, as urban scholar Xuefei Ren has pointed out, while the Wuhan lockdown and the city's ability to build hospitals from scratch in no time impressed the world's population, the epidemic "exposed many core issues of the Chinese model of governing: the habitual tendency of government officials to cover up problems, the lack of information disclosure to the public, and tightened media censorship" (Ren, 2020b).

At the outset of the pandemic, in the United States, the majority of COVID-19 infections and deaths were in large urban centres such as New York City, Detroit, and Los Angeles until all parts of the country were affected, as the *New York Times* concluded when it ran a commemorative article on the one million lives lost in the US: "What began as a crisis in cities spread to rural areas and back again, until the path of the virus traced the full geography of the country" (White et al., 2022). The particular challenges faced by a densely packed urban population that is divided by class and race at the best of times were thrown into sharp relief under pandemic conditions. Cities, however, were also sites of governance innovation. The utter failure by the American federal administration under President Trump to provide protection for its population forced cities (and states) to introduce what could be called an internal post-Westphalian system of governance to provide a modicum of safety for their people. As urban centres and suburbanized regions saw the death toll rise in their racialized neighbourhoods and institutions such as long-term care homes, hospitals, and the like, municipal and state governments filled the gap and provided the assistance that an incompetent, uncaring, distant, and cynical government at the national level could not or would not provide. This kind of tension highlighted a larger set of issues and fissures exacerbated by the pandemic in democratic societies more generally, opening questions about political sovereignty, multi-scale responsibilities for an infrastructure of care, the efficacy of the architecture of federal systems, the specific role of the city in these arrangements, and the perennial redefinition of state–market relationships (Davis, 2022; Acuto et al., 2020).

During the pandemic, scholars of urban and regional governance assessed the changing city-regional landscapes, between the enthusiasm for working from home and bicycle infrastructure on the one hand and the realization that many residents in cities found themselves trapped in substandard, overpriced housing and dangerous, precarious, and underpaid employment on the other (UN Habitat, 2021). As discussed in chapter 5, while some had the luxury of drawing a salary by staying at home and continuing their work or schooling online, others had no choice but to expose their bodies to the potential threats of public spaces, essential workplaces, and transportation. McGuirk and co-authors (2020: 2) found at one end "an atmosphere in which ecosystems of urban governance can be transformed, repertoires of practices expanded, state capacity revived, long-sought-after reforms advanced, agendas reset, and new governance ends and dispositions included," and at the other a cementing of usual practices of neoliberal governance, but these authors noted the importance of making any future option subject to critical reflection.

Perhaps not surprisingly, given the need for decisive public policy action and planning, cities, regions, networks of cities, private-led initiatives, philanthropists, and civic groups have been involved in pandemic response and post-pandemic planning, including innovation in government and politics. Focusing on "experimental, data driven, and crowd sourced" mechanisms, McGuirk and her co-authors concluded that "COVID-spurred urban governance innovations invoke new skills, capabilities, agendas, and value sets ranging from surveillance, control, and profitability to welfare, care, and mutuality" (McGuirk et al., 2020: 6). The authors believe COVID-19, already generative of stronger state capacity, has also potentially evoked change both in society–state relations and in urban governance beyond the scale of the city (see also Biglieri et al., 2022).

Certainly, the case has been made for a stronger role for metropolitan – or one might say regional – government and planning in the management of the crisis (Angel and Blei, 2021; Rubin, 2020; Harrison, 2020). Metropolitan governance was proposed as a lever and level of governance overall, not just the governance of municipal affairs. We were able to observe here a debate that goes back at least to the SARS crisis of 2003, when large global cities and city-states were most affected and their governance played a crucial role in the overall defeat of the epidemic. As discussed in chapter 3, the 2003 SARS outbreak hit predominantly large – global – city-regions, most prominently Hong Kong, Singapore, and Toronto, which led to the insight that the connectivity of the global city system might also make those regions particularly vulnerable to infectious disease outbreaks like the one the world has experienced in the past couple of years (Ali and Keil, 2008; Ng, 2008; Teo et al., 2008). This insight was linked to the perceived shift towards a post-Westphalian (meaning post-national) world order and the perception of SARS as the first post-Westphalian virus (Keil and Ali, 2007). Political theorists and international legal scholars had promoted the idea for years that in a globalized world of perforated boundaries, the international order built on nation states may need to be reviewed or even revised in the face of growing threats from emerging infectious disease (Fidler, 2004a; 2004b; 2004c). In this sense, international relations would need to be partly redefined as constituted through municipal rather than national networks of actors (Acuto, 2020). Municipal and metropolitan government and local and regional planning often appeared as the buffer between upper-level neoliberal government policy and global austerity tendencies. No wonder that metropolitan and regional governments were often portrayed as protecting the people from the ravages of national and global failure to contain the pandemic, and as reliable partners of communities in a much-noted return of big government during the crisis, even when calls for a re-establishment of "big government" got louder during that period (Carter, 2021). Seeing COVID-19 through an urban lens therefore draws attention to the social and political divides within and between our globally networked cities (Acuto et al., 2020).

Much of the experience of the pandemic was universal, although it was far from the same in cities around the world. If we understand global governance as growing from below, from the politics of the streets on upward, this pandemic has been shaped by urban governance as governance of the global city. Urban planners and designers grapple with the literal and metaphorical blueprints of urbanism beyond the pandemic. At one end, there has been an urge to revert to known categories of urbanism, and at the other end, wild speculation about the urban future, as if the present conditions and constraints could be wiped off the earth by this pandemic. The moment has been recognized by all as one in which change is not just a good idea but a necessity, although the direction of that change is not clear. "Seeing COVID-19 through an urban lens" often occurs on a register of progress and modernization, but there are also more modest subtexts of preparedness, prudence, and persistence (Acuto et al., 2020).

The times and spaces of the pandemic deserve more reflection as shifting dimensions and modalities of governance. The central and the peripheral – both in time and in space – in our urbanized world have occupied much of the conversation on the new "afterlife" in which we hope to find ourselves following the virus. Linear, and often colonial, narratives of modernization have been discredited in the current crisis as social, spatial, and institutional peripheries have been found in the "most advanced" centres of the global city hierarchy, like New York, and as some urban spaces perennially considered marginal to that hierarchy have been found to be resilient to the pandemic's onslaught (Plageman et al., 2020). As Xiang (2020) observes in response to yet another wave of anti-Chinese stereotyping: "The existence of those 'conditions of rudimentary hygiene' of these markets is not because of some 'irrepressible taste' or 'older custom.' It is first and foremost an economic condition, a dire economic condition at the center – not periphery – of global capitalism."

Space has provided an important lens through which the pandemic gained its profile. Some major academic journals in geography, planning, and territorial governance made statements early in the pandemic that are part programmatic, part collective admission that we are at a point where confusion reigns supreme and new thinking may need to be mobilized. *Dialogues in Human Geography* ran an early collection of comments in which space and governance were a major theme, as the editors contend: "Within a relatively short period of time, the COVID-19 pandemic has become a truly global event with consequences that span every facet of daily life in ways that are profoundly geographical. The spread of the disease demanded a spatialized response that recognized the vectors and clustering of diffusion within localized settings as well as across space and borders" (Rose-Redwood et al., 2020: 99). Geographers have pointed to the multi-fold "territorial traps" encountered by pandemic governance at all governmental scales from the local to the global (Wang et al., 2020). The editorial collective of the journal *Regional Studies* calls the current crisis "undoubtedly a regional one, with important consequences for economies, well-being, transportation, everyday life, and even the practice and publication of regional studies research itself" (Bailey et al., 2020: 1). The editors of *Territory, Politics, Governance* take the terms in the title of their journal under scrutiny and wonder what, at "a moment of crisis and long-term discombobulation, … can our key terms tell us about the contemporary and possible future state of the world?" (Dodds et al., 2020: 290).

But space has not just been subject to scholarly contemplation. It has also been a dimension of pragmatic pandemic response and governance. The two-metre social distancing rule and the chalk circles in parks and at beaches stand as a new spatial grammar of human behaviour and will, to some degree, be envisaged by many to have persistence beyond these quarantine times. They may also be indicators of new forms of societal alienation and the sign of a decollectivization with secondary, unintended consequences (Hartt, 2020). Urban residents will use space differently. When able, they will cycle and walk. Yet they have been more hesitant to reboard public transport, although our buses, trams, and underground railways have not been proven to be superspreader sites of infection. Most systems saw disastrously low user numbers that are only slowly rebounding. While many, especially essential workers in cities, were reliant on public transportation, passenger numbers across municipal transit systems fell dramatically after isolation measures were implemented (see, e.g., CBC, 2020, and chapter 5 above). Perennial points of contention have been the intertwined issues of density, crowding, and mixing. What we think the virus has to do with those markers may depend as much on what we expect normatively to be good urban life as on measurable parameters such as density gradients and people per square metre.

To most people, social distancing as a spatial strategy means a challenge of staying two metres clear of other humans, wearing a mask, and limiting your interaction with others to a bubble of one size or another. But right from the start of the lockdown, another phenomenon received a lot of attention. The "escape" of urbanites to their summer homes (Andrew-Gee and Bula, 2020) fits well into an already existing pattern of isolation and reclusiveness of elites everywhere (Atkinson, 2020). This confirms a pattern of spatial distancing that is reminiscent of the Alpha City super-gentrification of the world's elites: seeking refuge on islands they considered isolated enough to give them shelter (O'Connell, 2018).

THE GOVERNANCE OF THE URBAN PERIPHERY DURING THE PANDEMIC

We have posited hypothetically throughout this book that the relationships of cities and disease are shifting during the COVID-19 pandemic. Researchers have taken up this hypothesis in situated empirical studies as urban regions around the world were buckling under the onslaught of wave after wave of infection. Governance, in particular, was under scrutiny by comparative studies in order to gauge the various responses across the globe. Researchers and practitioners of urban governance called for an "ontology of justice" in order to move the needle of urban politics away from the mainstream urge to build back structures of inequality and equate pandemic resilience with a reconstitution of the pre-pandemic city (Golubchikov and DeVerteuil, 2021; see also Brail et al., 2021). Connolly (2022: 41) found that "[u]rban governance proved to be a critical element of how successful cities were in responding to the COVID-19 pandemic, particularly with regard to the role of civil society and community support," but insists that it was often spontaneous initiatives on the side of civil society actors that supplemented government action and made up for governance failure in institutional settings.

In the future, Connolly concluded, urban governments will need to collaborate more effectively with regional and national levels of government as well as with residents and civil society groups to decrease inequality in urban services. As he wrote, "Politics in municipalities, between cities and other jurisdictions, and between municipalities, civil society actors, and local communities will be crucial to under-standing the role urban health governance plays in an increasingly urbanised and globalised society" (Connolly, 2022: 42). In all questions of pandemic governance, it was obvious to keep in view, as Allahwala and Keil observed, "the creaky mechanics of cooperation between central-regional-local governments, especially in federal countries but also in centralist regimes where regional, class, and other differences erupted during the pandemic" (2021: 238).

Expanding on our initial hypothesis, our ongoing research into the pandemic spread revealed growing evidence that COVID-19 has had its most destructive effects in the peripheries of global urban society. We used the focus on the peripheral here as a heuristic device rather than a determination on a map, and we stressed that the peripheries could be social, spatial, and institutional (Biglieri et al., 2020; Keil et al., 2022; Mullis, 2021). In comparative work on Milan and Toronto, two heavily affected global city regions in Europe and North America, different governance models took shape in light of the overall tendency towards "governing cities through regions," as the subtitle of a topical book suggested (Keil et al., 2017). The focus on the peripheral means that governance must also be thought from there: what are the pandemic preparedness priorities after COVID-19 in neighbourhoods where vulnerabilities are compounded across work, residence, and mobility? How can health services be improved across a territorial jurisdiction? How can (health)care work be made less precarious? How can vulnerable communities be integrated better into mobility services? Biglieri and her co-authors (2022: 16) concluded: "Governance decisions about location, funding, and supports affected these areas, which ended up being hotspots during the COVID-19 pandemic in Toronto and Milan."

Future studies on extended urbanization and infectious disease will need to examine the role of smart technologies in pandemic governance (Datta, 2020; Chen et al., 2020). Logistical issues and boundary questions in urban regions warrant particular attention (Jamieson, 2022; Koh, 2022). It will also be important to ask how government policies might seek to regulate patterns of sub- and ex-urbanization in the interests of "healthy cities." One area of focus here should be the changing composition of suburban populations and communities, including the phenomenon of the "suburbanization of poverty," which brings new health concerns to areas that had traditionally been seen as privileged and well served by public health agencies and private providers of health care (Kneebone and Garr, 2010). Highlighting spatial inequalities in healthcare provision and response in urban areas is a topic which is well suited to urban political

Figure 6.3 Municipal COVID-19 vaccination campaign in a Toronto tower neighbourhood, 2021
Source: Roger Keil

ecology frameworks, given the field's focus on environmental injustice. This structural problem of social injustice built into the extended city is not just a problem that affects people during emergencies, although the pandemic shone a bright light on the fissures our extended urban regions face.

CONCLUSION

The (re)assessment of the role of health governance on an urban planet after the pandemic comes at a time of a general reckoning regarding the governance of global (public) health more widely (Hellowell and Nayna Schwerdtle, 2022). Pandemicity, which Richardson (2020: 142) calls "the linking of humanity through contagion," is now embedded in an unprecedented global urban connectivity. For an urban governance take on COVID-19, we can isolate four possible lessons.

1 We all live in an urban society, and the diseases we have are most likely diseases in and of that urban society.
2 The urban is not a collection of distinct towns and cities but a set of built, social, and natural environments that are connected through urban lifestyles and their corresponding priorities.
3 In this urban world, local and regional jurisdictions remain important, perhaps more than ever, as bounded forms of territorial decision-making and governance areas that are also connected to other such areas regardless of their location in a particular nation state.
4 The urban society, or this urban world, produces new types of social conflict and politics which will demand responses from authorities far and wide.

In the end, as West African states learned during the 2014/15 Ebola outbreak, it is the collaboration of multiple levels of government and society, from the local community to international organizations, that will save the day (Richards, 2016). We have seen in the climate emergency, and with movements such as Extinction Rebellion, what such a decentralized yet global urban movement can look like. In the COVID-19 pandemic, worldwide movements for rent strikes and against evictions, measures against racialization of the disease, financial support and improvement of labour conditions for critical workers, and demands for free public transport have been voiced. In this way, perhaps, the first pandemic of an urbanized planet will lead to stronger ties of the world's urban communities in the struggle for a better city.

7 Urban Planning and Infectious Disease Revisited

URBAN PLANNING: THEORY AND PRACTICE

In many ways, urban planning in most parts of the world experienced a major moment, some would say an insurgent moment, during the pandemic years of 2020 and 2021 (Hertel and Keil, 2020). Speculative calls to action and for changes to the theory and practice of planning and urbanism in the post-pandemic city were ubiquitous and came early (Batty, 2020). Mayors and citizens from Barcelona to Milan and almost everywhere else marked the pandemic condition as a point of departure for a different urbanism (Paolini, 2020; Sala, 2020; Sisson, 2020). Prominent mainstream urbanists in the city where two of the authors live, Toronto, issued a manifesto of sorts to rally urbanist practice around new priorities set by the pandemic as early as May 2020 (Keesmaat et al., 2020). Reframed as an online petition, this manifesto explicitly appealed to the urgency of the situation as the "COVID-19 pandemic provides a once-in-a-lifetime responsibility to accelerate the change we require in Canadian cities" (2020 Declaration, 2020). Some of the genesis of this moment lay in the particularities of the pandemic itself; some of it was tied to the world-moving events following the murder of George Floyd by Minneapolis police on 25 May of that year, which changed the way planning and planners – in the pandemic and beyond – had to answer questions about the structuring and politics of urban space (Worthington, 2020). Again, in Toronto, Jay Pitter, an internationally renowned author and place-maker, issued

"A call to courage: an open letter to Canadian urbanists" in June 2020, calling upon her planning colleagues to move "beyond polite platitudes and guilt to boldly chart a course forward" and "to help do this work, which is at once personal and systemic" (Pitter, 2020b).

The interventions, both ideational and practical, put forward by planners and planning during the extraordinary experience of lockdowns, social distancing, and quarantines were a mix of reactive emergency measures and long-term visual recalibrating. Planning found itself in a rare moment of potentially becoming an agent of change rather than a process through which the status quo was projected into the future. The particular mix of ad hocism and continuity that characterized planning discourse and practice, especially in 2020, set planners free to both make immediate changes and think differently about demographic and infrastructural innovation and the governance processes by which to guide those. Planning had recently begun to seek to reorient its fundamentals under the impression of climate change, which required similar mixes of emergency measures (as yet another flood or fire had to be reacted to) and long-term measures (as people had to be convinced to change their lifestyles, technologies had to be adjusted, and new processes of decision-making needed to be invented to stave off the long-term effects of a warming world on our cities) (Carlson et al., 2022; Witt, 2022).

But the pandemic impressed an urgency on the profession and the process of planning that was unprecedented. *Demographics* (in terms of both mounting and more diverse populations and the sprawling nature of settlement common to most urban expansion), *infrastructure* (making more of the world accessible to urban settlement in closer proximity to previously uninhabited ecological environments while creating higher mobilities at all scales), and *governance* (as the deliberative, democratic turn in the profession was confronted with challenges of emergency government in a moment where decisions could mean life or death) in the emergence of and response to the pandemic were central pillars in how urban planning had to position itself, following the declaration of the pandemic by the WHO in March 2020 (Hamel, 2022).

Progressive planners, on the one hand, recognized the opportunity to shape the urban environments under their responsibility more decisively into more environmentally sustainable, socially just, and democratically open places by moulding populations where they lived, worked, and played, shifting their habits of getting around the city, and opening the arena of decision-making to oppressed voices. Corporate and government actors, on the other hand, used the emergency powers invested in the governance of public health to introduce new technologies of biopolitical and infrastructural control to govern populations, with less than democratic intentions (Allahwala and Keil, 2021; Kipfer and Mohamud, 2021). In all cases, the interplay of demographic, infrastructural, and governance changes was on the agenda of planning and planners, as urban life as we thought we knew it was dramatically retooled in the short term, and in many ways also with a horizon beyond the pandemic response itself.

This chapter will first give some background regarding the role of urban planning in infectious disease management, some of which was introduced in chapter 1. It also discusses how the urban planning profession, and cities in general, were unprepared for the challenges posed by the COVID-19 pandemic, and how they sought to adapt, even though there had been forecasts of the increasing threats posed by emerging infectious diseases in major urban areas. We then turn to a discussion of planning theory, in particular how it is starting to approach the needs of "post-pandemic planning," and also how this differs between Northern and Southern cities. This includes a discussion of the "density dilemma" and overcrowding that have been heavily debated in both academic and popular writing, as well as touched on in chapter 5. We conclude with some open questions that urban planners must grapple with in designing the post-pandemic city, and suggest that the COVID-19 pandemic can be used as an opportunity to build more socially and environmentally just and sustainable cities. This will be vitally important, as cities and urban regions will probably bear the brunt of climate change, social inequalities, and future health emergencies in coming decades. Such changes will largely be made at the landscape scale, recalibrating the amount of open and green space in cities, modes of transport, housing, and urban design.

PANDEMIC PLANNING: URBAN SPACE AND INFECTIOUS DISEASE

Although some had anticipated the significance of the urban as origin, site, and theatre of a possible pandemic before 2020, pointing to the particular significance of the changing urban political ecologies and pathologies of demographic, infrastructural, and governance change, there was still surprise that cities and city planning became matters of popular conversation when the virus hit (Connolly et al., 2021). In fact, cities became a true focal point of societal adjustment. Urban planning, public space, and urban space became indicators of the ways we reorganize our lives and pointed towards thinking about urban life worth living: the increasing tendency to work from home and the closure of restaurants and other entertainment spaces initiated a push towards a re-evaluation of everyday life – a shift in focus on use values and care, on housing, children, the elderly, the neighbourhood.

At the same time, of course, the focus on the home and the boom in online work, entertainment, shopping, and communication created blind spots in the real city outside where more than half of the workforce kept the circuits of urban life connected (Black, forthcoming; Loreto, 2021). The orders for the commodities one wanted while stuck at home had to be filled, packed, and delivered by workers who continued to populate the urban roads, travel to work by public transport, and put themselves in harm's way in "shoulder-to-shoulder" work in warehouses and "fulfilment centres" (as discussed in chapter 5). At each intersection of the supply chain of the suddenly virtual urban world were physical interactions among living bodies and technologies that were not in lockdown or quarantine. These include the so-called "dark stores," neighbourhood-based micro-warehouses and distribution centres with no physical public interface that have started changing the urban landscape significantly (Schorung et al., 2022). Online shopping is just one example among many in the often precarious world of "essential" services those privileged enough to stay at home silently relied upon in this crisis.

Related to the recognition of the unseen in a world receding from public life was the attempt to use the restriction of public life by governments to fast-track politically motivated planning projects. In Ontario, Canada, the provincial government, which reigns supreme over municipal affairs and planning, intensified the use of so-called Minister's Zoning Orders which allowed the government to push through development projects without the usual planning restrictions, environmental assessments, and community hearings. While urban life changed in ways that disadvantaged residents and workers, those responsible for planning, for guidance and assistance to those groups left behind, appeared to push agendas benefiting others closer to their political camp and social class (Benzie, 2021; BLG, 2020; Crawley, 2021; Westoll, 2021).

The naming of spaces, communities, and their practices as problematic during the pandemic could have the unintended consequences of submitting certain land uses and activities to public scrutiny while exempting others, blaming some for their conditions and behaviour while idolizing or making excuses for others. For instance, while it was necessary to point to the unsafe labour conditions in Amazon warehouses as drivers of infection, while multigenerational housing in some immigrant communities gave cause for pragmatic concern, and while conditions in long-term care facilities were abhorrent, the workers in those facilities and the members of those communities deserved protection from elitist notions of work and veiled racism as the marginalized people associated with these locations and activities were being blamed for the disease spread, instead of the blame being attributed to the work and life conditions that such people were forced to occupy. The plight of these marginalized communities contrasts sharply with the life of those less marginalized who were in the privileged position of being able to use the public skating rinks, parks, and walking paths ostensibly open to all (Herhalt and Wilson, 2021; Loreto, 2021; Popal, 2021).

When the global pandemic was declared by the World Health Organization in March 2020, and the changing rhythms and confined spatial patterns of urban life became experiential (and largely experimental) almost overnight, urban and planning thinkers and practitioners reminded themselves of the baggage that planning carried when it came to the history of infectious disease in cities. Arguably, the entire history of planning thought and practice has been caught up with the health of urban life, especially since what Gandy called "the bacteriological city" took shape at the start of the twentieth century (Gandy, 2006; see also chapter 1). After all, the first attempts at creating order in built and social environments through zoning, parks, slum removal, and so forth, starting in the nineteenth century, were aimed at cleaning up the excesses of the industrial city (and at disciplining its often racialized proletarian residents). This was as much true for Victorian London as for the Paris of Haussmann or the Berlin of the pre-World War I years, and certainly for the colonial urban world. Special zeal was reserved for the ordering of colonial spaces through racialized biopolitics, particularly in Africa and Asia, promoted by a racist "conception of the black population as a barbaric collective that threatened the order and health conditions in the 'European' city" (Bigon, 2012: 2; Harrison, 2020; see also chapter 1). Yet, especially during periods when health emergencies occurred as urban phenomena, as was the case during the global SARS epidemic of 2003, urban planning came under scrutiny by professionals and scholars alike, in order to assess the particular intersections of planning practice with disease outbreaks and interventions (Matthew and McDonald, 2006).

Planning is often understood as a tool of modernization (Bollyky, 2018; 2019). The professional practice did indeed see the light of day at the time when industrial cities started to order their development through zoning and hygienic measures at around 1900. That this kind of hygienic progressivism has somewhat failed because it has been tangled up in histories of modernization and colonialism is no surprise. The stated ideal of the modern city got in the way of the realities of majority informal urbanism in many parts of the world. Writes Abigail Friendly about the favelas of Brazil: "Social distancing rules in response to COVID-19 are challenging to implement from the perspective of informal settlements, where there is no alternative other than for residents to live in close proximity to their neighbours" (Friendly, 2020: 4).

COVID-19 AND PLANNING THEORY: TOWARDS POST-PANDEMIC PLANNING

While the last word on urban planning and the pandemic has not been spoken at the time of this writing in the first half of 2022, there were some early signs that planners took an interest in looking at the health emergency through the eyes of the theories that undergird their practice. Much of that interest was spurred by what seemed to be planning *failure* at the outset of the pandemic, particularly in the United States. Year-end reviews of planning in 2020 gave a stern assessment of unpreparedness among the profession. The influential American blog *Planetizen*, for example, concluded that "Whatever it was that blinded us to the threat – blind faith, ignorance, a deeply ingrained belief in American exceptionalism – the country's response since the pandemic arrived on these shores has been unequivocally catastrophic, exacerbating every symptom and cause of American dysfunction along the way" (Brasuell, 2020; see also Brasuell, 2021).

Yet, in commenting on this type of assessment, leading planning thinker Bob Beauregard reminded readers as early as July 2020 that:

> In fact, however, the government had planned. Masks, ventilators, and other equipment had been stockpiled. Experts in federal health agencies and state and local departments of health had been assigned to track infectious diseases and develop protocols for halting their spread and treating those who became ill. Knowledge of "best practices" and plans for a response were available for elected officials to consult. (Beauregard, 2020)

The source of planning's apparent failure, in Beauregard's eyes, needed to be sought in the inability of planners to extend their influence from an advising role to an acting role. Beauregard defines planning theory as "an academic project that reflects on the nature and meaning of planning as it is practiced by governments and done so [sic] around issues of urban and regional development," and he takes the outsized impact of COVID-19 on American urban society as a sign that planning was unable to exert political influence when it counted, which casts responsibility back into the court of planning practice: "Central to planning theory is the relationship of planning to politics and thus to power. The COVID-19 indictment leads us to politics, but in a way that makes planning theorists uncomfortable" (Beauregard, 2020). Failing to recognize the political nature of planning leads to lack of implementation and falsely blaming political leadership for the obvious cracks in the responsive shield.

In terms of planning *practice*, emphasizing the growing role of cities as human habitat, Sharifi and Khavarian-Garmsir (2020: 3) conducted a thorough overview of the evidence from almost a year of analysis in urban and planning research in the areas of: "(1) environmental quality, (2) socio-economic impacts, (3) management and governance, and (4) transportation and urban design." They are led to the preliminary conclusion that COVID-19 exposed the anthropogenic activities that threaten urban life as well as the socio-economic cleavages that have plagued cities since before the pandemic and that were exacerbated in 2020. Specifically, they predict that the "pandemic is expected to fundamentally alter how cities are managed/governed in the future" and that the crisis in (public) transportation, brought on by a relapse into increased automobile use, might also have the unexpected benefit of heightened and sustained bicycle ridership in cities. Importantly, they summarize: "developing context specific integrated approaches is essential for developing and implementing effective planning, response, recovery, and adaptation actions" (Sharifi and Khavarian-Garmsir, 2020: 12).

When assessing its discipline's potential post-pandemic role, planning theory predictably started from the core of its past practice. In the first instance, Max Nathan notes that such post-pandemic "framing is unhelpful, not least because COVID-19 is likely to be one of many endemic globalised diseases. Rather we need to focus on 'pandemic-resilient' urban places, and develop economic, social, physical and governance systems accordingly" (2021: 2). Yet, as Jill Grant noted in an overview article at the end of 2020, when it came to the pandemic, planning scholars were "having a field day considering its implications and writing about its impacts" (Grant, J., 2020: 659). Grant continues her overview with a concise description of some of the impacts of the pandemic on built environments, land use, and housing – a tendency towards more use of space per person for those who can afford it, and more crammed space for those who can't – but also admits rather mixed effects on various commercial and residential sectors. As for population dynamics, Grant notes major changes in age structure, life expectancy, family patterns, and, most importantly, political reaction

Figure 7.1 Temporary road closures in Toronto neighbourhood, 2020
Source: Roger Keil

to "economic distress, unequal impacts, and videographic evidence of state brutality" (Grant, J., 2020: 661).

In line with other critical observers (Keil and Hertel, 2020; Pitter, 2020b), Grant also notes criticism levelled at planning for its historical "practices that contributed to racial segregation and environmental injustice, and for recent initiatives that promoted gentrification and displacement" (Grant, J., 2020: 662). Speaking of the need for re-evaluation and recalibration of planners' "assumptions," she warns against "dust[ing] off favorite prescriptions." Seeing planning thought caught in a Kuhnian predicament, she notices that "even as data incongruities accumulate, we find it hard to desert the theoretical paradigms that dominate practice" (Grant, J., 2020: 662). In order to break these patterns, Grant does not prescribe new theory but instead offers three scenarios that range from quick and successful recovery with a role for progressive planning, to stunted recovery and little political space for planning, to a darker vision of endemic disease and a diminishing of planning as governments focus on law and order. Grant concludes that "Post-pandemic planning will require clear thinking that begins from first principles, draws on solid evidence, and envisions realistic possible futures" and ends on an emphatic appeal for paradigmatic and pragmatic change in an era "where climate change and social justice constitute significant threats" (Grant, J., 2020: 663). In a similar vein, Pauline McGuirk and co-authors found at one end "an atmosphere in which ecosystems of urban governance can be transformed, repertoires of practices expanded, state capacity revived, long-sought-after reforms advanced, agendas reset, and new governance ends and dispositions included," and at the other a cementing of usual practices of neoliberal governance, but noted the importance of making any future option subject to critical reflection (McGuirk et al., 2020: 2).

DENSITY, OVERCROWDING, AND PERIPHERAL URBAN LIFE

An overwhelming amount of consideration at the beginning of the pandemic was focused on matters of density. It was the original lens through which the progression and proliferation of contagion came to be viewed (Hamidi et al., 2020). Simplistic notions of density gradients being reflected in rates of COVID-19 infections were quickly cast aside as, to take a telling example from the United States, the hotspots of contagion moved from the perceived crammed quarters of New York to the perceived realm of low density, air, and sunshine, Los Angeles, during 2020. Urbanists who had a stake in defending a positive image of dense urbanity continued to study this connection in order to reveal its fallacy (Fairs, 2020). Fears of the coronavirus ravaging the dense informal settlements of the South were well founded but proved equally one-sided, mostly for two reasons. First, projections of unpreparedness from the formal, planned, ordered, sanitized urban North onto the allegedly informal, unplanned, disorderly, and unsanitary cities of the urban South were quickly dispelled when, for instance, the urban centres in West Africa where Ebola virus disease had been confronted with concerted community action proved to have effective defences against the novel coronavirus, while their Northern counterparts faltered under the pressure (see chapter 4).

Second, density showed itself to be more complicated a term and a reality than could be measured in linear relationships of people to space (AbouKorin et al., 2021). In fact, as an activist in an informal settlement north of Rio de Janeiro told Abigail Friendly in an interview: "In the peripheries and mainly in the favelas, there are smaller spaces, houses on top of each other, verticalization ... So the family grows up to be able to cope with growth, and consequently, several families have no space to be able to do isolation" (Friendly, 2020: 4). Peripheral settlements like the ones found in the Brazilian favelas are mixes of densities in a landscape of horizontality and verticality. Density remains an insufficient factor and presents many dilemmas (Keil, 2020b; McFarlane, 2021; Pitter, 2020a).

Inspired by the conceptual frame suggested by Connolly et al. (2021; see chapter 2 of this book), Samantha Biglieri and her co-authors argued early in the pandemic that "vulnerabilities have been particularly pronounced in this new urban world where spatial peripherality has coincided with social marginality both in institutional and community contexts. Our argument is not that this is a suburban virus. Rather, we point to the fact that where the virus is concentrated, you find the peripheral, in the city and in society" (2020: 1). Related points were made in studies focused on the Netherlands (Boterman, 2020) and on Italy (Armillei et al., 2021). Indeed, in a related manner, the significance of the relationship of marginal peripherality and infectious disease more generally was noted by Paul Farmer (2001: 187), who notes that infectious diseases tend to "hide" amongst the poor because the poor are often socially and medically segregated from those whose deaths might be considered most significant (see, for instance, Ali, 2010, on social exclusion and tuberculosis among the homeless in Toronto).

In a sympathetic response to the argument by Biglieri et al. (2020), Daniel Mullis applies a focus on the periphery to the German situation, and critically adds generative points about centrality and politics. Accepting the general heuristic premise of locating the virus in the social, spatial, and institutional periphery of the urban world, Mullis also points to the limits of that strategy and proposes four "dimensions of centrality and how they matter when trying to understand the geographies of COVID-19: scale, mobility, economy, and governance" (2021). In another reply to Mullis, Biglieri and her co-authors restate their heuristic premise and add a strong emphasis on the urban periphery as a formative space of pandemic response and preparedness (Keil et al., 2022).

The particular challenges in informal settlements or Southern urbanism overall have consistently been brought up in the context of debates on density and overcrowding (Muggah and Florida, 2020a; 2020b; Wilkinson, 2020). In that case, it is not just a matter of practical consideration but also one that has inspired a fundamental rethinking of how urban planning, and especially pandemic planning, might need to be envisioned in a world where a large number, if not the majority, of urban dwellers are not likely to experience daily life in circumstances circumscribed by a clear separation of home and work, in conditions of modern sanitation and (auto)mobility and sufficient resources to separate themselves from harm. Inspired by South African Philip Harrison's (2014) "lament" that planning theory had left him unprepared to work in the complex environment of the real (Southern) city, India-based Gautam Bhan confronts Western-based planning thought and practice with the realities of, for example, "the squat" and the practice of "repair," and notes that incremental and temporally adjusted planning may be better suited to Southern urbanism than the conventional approach (Bhan, 2019).

As the pandemic struck in 2020, Bhan extended this planning theoretical approach to address the challenges of public health in a Southern urban environment. In collaboration with Teresa Caldeira, Kelly Gillespie, and AbdouMaliq Simone, Bhan set out to defy "the rush of planning and forecasting, projecting and flattening" present in common urbanist theory and practice, and argued that in Southern cities – the authors name in particular Delhi, São Paulo, Jakarta, Johannesburg, Cairo, Manila, Lagos, and Karachi – "lifeworlds that cannot be so clearly divided into 'before' and 'after' the pandemic, and 'crisis' and the 'everyday' are not so neatly separable" (Bhan et al., 2020). The implications of starting planning from the collective life of urbanism rather than with the blueprint of formalizing state action can be read as a fundamental departure from historical (and, one might add, colonial) approaches to planning and response in a pandemic.

Fear and concern that informal settlements would be dramatically devastated by the spread of COVID-19 were not fully borne out. As in the case of the spread of SARS, Africa and India were mostly spared. In actuality, the popular, peripheral communities of the urban poor were often places of the success not only of pandemic preparedness and planning but also of planning itself: how people organized themselves and designed and governed the spaces they inhabited came into focus. This relates back to Gautam Bhan and his co-authors, especially AbdouMaliq Simone's notion of people as infrastructure.

It highlights, as these theorists say, the collective life of cities as the element of importance that planners should focus on. Instead of bricks and mortar and mobility technology, in the pandemic, social technologies came into focus as important both for collective life and for how to plan cities post-COVID-19 (Bhan et al., 2020).

During the pandemic, the production of space proceeded in both a planned and an unplanned manner; and in ways that were both predictable and unpredictable. The attempted retreats to safety by the elites, and exposures of workers and residents through their home and work environments and the mobilities that connected them, show two sides of the same socio-physical urban form – that is, a form that has been planned and built to protect some and to leave others vulnerable. The pandemic posed a "conundrum" as it did not prove to be any less deadly in its effects even in those applications where planning was allegedly more formal, organized, institutionalized, and advanced (Mukherjee, 2021). Planning theorists, educators, and professionals now need to ask: to what degree did the planning of these spaces contribute to the exposure to viral threats through and in these spaces? Did these planning strategies facilitate or impede microbial traffic in ways that benefited or harmed people? How urban planning helped put people in harm's way needs to be part of the lesson to be learned, and will need to be fixed before the next pandemic.

PANDEMIC PLANNING IN THE WAKE OF COVID-19: REWILDING AND REIMAGINING URBAN SPACE

The appeal of the intervention proposed by Bhan and his colleagues is not just limited to giving Southern urbanism its rightful place as the relevant originator of both theory and practice of planning in the twenty-first century, especially under the condition of a health emergency. There may be more general lessons. In this pandemic we have seen both a *rewilding* and a *reordering* of the city not just in the South, but also in the Global North. We have seen urban planning failure at the institutional level as the usual ways in which cities were (infra)structured did not protect their citizens from disease. In fact, what made those cities work might have contributed to enabling viral spread. (Overcrowded) residences, (unjustly distributed) modes of transportation, (defunded) institutions of education, (unregulated and non-unionized) workplaces, all planned on proximity and mass mobility, turned out to be common traps and hotspots of outbreaks.

In most cases, such physical or infrastructural conditions were not solely responsible for viral proliferation. Those physical conditions were the mirror image of societal divisions and segregations: racial, socio-economic, settler, newcomer, and indigenous residents; white-collar and blue-collar work; high-end business service and personal support workers; essential work that could not be done from home. Our cities have been planned and built for these divisions. This is expressed in highly individualized and often private-property-based residential spaces, or public spaces that are either increasingly commer-cialized or restricted in access to various groups of residents. Planning has now been called to account over the inequities it has codified, and which have contributed to the effects the disease has had on cities and citizens.

In all places there was some political leadership at hand, but the experiences have been diverse. There has been progress and there have been success stories (Lusk, 2021). But the detrimental effects of the failures of central, jurisdictional, and political leadership and planning in cities and regions were also obvious in many cases. In order to address these, there has been a continuous outburst of non-institu-tional, community-based planning: thinking about planning, talking about planning, acting and planning by professionals and by regular citizens who have reused the streets and open spaces of their cities

Figure 7.2 Expansion of restaurant space into the street as part of the City of Toronto's CaféTO programme, 2020

Source: Roger Keil

and communities in innovative, and in some cases liberating, ways (see Huang et al., 2021).

One such aspect is the practice of what we could call "rewilding," which is a breaking of the mould that urban planning practice created for urban life (Lehmann, 2021). In many cities, citizens started walking on the streets as sidewalks proved to be too narrow for social distancing, compromising, in the act, the hegemony of automobility for which most cities (even in bicycle-friendly Denmark and the Netherlands) have been planned. Outdoor everyday and recreational activities like walking and cycling took over public spaces to unprecedented degrees. In some cities, sidewalks and lanes of traffic were refurbished and reused as restaurant patios and cycle paths, often under the political leadership of municipal government. The "rewilding" also meant that some activities that had previously taken place in tightly planned, zoned, and regulated commercial spaces, like bars, pubs, and dance establishments, spilled into public parks that were planned and regulated for activities that were usually ostensibly sequestered from the use of recreational drugs and alcohol (like children's playgrounds in parks). A new grammar of public space use became visible as individuals literally gave "a wide berth" when they encountered each other, or in the use of white chalk circles in parks to demarcate social distance. Also part of the "rewilding," of course, was the increased use of marginal urban spaces for previously non-existent activities: beaches for fires, winter volleyball courts and surfers on winter waves, even just walking everywhere on the coldest days, but also the massive, unplanned, and unregulated reuse of urban infrastructures such as boulevards for cycling.

On the one hand, you have stricter regulations being imposed on social life – enforcement of bylaws on social distancing, regulated seating on public transport, mask wearing. But on the other hand, you have less strict regulatory enforcement with respect to the rewilding and festivalization of social life under the pandemic. This likens the

Figure 7.3 Temporary street closures for bicycle use only, as part of ActiveTO municipal programme in Toronto, 2021
Source: Roger Keil

pandemic to times such as carnival/Mardi Gras when social sanctions are fewer and more is tolerated because it is seen as "temporary deviance" – a pressure-release valve of sorts. The enforcement is left with local municipalities, although the directives might come from higher-level governments (just like local public health in general), and this throws a spotlight on the relationship between planning and policing. Both are, to some extent, defined in terms of maintaining order – and the loosening of either might have consequences for the state. With the murder of George Floyd, policing came under public scrutiny and criticism, with social movements forming along these lines, and one can argue that this opening also allowed scrutiny and criticism vis-à-vis other municipal staff or planners (and their regulations); for example, how evictions of tenants from apartments and homeless people from parks were seen in the public eye. Thus, planning did at times become "politicized" (Hermer, 2021).

Such pandemic festivalization of public space was endured by authorities as long as it was outdoors and done in a safe way. When there were assemblies of people that were considered unsafe, as happened repeatedly in raves on Toronto beaches during the summer of 2020, crackdowns occurred, leading to occasional criticism of authoritarianism and fuelling the marginal opposition among corona-sceptics that also claimed city streets as their theatre of political dissent. The murder of George Floyd by Minneapolis police in May 2020 also brought a wave of protest in cities under lockdown and led to large-scale demonstrations in cities across the world. Typically respectful of each other's health and safety and in stark contrast to the corona-sceptics, participants in anti-racism protests painstakingly avoided the impression that they were contributing to pandemic spread through their actions.

But "rewilding" also showed the city's dark side of pandemic unpreparedness. It revealed the lack of services for and the vulnerabilities of marginally housed or unhoused residents. Homeless encampments have been popping up along the river valleys, in parks and forests, in cities everywhere, with people in tents and makeshift housing that have spread across more spaces than before the pandemic. These shifts demarcate a difference in how residents have populated the city. It is an opening of the horizons of what urban life might be, and that is of course exactly what urban planning is about.[1] These shifts will also recalibrate traditional planning discussions as new types of "rewilding" and "reordering" will vie for attention and implementation, and reregulation.

CONCLUSION

In a recent provocation, Ihnji Jon takes us back to Bob Beauregard's point, elaborated above, that planning needs to be understood and practised as politics. In light of the pandemic challenges to academic planning, Jon reminds us that "the production of knowledge itself cannot be dissected from the social, political, and economic fabric of our society" (2021: 2). In another – related – contribution that deals more specifically with planning's legacy after the pandemic, Jon notes that because "[t]he political power of COVID-19 has become evident," now we can talk about things that would otherwise have been considered "socialist," like guaranteed minimum income, socialized health care, and protection for tenants (2020: 331). Clearly, in the realm of physical planning practice, widened pavements, extended bicycle networks, and more park space became de rigueur. Those physical changes can make a difference to how we organize our societal relations, too. But are they enough? If this is, as Hertel and Keil have argued, urban planning's insurgent moment, we might extend the question as Jon (2020: 332) asked: *"can cities also harness this new condition as a momentum to validate and proclaim the importance of creating more inclusive and just urban futures?"*

Ultimately, urbanization is a chief condition and process from which the origin, spread, and trajectory of the pandemic have to be understood. Urban planning was central to how the COVID-19 pandemic developed and how interventions in urban life took place. Demographic dynamics, mobility patterns, and processes of governance were aspects to be considered. Urban space became the prime terrain of behavioural social distancing measures – regulated seating in public transit, mask wearing, two metres distance, etc. Immediately, urban planning rolled out post-pandemic blueprints, at times buoyed by the taking of the streets by protesting masses in the wake of the George Floyd murder, for a city built for people, not cars, for care, not profit, and for responsible mutuality instead of oblivious isolation.

The pandemic may recalibrate the relationship of the day-to-day "informal" aspects of urban life with the "formal" or institutional aspects (e.g., schooling, work). Will planning after the pandemic focus more on the informal aspects of urban social life? It is no coincidence that the social infrastructure of the type associated with the informal settlements is about day-to-day informal life where official planning has little meaning. Following the "planning codes" is an illusion. In the post-pandemic city, are we moving to a new planning culture, with an orientation to other aspects of urban life?

To answer these questions, it may be wise to revisit the categories of conceived (planned), perceived (experienced), and lived (imagined) aspects of the production of space in rebuilding the post-COVID-19 city in order to capture the complexity of the task ahead, as French urban thinker Henri Lefebvre (1991) suggested some time ago. Planning may also need to take on board experiences that explode the usual canon of professional knowledge, in theory and practice, in the discipline. Accordingly, and appropriately, the Australian planning scholar Matt Novacevski (2021: 333) recently proposed to planners that they should take lessons from Camus' *The Plague* when charting a post-pandemic course. For that, "planning must stage its own radical reconnection with place ... pay more attention to empirical observation and fuse it with expert knowledge ... move beyond the crassness of utilitarianism and the obduracy of bureaucratic systems, towards placing a radical compassion and renewed sense of decency." Those are good lessons to live by.

Nearly three years after the pandemic emerged, we cannot be sure we collectively made enough of this moment, pushed ourselves hard enough to succeed in helping to build a better world with the modest means of our planning scholarship and professional practice. We need to keep pushing to make our cities and regions, and especially their most vulnerable, racialized, economically exploited, and socially marginalized communities, less susceptible to the damage done by emergencies, pandemics, financial crises, and the like. This does not mean subscribing to a weak appeal to the mantra of resilience; it means committing to meaningful, structural change where we can help effect it through our thoughts and actions. In 2020 and 2021 we learned that the *new* normal has been the *always* normal for many and the *old* normal is something we cannot accept going back to. The status quo ante is not an option. Planning must measure its mission by that fact.

8 | The City after the Plague ———————

In an age of mega-urbanization, city-regions will need to develop efficient and innovative methods of confronting emerging infectious disease without relying on drastic, top-down state measures that can be globally disruptive and often ineffective. This book has, in part, sought to provide an innovative framework of post-pandemic governance that might engender new ideas for more healthy, equitable, resilient, sustainable, and participatory metropolitan regions. This has required providing an account of the specific role of urban governance in the overall structure of global health governance during the COVID-19 pandemic, including municipal response strategies, smart governance and planning innovations, and community response mechanisms.

This concluding chapter will reflect on the key arguments advanced in the book and the significance of the current pandemic for our global society. Subsequently, it will suggest some possible future avenues for urban researchers to develop new and better explanations for the relationships of extended urbanization and the spatialities of emerging infectious disease along truly interdisciplinary lines, including geographers, health scientists, and sociologists. While the book's earlier chapters focused on the causal factors giving rise to the (post-)pandemic society that we now live in, this chapter will continue with the focus on how a more socio-ecologically just urban future might be assembled: one which can address the social and ecological consequences of the pandemic's various impacts. As cities are now ubiquitous and global in their reach, we argue that institutions and actors of urban governance will be central to any efforts that inform future public health initiatives across political boundaries and geographical continents.

THE COVID-19 PANDEMIC: THREE YEARS ON

When 2021 drew to an end, the first full calendar year under the pandemic, more tallies were made and they were contradictory: excess deaths, vulnerability to infection, "Long COVID," mental health issues, triggered co-morbidities, and trauma from the loss of loved ones to the pandemic continue to haunt and hurt communities and individuals unevenly. As this book has shown, this pandemic, as all pandemics, will end, but the victims will be accounted for in unequal terms. The *Economist* speculated that by 2023, COVID-19 "will no longer be a life-threatening disease for most people in the developed world. It will still pose a deadly danger to billions in the poor world. But the same is, sadly, true of many other conditions. COVID-19 will be well on the way to becoming just another disease" (Carr, 2021). And as the same magazine confirms in its constantly updated tracking system, "the pandemic's true death toll" far exceeded the confirmed 6.3 million COVID-19 deaths at the time of writing.[1]

We have argued throughout this book that there was an uncanny relationship between the spread of global urbanization and the spread of disease. We followed this relationship through the lenses of three epidemic events – SARS, Ebola, and COVID-19 – which we associated with three distinctive, yet interlaced types of planetary urban growth: the emergence of the global city system, the rise of Southern urbanism (exemplified through the case of African urbanization), and extended urbanization as a generalized phenomenon. In doing so, we have focused attention on the ways in which processes of planetary urbanization are remaking the (non-)human geographies of more-than-urban spaces, triggering the potential for new infectious pathogens to be introduced into society through processes of territorial (urban) expansion and socio-ecological disruptions. The three key themes of demographic change, infrastructural expansion, and modalities of (urban global) governance provided the methodological and empirical core of most chapters, and we will reflect upon these here.

The urgency of our writing was prompted by the shared planetary experience of COVID-19, the first pandemic since that of the flu of 1918 to affect all of humanity, if not in equal measure. One tremendous difference between the 1918 and 2020 events was that the more recent pandemic hit a world that was majority urban (something unimaginable even at the beginning of the twentieth century). But the quantitative growth of urban populations only tells part of the story. As we have emphasized in this book, demographic change has been dramatic, with major population movements across continents and more diverse populations in many urban areas. Cities are also more connected through ever-more powerful and far-reaching infrastructures; and new forms of governance in and beyond nation states, inside and at the scales of cities, have changed the modalities of pandemic governance, response, and preparedness. Planetary urbanization thus involves not only the growth of cities, but also the reshaping of territories and political ecologies beyond metropolitan centres, processes which we have sought to capture through the concept of landscape political ecology (see chapter 2).

Since 11 March 2020, when the World Health Organization (WHO) declared COVID-19 a pandemic, the disease has been ruling our lives and our cities. In the meantime, what was considered "normal" urban life was under constant redefinition and tied to both the waves of variants and the rollout of vaccines in response. But beyond the "natural" evolution of the virus and the technology of mRNA vaccines, the urban world churned and changed as people adjusted, local government reacted, and unanticipated outcomes took place. At the same time, human life itself – although encapsulated for the most part in modern, and now often digital, technologies – appeared vulnerable. It was a common experience of urban living that the safety and security of the human body could be compromised in ways that had often been overlooked in the victorious representations of urbanism that had informed the field in the first two decades of this century (e.g., Glaeser, 2011; Florida, 2002).

The idea of a post-pandemic urban life was most directly related to the availability of widespread and repeated vaccination. By mid-December 2020, many countries in the world began to roll out COVID-19 vaccination programmes, with others to follow in early 2021. By the beginning of 2022, almost 10 billion doses of vaccine had been administered worldwide, albeit very unevenly. This in itself indicates the changing nature of pandemic urbanism in the current era, as the dynamics of and responses to emerging infectious diseases are now increasingly macro in scale. Diseases are no longer to be fought at the intra-local scale, focusing on neighbourhoods and specific cities, but must now be addressed through the lens of globalized urbanization and deeply uneven landscapes of viral circulation. In sum, global urbanization and increasing urban–rural connectivity pose new challenges for the management of emerging infectious diseases, which have rendered inadequate some of the previous methodologies for the control of infectious disease.

Just as the outbreak itself had come with a distinct new urban spatial grammar, the administration of the vaccine came with its own biopolitical or necropolitical landscape of fear and hope. First, the world looked in fascination towards Wuhan, where ballets of cater-pillar vehicles and cranes constructed hospitals in record time in the winter; towards New York in the spring, where mass graves swallowed the overwhelming waves of the deceased; and towards India in the summer of 2020, when migrant workers returned from cities to their home villages. As the disease returned in waves during winter 2021 in the northern hemisphere, gymnasiums, stadiums, and fairgrounds

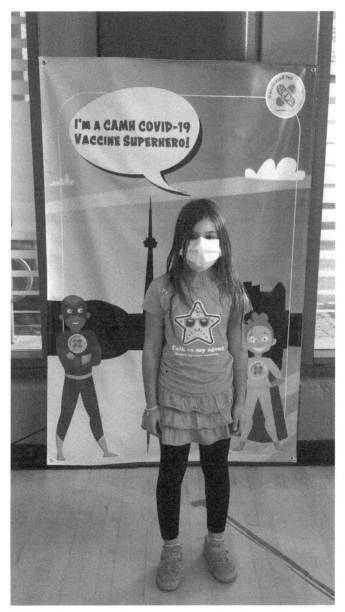

Figure 8.1 Superheroes: vaccination campaign aimed at children in Toronto
Source: S. Harris Ali

were turned into stations of mass inoculations evoking, for those old enough to remember, earlier mass vaccination events: polio, the flu, and other diseases that had caused havoc during the twentieth century. The vaccination centres that were set up quickly had all the accessories of mass social and spatial engineering reminiscent of other such architectures of state control, decisiveness, and representation in the past (Morris and Beck, 2020).

The vaccine came when the trajectory of the pandemic was far from clear. In early 2020, it looked as if COVID-19 would get out of hand in China, where, for all that we know, the virus originated. But the drastic lockdown measures in Wuhan and Hubei province – enacted through a system of central planning with neighbourhood-based structures of surveillance and contact tracing – that impressed the world almost as much as the virus itself seem to have protected the rest of the most populous country on the planet from much further harm. This proven strategy became the go-to method for China to stick to its "zero-COVID" strategy in subsequent waves caused by variants such as Omicron, which returned megacities like Shanghai to lockdown in the spring of 2022 (McCarthy et al., 2020; Ren, 2020a; 2020b).

Early in the outbreak, Italy (where the virus initially ran rampant despite attempts to contain it) and Sweden (where the virus was given freer rein to move among a barely restricted population) seemed at opposite ends of the experience and strategy of battling the disease. Later, in the summer of 2020, both countries were lauded for bending the curve consistently downward (Laurent, 2020). Yet both have suffered severe upticks again during subsequent waves, and Sweden experienced extremely high rates of excess deaths in the winter of 2021. The most powerful and richest nation state on the globe, the United States, has failed to contain the virus, as it has fallen short in so many other things most capitalist democracies were able to provide and deliver to their citizens, especially the socially weaker ones – with very little compensation for workers or small businesses that were suffering. American cities in particular also suffered from a historical abandonment of public health principles that had once emanated from those very same places (W. Davis, 2020; see also Kreisel, 2020, for an alternative view; Yong, 2020a; 2021). In a signature article entitled "How public health took part in its own downfall," the *Atlantic*'s Ed Yong noted that the public health system, "with its overstretched staff, meager budgets, crumbling buildings, and archaic equipment, could barely cope with sickness as usual, let alone with a new, fast-spreading virus."

As the COVID pandemic seemingly nears its end, we are left with the important insight that *proactive* approaches, such as upstream preventive measures rather than downstream curative responses to health problems, worked better than reactive ones, a view long shared by environmentalists, progressive public health and medical officials, disaster managers, and engineers. What urban scholars and planners can take from this is two-fold. One lesson is that planning, by its very nature, must have an element of future orientation, and if, as John Friedmann taught us, planning is the "application of knowledge to action" (Sanyal, 2018: 9), this knowledge must always be ready to point to a pathway for a better tomorrow rather than being reactive, merely guarding and reaffirming the codified status quo; and, to stick with Friedmann, such "effective planning action require[s] a symbiotic relationship between professionals and citizens – that is, between professionals' codified knowledge and citizens' tacit knowledge" (Sanyal, 2018: 2).

The second point to remember is that planning must not get stuck in confirming the obvious, revert to the comfortable, and prioritize the physical aspects of urban change (such as widened sidewalks, paint circles in parks, and bicycle paths that should be built as a matter of course). Instead, planning post-COVID must strive to expand its mandate and portfolio to challenge and change the fundamental injustices that led to a grossly uneven distribution of damage caused by the virus in the first place. Future emerging infectious disease outbreaks might be different from this particular respiratory syndrome, and the technical, physical focus of planning might have to change when the next contagion hits. But that cannot be the main point of pandemic preparedness planning. Instead, before the next outbreak hits, planning must help create the structural conditions from which we can fix the social and spatial injustices that resulted in so many excess deaths this time around.

VACCINATED DREAMS, OSCILLATING REALITIES

Throughout 2021, in the dreamscape of widespread vaccination, the world began to imagine once more that streets and restaurants were teeming with people, swimming pools could be filled, beaches could be populated, and football stadiums resound with the battle songs of the faithful. Liverpool Football Club's slogan, "you'll never walk alone," had an entirely new meaning now: families could have gatherings, young people could date, old people could be visited by their loved-ones, and essential workers everywhere did not have to put their lives on the line as they went to work. While urban life started to be imaginable again in its complex, contradictory shape, the real work of rebuilding and reorienting had only just begun, and that work is built on an oscillating reality with no fixed parameters.

For, despite the vaccine, there is no imminent rescue from this health emergency. The immediacy and novelty that characterized the pandemic in March and April 2020 have made way for an exhausted acceptance of the inevitable. It now structures our life in ways we will not forget. Boundaries between the normal and the emergency begin to blur. Everyday experiences of crisis that were identified with the Global South are now more common here and everywhere (Bhan et al., 2020). And for many among the most vulnerable in our cities, the pandemic is only one of many simultaneous, overlapping crises in

THE CITY AFTER THE PLAGUE

an age of climate change and neoliberal globalization (Sultana, 2021). It seems as though the "before time" of a "pre-postapocalyptic world" is even more difficult to remember now than it is to envision the "after time" of a post-pandemic future (Schermer, 2020).

An article in *Nature* noted as early as August 2020: "COVID-19 is here to stay, and the future depends on a lot of unknowns, including whether people develop lasting immunity to the virus, whether season-ality affects its spread, and – perhaps most importantly – the choices made by governments and individuals." In addition to this uncer-tainty, the article concludes: "The world will not be affected equally by COVID-19" (Scudellari, 2020: 23, 25). The uncertainty is, of course, not helped by a pervasive sense of the instability of institutions at all scales, from the protocols that govern the local daycare and long-term care centres to the advice given to governments by the World Health Organization.

More than two years into the pandemic, and way past that once futur-istic vantage point, exasperated scientists continued to educate a public tired of learning about yet another new aspect, or even new strains, of this unpredictable and unprecedented virus, SARS-CoV-2, and the disease it causes, COVID-19. As early as in the summer of 2020, Laura Helmuth, the editor of the popular science magazine *Scientific American*, bemoaned the "anchoring bias" that locks people in a state of knowledge of COVID-19 and prevents them from learning about the new and often surprising turns our familiarity with the disease has taken. In nine terse paragraphs, she dissects the myths and made-up "facts" on the pandemic, from masks to racism, and leaves us with a list of certainties hard come by through experience and science. "Racism, not race, is a risk factor" and "Spreading lies has spread this disease" are among the memorable aperçus Helmuth is leaving us with (Helmuth, 2020).

That same lesson is taught by the situation on the ground in most urban communities worldwide. To Neethan Shan, executive director of the Urban Alliance on Race Relations and the chief executive officer of Tamil Civic Action in the Toronto suburb of Scarborough, it is not the *virus* that kills people but the *conditions under which they live* in the part of the city he calls home, where class oppression and racialization melt into a concoction of heightened vulnerability (Pelley, 2020). With many outbreaks occurring at workplaces where shielding individuals from the virus is difficult, and with insufficient protection in terms of sick leave in many countries including Canada, workers are confronted with the choice of no income or increased risk. This is indeed one of the main lines of inquiry that has been taken up by scholars in the wake of the COVID-19 pandemic, as it has become increasingly clear that geographies of class and ethnic or racial division are being exacerbated and reconfigured in the wake of the numerous crises posed by the pandemic (see Pitter, 2020a). This is a theme that we have tried to address in this book, along with the related issue of how such inequalities have been responded to by community organizations and democratic politics.

WHAT WE NEED TO KNOW. WHAT WE CAN DO. WHAT WE MUST DO.

Beyond the allegedly neutral rational microscopical certainties and uncertainties of natural and medical science lies a vast field of social and cultural realities that are emphatic and political in an unapologetic way. David Napier and Edward Fischer concluded that:

> If lasting immunity doesn't happen soon, we need to rethink the social contract in ways that run counter to those who advocate for biodeterminism or xenophobic scapegoating or maximising self-interest. Otherwise, when the pandemic abates even temporarily, we risk going back to "normal," forgetting what we might have learned until the next infectious disease outbreak, when we will again be completely

surprised by what we should have expected. We need to consider the needy before that happens – to put heart and soul into thinking about both how we live together with uncomfortable uncertainty, and how we address together the social and cultural drivers of health vulnerability. (Napier and Fischer, 2020)

Most urban scholars and many planning practitioners are progressives. Some believe that this crisis provides a window through which to look beyond the status quo (Fanelli and Whiteside, 2020; Luxemburg Foundation, 2020). Others have commented also about the openings related to the simultaneous "defund the police" and "cancel rent" movements that emerged in the wake of the George Floyd murder and the pandemic relief process (Akbar, 2020a). But clearly, the spectrum of critical takes ranged from seeing COVID-19 as "a portal," to imagining and constructing a new world (Roy, 2020), to warning against such "monumental terms" and looking for political opportunity in majority urban life instead (Bhan et al., 2020).

FROM PANDEMIC TO THE ENDEMIC URBANISM?

Although some reminded us that "our endemic future is not around the corner" (Gonsalves, 2021), in early 2022 the conversation shifted from a pandemic to an endemic framework. Notably, this occurred at a time when regional differences persisted in relation to COVID-19 exposure, morbidity, and mortality; that is, at a point in the pandemic where socio-economic, socio-demographic, and political factors combined to create massive discrepancies in the rates of infection and death. Vaccination rates figure centrally in influencing these outcomes. As Gonsalves (2021) observed shortly before Thanksgiving weekend in 2021 in the United States: "While here in the Northeast we may be able to live with relatively lower levels of hospitalizations and deaths achievable through high vaccination rates, we will have towns and neighborhoods – mostly poor, some just politically conservative in a sea of blue – that will remain at higher risk than others."

We can already sense a danger that the rebuilding of cities will occur at the expense of the poor and unwanted, as the political will of the powerful comes to regain full domination over the temporary power afforded to essential workers, precarious tenants, the racialized, and the disabled during the extreme and urgent circumstances of the early pandemic period. So far, such sublimation in the politics of the city that had been radicalized in the pandemic is still a matter of speculation, but it is real nonetheless. Turning to Anne Helen Petersen (2021), we might agree:

> I'm not sure if we'll see widespread COVID-related clearing out of neighborhoods; I think more so we've seen the benign to malignant neglect of hotspot areas when it comes to their environmental conditions, without a lot of recognizance that those hotspots also had a lot of predisposing conditions for COVID severity like air pollution, lack of public space, and substandard housing due to histories of environmental injustice. There are also certainly other smaller scale troubling patterns that have already come out of the pandemic like increased policing of parks and public space.

Relatedly, but viewing the pandemic from a different angle, some have noted the emergence of a state of affairs in which certain "states of acceptance" have influenced the "necropolitics" of the pandemic. With this comes the recognition of the troubling possibility that "slow death" may have become a marker of the pandemic's trajectory into endemic normalization (Sandset, 2021). The dystopian automatism of despair will still have to contend with the growth of urban democratic potential which has grown and shifted in adversity and suffering, as Jacqueline Rose (2021) insists:

The misery of impoverished peoples, black men gunned down by police on the streets, women trapped in their homes during lockdown, assaulted and murdered by their partners – all these realities, each with its history of racial and sexual violence, are pressing harder on public consciousness, as they move from the sidelines on to the front page. The psychological terrain is starting to shift. Alongside the terror, and at least partly in response, a renewed form of boldness, itself relying on longstanding traditions of protest, has entered the stage – a new claim on the future, we might say.

Surely, there was plenty of urban democratic potential to go around as the pandemic opened up avenues for new claims to the Right to the City.[2] Italian scientists observed that in the absence of an effective state response to the pandemic in early 2020, "the civil society of Bergamo organised itself into a grassroots justice movement" (Alfieri et al., 2022). Emphasizing the democratic potential for change in and after the pandemic, Allahwala and Keil (2021: 241–2) have noted that early in the pandemic there was "a renaissance of societal discourses of solidarity at various scales, ranging from the neighbourhood to the nation," which stood fast against the mostly conservative populism that claimed the urban streets for an unhealthy display of amorphous conspiracy narratives and organized right-wing forces that may change the urban polity in ways not deemed possible before COVID-19. The crisis of democratic governance deepened during the pandemic as a "federal jumble" (*föderales Kuddelmuddel*; Vooren, 2021) took hold in many countries and regions. While cities have been the predominant theatres of this largely anti-democratic movement, it has been a tendency everywhere, including their peripheries and in the countryside. In a small Ontario town caught in COVID's rural–urban divide, "people don't even talk to each other" over the pandemic-related issues that separate them, including vaccinations, social distancing, and other measures (Daubs, 2021).

Figure 8.2 "We're all in this together": the appeal for social solidarity between municipal directive and everyday vernacular

Source: Roger Keil

But the situation of political confusion and indecisiveness also called to action the most absurdly incoherent amalgam of political forces that tested the democratic consensus mostly at the right-hand end of the spectrum. Cities became stages, and in some cases breeding grounds, for these "corona-sceptical" politics (Vooren, 2021). Scholars of far-right movements saw reason for concern as they noted systematic correlation and political alliances of anti-democratic groups and COVID sceptics in many parts of the world: "Even if questions concerning the connections between COVID-19 deniers and the far right remain, it is clear that where the virus is concentrated not only reflects patterns of peripheralization but also political geographies of the (far) right" (Mullis, 2021: 4). This "revolt against reason" has evoked the worst nightmares of democratic failure and the fault lines of Enlightenment thought in Europe and other parts of the world (Misik, 2021). In turn, cities were also increasingly ruled by governments that held societies hostage to their ostensibly indisputable demands to introduce states of emergency, ruling through measures that had often been well rehearsed in the colonial and imperial histories, especially in Western countries: "creeping authoritarianism such as executive rule, administrative discretion, preventative justice, and the militarization of policing" (Kipfer and Mohamud, 2021: 279).

THE SMART CITY AFTER PANDEMIC URBANISM

Beyond the technologies of power and democratic discourse, one of the most pervasive themes of post-pandemic urbanism was linked to issues pertaining to the transformative potential of the smart city. Such a focus is important to an understanding of the full spectrum of more-than-urban transformations that constitute contemporary urban geographies and political ecologies in the wake of the COVID-19 pandemic (see Brenner and Ghosh, 2022). As Brenner and Ghosh note, such processes have important implications for the industrial and agricultural making of urban, peri-urban, and rural areas in response to socio-economic changes arising from the pandemic. Smart cities are one of the key examples of this, as digital technologies have become increasingly important to mitigating the threat of disease in our urban age.

As for smart city futures, it is not entirely clear what the post-pandemic future holds. Artyushina and Wernick (2021) observed that "on the face of it, the smart city market is bleeding" as a number of high-profile projects were cancelled. But there is, as these authors argue, a "small-scale, green and over-policed" future on the cards for the smart city (Artyushina and Wernick, 2021). While it was counter-intuitive to see Google's Sidewalk Lab call it quits on the proposed smart Quayside waterfront development in Toronto, just when there might have been a need for urban intelligences of the kind the Lab imagined in outbreak response and preparedness planning, the smart city as a concept made a showing throughout the pandemic period in cities everywhere (Keil, 2020a; Mattern, 2021). German planner Klaus Kunzmann identifies ten narratives spun around smart cities after COVID-19 and concludes that the "biggest winner of the COVID-19 crisis will be the digital industries that provided the software and all the information and communication services for teleconferences, home-office services, digitalised culture and entertainment, education and research" (Kunzmann, 2020: 29), effectively sidelining other sectors that had previously dominated urban economic life. Facebook's rebranding and renaming as Meta kindled a particular interest in urban smartness as cities already began to join the race for inclusion in the metaverse that is as yet more fictional than real.

Relatedly, there are now concerns as to how the digital retail sector, one many urban dwellers started to rely on for both jobs and delivered goods, will restructure the design and fabric of cities. This has had dire implications for the working classes and racialized populations of cities and urban regions worldwide. One such development is the growth of what could be called "shadow infrastructures," which has been accelerating during the pandemic. We use this term to refer to the "dark stores" – mini-warehouses stocked with groceries to be delivered within 15 minutes – and "ghost restaurants" which provide delivery services to customers without a physical retail location or restaurant in the vicinity (Kushner and Lindsay, 2021; see also chapter 7). This "ghosting" of urban life relates back to a core concern voiced throughout the pandemic. Immediately, in early 2020, a central question about urban post-pandemic futures was: "Will coronavirus cause a big city exodus?" which was answered readily by scholars and practitioners, often led by ideological or political agendas linked to particular futures of the city (Nathan and Overman, 2020; Florida et al., 2021). Increasingly, this is a future that can be characterized by platformization, informalization, and other forms of marginalization that are associated with fiscal austerity in cities (see Brenner and Ghosh, 2022).

In the bigger, regional picture, speculations abound as to how the urban–suburban relationship will develop in the future. Our three narratives of demographics, infrastructure, and governance, pursued throughout this book, come together in this story. The new landscapes of warehousing that supply the "dark stores" in the city have already profoundly reshaped what we may recognize as a future city (MacGillis, 2021). In a perceptive essay, Dan Hill (2021) sees "underlying shifts in technology, environment and culture" that got exacerbated and gained profile during the pandemic. He also sees flows, dispersion, and new relationships to "nature" as elements of a renewed regional urbanism that is both resilient and sustainable (Hill, 2021). In many ways, this can be understood by relating the story of Brampton, the suburb of Toronto that we have frequently visited in this book: that is, how Brampton went from a COVID-19 hotspot to one of Canada's most vaccinated communities, and the ways in which the often-maligned socialities of the suburban were redeployed through social sharing and other solidarities to change the trajectory of the pandemic itself.

Urban form and process have undergone tremendous spatio-temporal shifts and so have the biopolitical and infrastructural politics that have undergirded them. Brampton became the site of several COVID-19 hotspots starting in the summer of 2020 when the second and third waves of infections hit Canada. In terms of comparative urban research, the hyper-diverse immigrant city has indelible lessons to teach. It is the kind of place that points to the future of urbanization and urbanism across several registers. Brampton is at the forefront of the kind of extended urbanization that is typical of the twenty-first century, now and in the foreseeable future. It is an under-served immigrant city at the periphery of a large, growing metropolis and has new and often ill-understood challenges linked to culture, economy, and infrastructure. It has a majority racialized population. It is a centre for a new urban economy structured around low-wage employment in the service economy, especially in logistics and e-commerce. It is the type of place where the infrastructure turn – referring to the increasing centrality of infrastructures in urban life and development beyond the mere engineering and physical qualities they add – becomes physical reality, rivalling the traditional inner city for connectivity.

Generally, the question of urban in/equalities is central to this story and relates back to what has been said about the warehousing supply-economy landscapes Alec MacGillis introduces us to in *Fulfillment*, a book about the history and geography of Amazon (2021). In her award-winning reporting on "Inequality's deadly toll" in those exact landscapes, Amy Maxmen (2021) lays out the spatial dimensions of the social determinants of health that have steadfastly been at the foundation of the increased structural vulnerabilities of peripheral and marginal groups. She notes that these vulnerabilities are both tied in to and severed from the rapidly changing infrastructural connectivities that characterize urban regions today: pandemic hotspots tend to be places that are both central to the emerging transportation and warehousing economy of the time and marginal to the mobility needs of the precarious workers and residents that inhabit and labour in them. As we have argued, these changing connectivities – particularly in peri-urban areas – are one of the primary factors that have made emerging infectious diseases much more difficult to contain than they were at the start of the twenty-first century.

So, what should cities do to build a better post-pandemic future? Laia Bonet, Barcelona's deputy mayor, and Sameh Wahba (2021) advised in September 2021 a focus on three items: fix the digital divide, restore a healthy balance between tourism and housing needs, and enshrine the right to green spaces and public squares. They conclude:

> The pandemic has turned catastrophic scenarios that once seemed far-fetched into reality for countries around the world. As they emerge from the health crisis, people and governments realize that climate change prophecies may well materialize. Investing in nature-based solutions to protect cities from extreme events such as heat waves, flooding and mudslides should now be at the top of cities' to-do lists.

Others have suggested the prospect of developing a new municipalism that is driven by the contradictory but progressive dynamics of urban social movements and local government (Zarate, 2020).

THE CITY AFTER THE PANDEMIC

This pragmatic turn is necessary and welcome, and discussions are happening in every city and town around the globe. But we want to end here with an appeal for us to continue to make articulations between how we view and organize the recovery from the pandemic and the reconstitution of just urban life. It is important to recall that the conditions of inequality and oppression that led to the explosion of urban protest after the killing of George Floyd were related to the social, political, and economic fissures that were revealed by the pandemic. There is some indication that social movement activity globally was not stifled entirely and such activity bloomed in this "peculiar 'global moment'" as "movements for social justice adapted to unexpected circumstances and were actually very active in this challenging period" (Pleyers, 2020: 307). In this sense, the pandemic and democracy were articulated in ways that created opportunities to mobilize for an expansion of social rights and social justice as the necessary preconditions for a substantive democracy in everyday life and a democratic political economy (Akbar, 2020a; 2020b).

Warren Magnusson notes that an "obvious fact about the city is that it has no clear boundaries and no particular scale. … The city as city is a series of tracings and scalings, unmappable except from within" (Magnusson, 2011: 155). The challenge of building a good city is not guaranteed to be met by the political processes emerging from democratic movements, which remain open in their result. But self-government following an urban perspective is an imperative in this world of the global city. The pandemic taught us the utility of this perspective as urban life in its most visceral form became the matter of political concern. As the first two waves of the pandemic kept washing over the urban world, some researchers began to look ahead and argued that, inspired by Magnusson's work, the recovery should be guided by a perspective that "sees like a city." As Acuto et al. (2020: 978) argued: "Re-building cities post-COVID-19 requires negotiating multiple, concurrent needs in order to meaningfully address the complexity of how contagion, sustainability and economic recovery work in urban settlements."

Acuto and his co-authors (2020) identified four advantages that are associated with this perspective on "seeing COVID-19 like a city." First, it opens the perspective up to the role of extended forms of urbanization in accelerating zoonotic events like COVID-19 at a planetary scale. Second, it sharpens the focus on the specific "forced experimentation" experienced in specific cities, and provides a reality check guarding against the universalism of the urbanist agenda that had become a travelling roadshow of policy advice since the turn of the century. Third, it "values the active role played by citizens and urban communities in crisis response" (Acuto, 2020: 978). Lastly, it reminds us that the local state consists of multiple scales and always includes the residents. As the authors concluded: "An urban lens on the COVID-19 crisis underscores the window of opportunity we have to inform recovery plans before they are locked-in unsustainably" (Acuto, 2020: 978).

With this in mind, we return to the murder of George Floyd and its impact on urban and pandemic politics. Black Lives Matter (BLM) after George Floyd was a disruption to normal democratic exchange, especially institutionalized politics of the municipality. Particularly, the demand to "defund the police" struck at the heart of the property–order complex that had institutionalized racialized violence in many urban communities (Walcott, 2021). Demands were made. Differences and identities were challenged. Monuments were toppled. Local politics put to the test the global order at a time when the pandemic had provided the stage for a different planetary experience.

When we argue that COVID-19 was a disease of the periphery, we note, among other things, that the political spaces and subjects affected by the pandemic are not central in the conventional sense, but make necessary a shift of attention that comes with microbial traffic and the territory of the disease spread itself. This involves examining the political ecologies of urban metabolism, the landscapes of extended and planetary urbanization, and forms of marginalization that are central to the processes that have emerged in the past two decades of global (and pandemic) urbanism. Such a shift is, of course, not a natural occurrence but reflects the political economies, political ecologies, and political pathologies that structure urban space and result in some spatial, social, and institutional domains being predisposed to higher vulnerabilities. Those could be racialized, classed, gendered, influenced by immigration, or produced by urban dynamics such as gentrification. In the Toronto area, the suburban municipality of Brampton and the northwest of the City of Toronto were such "hotspots," spaces of heightened and compounded vulnerability that led to cascading health and associated crises. From those peripheral spaces, a new local politics springs that will specifically speak to the urban agenda. At a minimum, we need to better understand the suburban municipalities of this world in order to learn about the possibility of post-pandemic urban democracy in an urban society. This underscores the utility of the landscape political ecology framing that we have developed in this book, as it combines the political (governance) and socio-spatial dimensions that are essential to understanding and mitigating the impact of infectious diseases as they emerge and proliferate along the urban edge.

As Magnusson reminds us, "a multiplicity of political authorities in different registers and at different scales is characteristic of urban life," and "transformations are non-linear and hence inherently unpredictable" (2011: 168). We pick this idea up with the help of Doug Saunders, one of the writers who have intervened regularly in the debate on what will happen to cities in and after the pandemic. Saunders, who had previously summarized important municipal and urbanist initiatives at the end of 2020 (Saunders, 2020), more recently took the sixtieth anniversary of the publication of Jane Jacobs' *The Death and Life of Great American Cities* as an opportunity to reflect about the issues we have discussed here, especially the changing form and function of the modern city in an age of extended urbanization.

Saunders observes and underlines a necessary shift in attention from the kinds of central neighbourhoods Jacobs took as the model of good urbanism to "the grassy slab-apartment districts of the inner 'burbs'" (Saunders, 2021). While mayors like Anne Hidalgo in Paris and Sadiq Khan in London may be tempted to structure post-pandemic recovery along the lines laid out in Jacobs' masterwork – such as the 15-minute city, for example – Saunders points to the need to integrate the post-war suburbs into the calculation if such a recovery is to be successful. Not only did the patterns of postwar suburbanisation prefigure this shift, but it is also necessary due to the ongoing "suburbanisation of immigration and poverty," which means "the districts that most need to shift and evolve are the ones least able to do it on their own, without large-scale rescues" (Saunders, 2021).

As Saunders notes, the politicians who make the speeches and the decisions have come to celebrate Jane Jacobs in their own interest. The often-celebrated diverse Jacobsian city, however, has calcified into a stasis of gentrified sameness. The neighbourhoods that served as models to the great writer are now the whitest, most super-gentrified districts with the lowest COVID-19 infection rates and the highest vaccination rates. Saunders ends his ruminations with three pointed comments on how to move forward. Certainly very much with his home, Toronto, in mind, and reiterating the fact that they were the prime locations for COVID infections, he first recommends that "all-housing apartment districts need to become real neighbourhoods." Second, he claims that "there needs to be a lot more high-density housing in neighbourhoods that think they don't want it," making particular reference to the "huge single-family-housing swaths of Toronto and Vancouver" protected by zoning. And third, "there needs to be a mass knocking-down of boundaries, both physical and psychological – the barriers to human activity and community connection that slow and patient change won't fix. But the worst of those boundaries are no longer found in the historic urban core; they're planned and designed into the very shape of today's most challenged neighbourhoods" (Saunders, 2021).

BLM directed the post-pandemic city, still a mirage in the summer of 2020 of course, down a path towards revolutionary change to the way cities are policed, justice and wealth are distributed, property is owned, and work is divided. The triple crisis of the climate emergency, racial injustice, and the pandemic needs such revolutionary solutions in thought and practice, and it needs permanent mobilization of urban diversities in the agoras of our urban regions, central and suburban. In the end, the post-pandemic city must live up to the demands of a substantive, redistributive democracy and emerge into a globalized world of cities where multi-scalar, multi-level connectivities define the parameters of urban politics.[3] In political theory, Ross Beveridge and Philippe Koch leave us with a fine strategy to charge ahead: "When we think about democracy, we should therefore start a discussion of its merits by asking: where are the people, the demos, in the making of cities and urbanisation, why are they only involved intermittently? Taking this simple approach to democracy, we might be able to overcome the fixation on the state" (Beveridge and Koch, 2022: 138).

The COVID-19 pandemic is now part of a long history of experiences that cities and urban residents have had with infectious disease. South African scholar Philip Harrison has observed, in his comprehensive account of epidemic history in Johannesburg, that: "the COVID-19 pandemic will soon become part of the historical account, and it is critical that we maximise the positive learning potentials from this traumatic happening." Harrison summarizes his own conclusive thoughts on such lessons, and we have already touched on this previously in this book. We need to pay particular heed to local and place-specific, but really urban, forms of governance that were affected by disease outbreaks and, in turn, created the conditions for future response. Harrison notes that such a local focus reveals the complexity of that relationship between place and disease over time, as his research shows that:

lessons of history need to be translated cautiously across temporal contexts, but that history does direct us to themes including: the unpredictable course of most epidemics (i.e. the constant surprises they throw in our path); the huge variability in the spatial patterning of epidemics;

Figure 8.3 "(Not) everything is possible": comment on graffiti by unknown Toronto artist

Source: Roger Keil

the significance of governance across all scales in shaping the course of epidemics, but also the effect of epidemics on shaping the continued evolution of governance; the economic and social consequences of epidemics; the political consequences, and more. (Harrison, 2020: 6)

Notes

1 Introduction
1 For a discussion of such matters in the context of the COVID-19 pandemic, see the special issue of the journal *Built Environment*, 47, 3, 2021.

3 SARS and the Global City
1 Using this particular definition of the global or world city is a heuristic device to focus on a certain type of financial centre that is often discussed in this manner and differentiated from previous types of cities (industrial; market towns) and from other types of cities today (regional centres; specialized industry towns; etc.). See Ren and Keil (2017) and Brenner and Keil (2017) for extended discussions on this topic. The focus on this type of city as a global city is also indicative of the state of the discussion in much of urban studies during the 1990s and into the 2000s, during the time the SARS crisis took shape (see, for example, Sassen, 1991; Taylor 2004; Brenner and Keil, 2006).
2 We are not arguing here that all global cities defined in the way we chose in this chapter are ethnoculturally diverse, and, in turn, we are not saying that cities not so defined could not be ethnoculturally diverse. In fact, many of the sites of globalized urbanization that were exposed in the COVID-19 crisis – inner suburbs, agricultural areas with migrant workers, meatpacking towns in the countryside, energy production centres like Canada's Fort McMurray – are more diverse than the centres of cities. We insist, though, that the critical mass of diaspora cultures is typically higher in what we here call global cities than in other types of urban settlement.
3 In 1998, Toronto was merged with its suburban municipalities of East York, Etobicoke, North York, Scarborough, and York to form the new "megacity" of Toronto.

4 Ebola and African Urbanization
1 One nuance in this discussion is the issue of whether the forests currently surrounding West African villages actually represent the remains of recently deforested areas or whether they are areas hosting the regeneration of previously lost forest cover from some time back (see Fairhead and Leach, 1995).

2 One of the fears for families was that if their deceased were taken away, they would not be properly buried in accordance with religious and traditional requirements. This fear was substantiated during the early stages of the response because those who succumbed to EVD had to undergo mandatory cremation (Abramowitz et al., 2015). This led some families to keep knowledge of the deceased private so they could conduct secret burials in accordance with their revered customs. In response, later on, based on community consultation, "safe and dignified" burials were conducted, in which family members garbed in proper personal protective equipment and following proper public health protocols could participate in a safe way in burial rites (Abramowitz, 2017).

5 COVID-19 and Extended Urbanization

1 https://www.statista.com/statistics/564717/airline-industry-passenger -traffic-globally/.

2 https://www.toronto.ca/city-government/data-research-maps /neighbourhoods-communities/neighbourhood-profiles/.

3 https://www.toronto.ca/home/COVID-19/COVID-19-pandemic-data /COVID-19-neighbourhood-maps-data/. See also Bridge and Roumeliotis (2021).

4 Arrangements involving multiple generations living together in one house became the focus of stigmatization and racism directed against the South Asian (and Asian) Canadian communities during the pandemic (Bascaramurty and Bhatt, 2021).

7 Urban Planning and Infectious Disease Revisited

1 In one response during winter 2021 in Toronto, Khaleel Seivwright, a local carpenter, built mobile shelters for unhoused people in city parks where camps of tents had begun to pop up. The city outlawed the practice on the pretext of fire safety and prevented Seivwright from continuing his work. But the event only highlighted the struggle about public space and what it means for whom, who has the access to it, and who has the resources to use it. In this light, planning for public space became an entirely different story. See Boisvert (2020).

8 The City after the Plague

1 https://www.economist.com/graphic-detail/coronavirus-excess-deaths -estimates.

2 See here, for example, contributions to a special issue of the journal *sub\urban* on urbanism after the pandemic: https://zeitschrift-suburban.de/sys/index .php/suburban/issue/view/46.

3 For an application of this thinking in the area of climate change and cities, see Goh (2021).

References

2020 Declaration for Resilience in Canadian Cities. 2020. [Online petition]. https://www.2020declaration.ca/.

Aaditya, B. and T.M. Rahul. 2021. Psychological impacts of COVID-19 pandemic on the mode choice behaviour: a hybrid choice modelling approach. *Transport Policy*. 108: 47–58.

Abdullah, I. and I. Rashid, eds. 2017. *Understanding West Africa's Ebola Epidemic: Towards a Political Economy*. London: Zed Books.

AbouKorin, S.A.A., H. Han, M. Gamal, and N. Mahran. 2021. Role of urban planning characteristics in forming pandemic resilient cities: case study of Covid-19 impacts on European cities within England, Germany and Italy. *Cities*. 118: 103324. https://doi.org/10.1016/j.cities.2021.103324.

Abraham, T. 2004. *Twenty-First Century Plague: The Story of SARS*. Baltimore: Johns Hopkins University Press.

Abramowitz, S. 2017. Epidemics (especially Ebola). *Annual Review of Anthropology*. 46, 1: 421–5.

Abramowitz, S., S.L. McKune, M. Fallah, J. Monger, K. Tehoungue, and P.A. Omidian. 2017. The opposite of denial: social learning at the onset of the Ebola emergency in Liberia. *Journal of Health Communication*. 22 (sup1): 59–65. https://doi.org/10.1080/ 10810730.2016.1209599.

Abramowitz, S., K. McLean, S. McKune, K. Bardosh, M. Fallah, J. Monger, et al. 2015. Community-centered responses to Ebola in urban Liberia: the view from below. *PLoS Neglected Tropical Diseases*. 9, 4. https://doi.org/10.1371 /journal.pntd.0003706.

Acuto, M. 2020. Engaging with global urban governance in the midst of a crisis. *Dialogues in Human Geography*. 10, 2: 221–4.

Acuto, M., S. Larcom, R. Keil, M. Ghojeh, T. Lindsay, C. Camponeschi, and S. Parnell. 2020. Seeing COVID-19 through an urban lens. *Nature Sustainability*. 3, 12: 977–8.

Adey, P., K. Hannam, M. Sheller, and D. Tyfield. 2021. Pandemic (im)mobilities. *Mobilities*. 16, 1: 1–19.

Adeyanju, C. 2010. Deadly fever: racism, disease and a media panic. *Canadian Journal of Sociology*. 35, 4: 676–8.

Akbar, A. 2020a. The left is remaking the world. *The New York Times*, 11 July. https://www.nytimes.com/2020/07/11/opinion/sunday/defund-police-cancel-rent.html#click=https://t.co/bLbOj8dnFZ.

Akbar, A. 2020b. Demands for a democratic political economy. *Harvard Law Review*. 134, 1: F90.

Alfieri, C., M. Egrot, A. Desclaux, and K. Sams. 2022. Recognising Italy's mistakes in the public health response to COVID-19. *The Lancet*. 399, 10322: 357–8.

Ali, S.H. 2004. A socio-ecological autopsy of the *E. coli* O157:H7 outbreak in Walkerton, Ontario, Canada. *Social Science & Medicine*. 58, 12: 2601–12.

Ali, S.H. 2008. Stigmatized ethnicity, public health and globalization. *Canadian Ethnic Studies*. 40, 3: 43–64.

Ali, S.H. 2010. Tuberculosis, homelessness and the politics of mobility. *Canadian Journal of Urban Research*. 19, 2: 80–107.

Ali, S.H. and R. Keil. 2006. Global cities and the spread of infectious disease: the case of Severe Acute Respiratory Syndrome (SARS) in Toronto, Canada. *Urban Studies*. 43, 3: 1–19.

Ali, S.H. and R. Keil. 2007. Contagious cities. *Geography Compass*. 1, 5: 1207–26.

Ali, S.H. and R. Keil. 2008. *Networked Disease: Emerging Infections in the Global City*. Oxford: Wiley-Blackwell.

Ali, S.H. and R. Keil. 2010a. Public health and the political economy of scale: implications for understanding the response to the 2003 Severe Acute Respiratory Syndrome (SARS) outbreak in Toronto. In R. Keil and R. Mahon, eds. *Leviathan Undone? Towards a Political Economy of Scale*. Vancouver: UBC Press, 195–208.

Ali, S.H. and R. Keil. 2010b. Securitizing networked flows: infectious diseases and airports. In S. Graham and S. Marvin, eds. *Disrupted Cities: When Infrastructure Fails*. New York: Routledge, 97–110.

Ali, S.H. and R. Keil. 2012. Global cities and infectious disease. In B. Derudde, M. Hoyler, P.J. Taylor, and F. Witlox, eds. *International Handbook of Globalization*. Cheltenham: Edward Elgar, 593–611.

Ali, S.H. and R. Keil. 2017. Global cities and the spread of infectious disease: the case of Severe Acute Respiratory Syndrome (SARS) in Toronto, Canada. In X. Ren and R. Keil, eds. *The Globalizing Cities Reader*. London: Routledge, 169–75.

Ali, S.H. and J.R. Rose. 2022. The post-colonialist condition, suspicion, and social resistance during the West African Ebola epidemic: the importance of Frantz Fanon for global health. *Social Science and Medicine*. https://doi.org/10.1016/j.socscimed.2022.115066.

Ali, S.H., A. Conteh, J.M. Macarthy, A. Sesay, V.N. Blango, and Z. Hrdličková. 2022a. Ebola, informal settlements and the role of place in infectious disease vulnerability: evidence from the 2014–2016 Ebola outbreak in urban Sierra Leone. *Disasters.* https://doi.org/10.1111/disa.12553.

Ali, S.H., B. Dumbuya, M. Hynie, P. Idahosa, R. Keil, and P. Perkins. 2016. The social and political dimensions of the Ebola response: global inequality, climate change, and infectious disease. In W. Leal Filho, U. Azeiteiro, and F. Alves, eds. *Climate Change and Health.* Cham: Springer International.

Ali, S.H., M. Fallah, J. McCarthy, R. Keil, and C. Connolly. 2022b. Mobilizing the social infrastructure of informal settlements in infectious disease response: the case of Ebola Virus Disease in West Africa. *Landscape and Urban Planning.* 217: 104256.

Alirol, E., L. Getaz, B. Stoll, et al. 2010. Urbanisation and infectious diseases in a globalised world. *The Lancet.* 10: 131–41.

Allahwala, A. and R. Keil. 2021. The political economy of COVID-19: Canadian and comparative perspectives – an introduction. *Studies in Political Economy.* 102, 3: 233–47.

Alwan, N., R.A. Burgess, S. Ashworth, R. Beale, N. Bhadelia, D. Bogaert, J. Dowd, I. Eckerle, L.R. Goldman, T. Greenhalgh, D. Gurdasani, A. Hamdy, W.P. Hanage, E.B. Hodcroft, Z. Hyde, P. Kellam, M. Kelly-Irving, F. Krammer, M. Lipsitch, A. McNally, M. McKee, A. Nouri, D. Pimenta, V. Priesemann, H. Rutter, J. Silver, D. Sridhar, C. Swanton, R.P. Walensky, G. Yamey, and H. Ziauddeen. 2020. Scientific consensus on the COVID-19 pandemic: we need to act now. *The Lancet.* 396, 10260: 71–2.

Amin, F. and M. Bond. 2020. COVID-19 disproportionally impacting Black communities, people of colour in Toronto. *City News,* 9 July. https://toronto.citynews.ca/2020/07/09/race-data-covid-toronto/.

Andrews, G.J., V. Crooks, J. Pearce, and J. Messina, eds. 2021. *COVID-19 and Similar Futures: Geographical Perspectives, Issues and Agendas.* Cham: Springer.

Andrew-Gee, E.A. and F. Bula. 2020. Urbanites run for country homes, cottages amid coronavirus outbreak, creating tensions with year-round residents. *The Globe and Mail,* 24 March. https://www.theglobeandmail.com/canada/article-urbanites-runfor-country-homes-cottages-amid-coronavirus-outbreak/.

Angel, S. and A. Blei. 2021. Why pandemics, such as COVID-19, require a metropolitan response. *Sustainability.* 13, 1: 79. https://doi.org/10.3390/su13010079.

Angel, S., R.M. Blei, D.L. Civco, N.G. Sanchez, P.M. Lamson-Hall, J. Madrid, F. Parent, and K. Thom. 2017. Engaging with the planet's urban expansion. In A.M. Berger, J. Kotkin, and C.B. Guzmán, eds. *Infinite Suburbia.* New York: Princeton Architectural Press, 164–77.

Angelo, H. and D. Wachsmuth. 2015. Urbanizing urban political ecology: a critique of methodological cityism. *International Journal of Urban and Regional Research*. 3, 1: 16–27.

Armillei, F., F. Filippucci, and T. Fletcher. 2021. Did Covid-19 hit harder in peripheral areas? The case of Italian municipalities. *Economics & Human Biology*. 42: 101018.

Artyushina, A. and A. Wernick. 2021. Smart city in a post-pandemic world: small-scale, green, and over-policed. *Spacing Toronto*, 8 November. http://spacing.ca/toronto/2021/11/08/smart-city-tech-post-pandemic-small-scale-green-over-policed/.

Asmelash, L. 2020. Philadelphia didn't cancel a parade during a 1918 pandemic. The results were devastating. *CNN*, 15 March. https://www.cnn.com/2020/03/15/us/philadelphia-1918-spanish-flu-trnd/index.html.

Atkinson, R. 2020. *Alpha City*. London: Verso.

Bader, N., C. Berndt, F. Flade, A. Ghassim, M. Grill, and J. Schreijäg. 2021. Das ungerechte Virus. *Süddeutsche Zeitung*, 4 March. https://www.sueddeutsche.de/wissen/coronavirus-ungleichheit-migranten-1.5224640?reduced=true.

Bailey, D., J. Clark, A. Colombelli, et al. 2020. Regions in a time of pandemic. *Regional Studies*. 54, 9: 1163–74.

Banta, J.E. 2001. Commentary: from international health to global health. *Journal of Community Health*. 26, 2: 73–6.

Barua, M. 2014. Bio-geo-graphy: landscape, dwelling, and the political ecology of human-elephant relations. *Environment and Planning D: Society and Space*. 32, 5: 915–34. https://doi.org/10.1068/d4213.

Bascaramurty, D. and V. Bhatt. 2021. Impossible choices: how this Brampton community explains Canada's Covid-19 crisis like no other. *The Globe and Mail*, 20 May. https://www.theglobeandmail.com/canada/article-l6p-brampton-english/.

Batterbury, S. 2001. Landscapes of diversity: a local political ecology of livelihood diversification in south-western Niger. *Cultural Geographies*. 8, 4: 437–64. https://doi.org/10.1177/096746080100800404.

Batty, M. 2020. The coronavirus crisis: what will the post-pandemic city look like? *Environment and Planning B: Urban Analytics and City Science*. 47, 4: 547–52.

Bausch, D.G. and L. Schwarz. 2014. Outbreak of Ebola virus disease in Guinea: where ecology meets economy. *PLoS Neglected Tropical Diseases*. 8, 7: e3056.

BBC. 2020. Coronavirus: London Tube passenger numbers fall during outbreak. *BBC*, 16 March. https://www.bbc.co.uk/news/ukengland-london-51910740.

Beauregard, R.A. 2020. Planning, politics and the pandemic. *Elgar Blog*, 8 July. https://elgar.blog/2020/07/08/planning-politics-and-the-pandemic/.

Benzie, R. 2021. Doug Ford says he's "proud" of controversial MZOs to fast-track development. *The Toronto Star*, 9 March. https://www.thestar.com/politics

/provincial/2021/03/09/doug-ford-says-hes-proud-of-controversial-mzos -to-fast-track-development.html.

Beveridge, R. and P. Koch. 2022. *How Cities Can Transform Democracy.* Cambridge: Polity.

Bhan, G. 2019. Notes on a Southern urban practice. *Environment and Urbanization.* 31, 2: 639–54.

Bhan, G., T. Caldeira, K. Gillespie, and A. Simone. 2020. The pandemic, Southern urbanisms and collective life. *Society and Space,* 3 August. https:// www.societyandspace.org/articles/the-pandemic-southern-urbanisms-and -collective-life.

Biglieri, S. and R. Keil. Forthcoming. Examining the spatial-temporal imaginaries of suburban landscapes of care. In J.P. Addie, M. Glass, and J. Nelles, eds. *Infrastructural Times.*

Biglieri, S., L. De Vidovich, and R. Keil. 2020. City as the core of contagion? Repositioning COVID-19 at the social and spatial periphery of urban society. *Cities & Health.* 5: suppl. 1, S63–S65. https://doi.org/10.1080/23748834 .2020.1788320.

Biglieri, S., L. De Vidovich, J. Iacobelli, and R. Keil. 2022. Health governance of COVID-19 in Milan and Toronto: long term trends and short term failures. *Studies in Political Economy.* 103, 1: 55–79. https://doi.org/10.1080 /07078552.2022.2047483.

Bigon, L. 2012. A history of urban planning and infectious diseases: colonial Senegal in the early twentieth century. *Urban Studies Research.* 2012: 1–12.

Black, S. Forthcoming. COVID, work, care, crisis. *Studies in Political Economy.*

BLG. 2020. Minister's zoning orders come to the fore in a pandemic. *BLG,* 20 November. https://www.blg.com/en/insights/2020/11/ministers-zoning -orders-come-to-the-fore-in-a-pandemic?utm_source=Mondaq&utm _medium=syndication&utm_campaign=LinkedIn-integration.

Bloch, R., N. Papachristodoulou, and D. Brown. 2013. Suburbs at risk. In R. Keil, ed. *Suburban Constellations.* Berlin: Jovis, 95–101.

Bloch, R., A. Mabin, and A. Todes. 2022. Africa's suburban constellations. In R. Keil and F. Wu, eds. *After Suburbia.* Toronto: University of Toronto Press.

Boisvert, N. 2020. Meet the Toronto carpenter building insulated, mobile shelters for homeless people this winter, 27 October. https://www.cbc.ca/news /canada/toronto/mobile-shelters-homelessness-COVID19-1.5777158.

Bollyky, T.J. 2018. *Plagues and the Paradox of Progress: Why the World Is Getting Healthier in Worrisome Ways.* Cambridge, MA: MIT Press.

Bollyky, T.J. 2019. The future of global health is urban health. *Council on Foreign Relations,* 31 January. https://www.cfr.org/article/future-global-health-urban -health.

Bollyky, T.J. and D. Fidler. 2020. It's time for an independent coronavirus review.

Foreign Affairs, 24 April. https://www.foreignaffairs.com/articles/china/2020
-04-24/its-time-independent-coronavirus-review.

Bonet, L. and S. Wahba. 2021. Taking three pandemic lessons to heart to build better cities. *World Bank Blogs*, 8 September. https://blogs.worldbank.org /sustainablecities/taking-three-pandemic-lessons-heart-build-better-cities ?cid=SURR_TT_WBGCities_EN_EXT.

Booth, C.M. and T.E. Stewart. 2005. Severe Acute Respiratory Syndrome and critical care medicine: the Toronto experience. *Critical Care Medicine*. 33: S53–60.

Boozary, A.S., P.E. Farmer, and A.K. Jha. 2014. The Ebola outbreak, fragile health systems, and quality as a cure. *JAMA*. 312, 18: 1859–60.

Boterman, W. R. 2020. Urban–rural polarisation in times of the corona outbreak? The early demographic and geographic patterns of the SARS-CoV-2 epidemic in the Netherlands. *Tijdschrift Voor Economische En Sociale*. 111, 3: 513–29.

Boterman, W. 2022. Population density and SARS-CoV-2 pandemic: comparing the geography of different waves in the Netherlands. *Urban Studies*. https:// doi.org/10.1177/00420980221087165.

Boudreau, J.A. 2017. *Global Urban Politics: Informalization of the State*. Cambridge: Polity.

Brail, S., M. Martin, J. Munasinghe, R. Ratnayake, and J. Rudner. 2021. Transnational experiences of COVID-19: Transferable lessons for urban planning between the Global South and the Global North. In P. Filion, B. Doucet, and R. Van Melik, eds. *Global Reflections on Covid-19 and Urban Inequalities. Vol. 4: Policy and Planning*. Bristol: Bristol University Press, 145–58.

Brasuell, J. 2020. Urban planning and the coronavirus: 2020 year in review. *Planetizen*, 31 December. https://www.planetizen.com/features/111719 -urban-planning-and-coronavirus-2020-year-review.

Brasuell, J. 2021. Planning and the pandemic: trends from 2020. *Planetizen*, 5 January. https://www.planetizen.com/features/111764-planning-and -pandemic-trends-2020.

Bratton, B. 2021. *The Revenge of the Real: Politics for a Postpandemic World*. London: Verso.

Braun, B. 2008. Thinking the city through SARS: bodies, topologies, politics. In S.H. Ali and R. Keil, eds. *Networked Disease: Emerging Infections in the Global City*. Oxford: Wiley-Blackwell, 251–65.

Brenner, N., ed. 2014. *Implosions / Explosions: Towards a Study of Planetary Urbanization*. Berlin: Jovis.

Brenner, N. and S. Ghosh. 2022. Between the colossal and the catastrophic: planetary urbanization and the political ecologies of emergent infectious disease. *Environment and Planning A: Economy and Space*. 54, 5: 867–910. https://doi.org/10.1177/0308518X221084313.

Brenner, N. and R. Keil, eds. 2006. *The Global Cities Reader*. London: Routledge.

Brenner, N. and R. Keil. 2017. From global cities to globalized urbanization. In N. Brenner, ed. *Critique of Urbanization: Selected Essays*. Basel: Birkhäuser, 69–84.

Brenner, N. and C. Schmid. 2014. The "urban age" in question. *International Journal of Urban and Regional Research*. 38, 3: 731–55. https://doi.org/10.1111/1468-2427.12115.

Bréville, B. 2020. The return of the city-state. *Le Monde Diplomatique*, April. https://mondediplo.com/2020/04/11cities.

Bridge, S. and I. Roumeliotis. 2021. Vulnerable Toronto neighbourhoods push for priority access to COVID-19 vaccines. *CBC News*, 27 January. https://www.cbc.ca/news/canada/toronto/vaccination-at-risk-communities-toronto-1.5886443.

Brisbois, B.W. and S.H. Ali. 2010. Climate change, vector-borne disease and interdisciplinary research: social science perspectives on an environment and health controversy. *EcoHealth*. 7, 4: 425–38.

Burton, A. 2021. Journaling the COVID-19 pandemic: locality, scale, and spatialised bodies. *Geographical Research*. 59, 2: 217–27.

Cabana, Y. 2021. Amazon's Brampton warehouse is back in business – but workers are still at risk. *Canadian Dimension*, 9 April. https://canadiandimension.com/articles/view/amazons-brampton-warehouse-is-back-in-businessbut-workers-are-still-at-risk.

Caldeira, T.P. 2017. Peripheral urbanization: autoconstruction, transversal logics, and politics in cities of the Global South. *Environment and Planning D: Society and Space*. 35, 1: 3–20.

Carey, B. and J. Glanz. 2020. Travel from New York City seeded wave of U.S. outbreaks. *The New York Times*, 7 May. https://www.nytimes.com/2020/05/07/us/new-york-city-coronavirus-outbreak.html.

Carlson, C.J., G.F. Albery, C. Merow, et al. 2022. Climate change increases cross-species viral transmission risk. *Nature*. https://doi.org/10.1038/s41586-022-04788-w.

Carr, E. 2021. Covid-19 is likely to fade away in 2022. *The Economist*, 8 November. https://www.economist.com/the-world-ahead/2021/11/08/covid-19-is-likely-to-fade-away-in-2022.

Carter, Z. 2021. The coronavirus killed the gospel of small government. *The New York Times*, 11 March. https://www.nytimes.com/2021/03/11/opinion/coronavirus-economy-government.html?smid=tw-share.

Castells, M. 1996. *The Rise of the Network Society*. Oxford: Blackwell.

CBC. 2020. Brampton, Ont., needs help to tackle surge in coronavirus cases, says mayor. *CBC News*, 14 September. https://www.msn.com/en-ca/news /canada/brampton-ont-needs-help-to-tackle-surge-in-coronavirus-cases -says-mayor/vp-BB191YSL.

CDC (Centers for Disease Control and Prevention). n.d. *2014–2016 Ebola Outbreak in West Africa.* https://www.cdc.gov/vhf/ebola/history/2014-2016 -outbreak/index.html.

Chalk, F. 1967. The anatomy of an investment: Firestone's 1927 loan to Liberia. *Canadian Journal of African Studies / Revue Canadienne des Études Africaines.* 1, 1: 12–32.

Charmes, E. and R. Keil. 2015. The politics of post-suburban densification in Canada and France: debates and developments. *International Journal of Urban and Regional Research.* 39, 3: 581–602.

Chen, B., S. Marvin, and A. While. 2020. Containing COVID-19 in China: AI and the robotic restructuring of future cities. *Dialogues in Human Geography.* 10, 2: 238–41.

CNN Editorial Research Team. 2022. COVID-19 pandemic timeline fast facts. *CNN*, 17 May. https://www.cnn.com/2021/08/09/health/covid-19 -pandemic-timeline-fast-facts/index.html.

Coburn, J., D. Vlahov, B. Mberu, et al. 2020. Slum health: arresting COVID-19 and improving well-being in urban informal settlements. *Journal of Urban Health.* https://doi.org/10.1007/s11524-020-00438-6.

Coker, R.J., B.M. Hunter, J.W. Rudge, et al. 2011. Emerging infectious diseases in southeast Asia: regional challenges to control. *The Lancet.* 377, 9765: 599–609.

Colgrove, J. 2011. *Epidemic City: The Politics of Public Health in New York.* New York: Russell Sage Foundation.

Collard, R.C. 2012. Cougar–human entanglements and the biopolitical un/making of safe space. *Environment and Planning D: Society and Space.* 30, 1: 23–42.

Connolly, C. 2017. Landscape political ecologies of urban "swiftlet farming" in George Town, Malaysia. *Cultural Geographies.* 24, 3: 421–39.

Connolly, C. 2019. Urban political ecology beyond methodological cityism. *International Journal of Urban and Regional Research.* 43, 1: 63–75.

Connolly, C. 2022. The urbanisation of spatial inequalities and a new model of urban development. In H.B. Shin, M. Mckenzie, and D.Y. Young, eds. *COVID-19 in Southeast Asia: Insights for a Post-Pandemic World.* London: LSE Press, 37–45.

Connolly, C., P. Kotsila, and G. D'Alisa. 2017. Tracing narratives and perceptions in the political ecologies of health and disease. *Journal of Political Ecology.* 24, 1: 1–10.

Connolly, C., R. Keil, and S.H. Ali. 2021. Extended urbanisation and the spatialities of infectious disease: demographic change, infrastructure and governance. *Urban Studies*. 58, 2: 245–63.

Corburn, J. and I. Karanja. 2016. Informal settlements and a relational view of health in Nairobi, Kenya: sanitation, gender and dignity. *Health Promotion International*. 31, 2: 258–69.

Cosgrove, D.E. and S. Daniels. 1988. *The Iconography of Landscape: Essays on the Symbolic Representation, Design, and Use of Past Environments*. Cambridge: Cambridge University Press.

Crawley, M. 2021. What's really behind the Ford government's push to pave protected wetland in Pickering. *CBC News*, 10 March. https://www.cbc .ca/news/canada/toronto/doug-ford-duffins-creek-wetland-pickering-ajax -warehouse-amazon-1.5942938.

Cribb, R. 2020. The public knew about a COVID-19 outbreak at Maple Lodge Farms. So how is it that a Mississauga business, where 61 employees have been infected, has not been identified? *Brampton Guardian*, 14 September. https:// www.bramptonguardian.com/news-story/10189899-the-public-knew-about -a-covid-19-outbreak-at-maple-lodge-farms-so-how-is-it-that-a-mississauga -business-where-61-employees-have-been-infected-has-not-been-identified -/?utm_source=twitter&source=bmptguardian&utm_medium=socialmedia &utm_campaign=&utm_campaign_id=&utm_content=.

Crowley, J.S., L. Gostin, and S. Halabi. 2017. *Global Management of Infectious Disease after Ebola*. Oxford: Oxford University Press.

Datta, A. 2020. Self(ie)-governance: technologies of intimate surveillance in India under COVID-19. *Dialogues in Human Geography*. 10, 2: 234–7.

Daubs, K. 2021. In a small Ontario town caught in COVID's rural–urban divide, "people don't even talk to each other." *The Toronto Star*, 6 December. https://www.thestar.com/news/canada/2021/12/06/in-a-small-ontario -town-caught-in-covids-rural-urban-divide-people-dont-even-talk-to-each -other.html.

Davies, J., I. Blanco, A. Bua, I. Chorianopoulos, M. Cortina-Oriol, A. Feandeiro, N. Gaynor, B. Gleeson, S. Griggs, P. Hamel, H. Henderson, D. Howarth, R. Keil, M. Pill, Y. Salazar, and H. Sullivan. 2022. *New Developments in Urban Governance: Rethinking Collaboration in the Age of Austerity*. Bristol: Bristol University Press.

Davis, D. 2022. Urban sovereignty in a time of crisis: territorialities of governance and the ethics of care. In R. Acosta, E. Durr, M. Ege, U. Prutsch, C. van Loyenm, and G. Winder, eds. *Urban Ethics as a Research Agenda: Outlooks and Tensions in Multidisciplinary Debates*. London: Routledge.

Davis, M. 2005. *The Monster at Our Door: The Global Threat of Avian Flu*. New York: New Press.

Davis, M. 2020. *The Monster Enters: COVID-19, Avian Flu, and the Plagues of Capitalism.* London: OR Books.

Davis, W. 2020. The unraveling of America. *Rolling Stone*, 6 August. https://www.rollingstone.com/politics/political-commentary/covid-19-end-of-american-era-wade-davis-1038206/.

De Vidovich, L. 2019. Suburban studies: state of the field and unsolved knots. *Geography Compass.* 13, 5: e12440.

Dodds, K., V. Castan Broto, K. Detterbeck, M. Jones, V. Mamadouh, M. Ramutsindela, M. Varsanyi, D. Wachsmuth, and C. Yuan Woon. 2020. The COVID-19 pandemic: territorial, political and governance dimensions of the crisis. *Territory, Politics, Governance.* 8, 3: 289–98.

Dorit, R. 2015. Breached ecological barriers and the Ebola outbreak. *American Scientist.* 103, 4: 256.

Doucet, B., R. van Melik, and P. Filion, eds. 2021. *Global Reflections on COVID-19 and Urban Inequalities.* 4 vols. Bristol: Bristol University Press.

Drexler, M. 2002. *Secret Agents: The Menace of Emerging Infections.* Washington, DC: Joseph Henry Press.

Du Bois, W.E.B. 1933. Liberia, the League and the United States. *Foreign Affairs.* 11, 4: 682–95.

Eckholm, E. 2006. SARS in Beijing: the unraveling of a cover-up. In A. Kleinman and J.L. Watson, eds. *SARS in China: Prelude to Pandemic.* Stanford: Stanford University Press, 122–30.

Elsey, H., I. Agyepong, R. Huque, Z. Quayyem, S. Baral, B. Ebenso, C. Kharel, R.A. Shawon, O. Onwujekwe, B. Uzochukwu, J. Nonvignon, G.A. Aryeetey, S. Kane, T. Ensor, and T. Mirzoev. 2019. Rethinking health systems in the context of urbanisation: challenges from four rapidly urbanising low-income and middle-income countries. *BMJ Global Health.* 4, 3: e001501.

Epstein, P.R. 1998. Global warming and vector-borne disease. *The Lancet.* 351, 9117: 1737.

Evans, R.J. 2005. *Death in Hamburg: Society and Politics in the Cholera Years.* London: Penguin.

Fairhead, J. 2016. Understanding social resistance to the Ebola response in the forest region of the Republic of Guinea: an anthropological perspective. *African Studies Review.* 59, 3: 7–31.

Fairhead, J. and M. Leach. 1995. False forest history, complicit social analysis: rethinking some West African environmental narratives. *World Development.* 23, 6: 1023–35.

Fairhead, J. and M. Leach. 1996. *The Making and Misreading of an African Landscape: Society and Ecology in the Forest–Savanna Mosaic.* Cambridge: Cambridge University Press.

Fairs, M. 2020. "No evidence" that urban density helps spread of coronavirus says

Richard Florida. *Dezeen*, 2 November. https://www.dezeen.com/2020/11 /02/coronavirus-cities-affordable-creatives-richard-florida/.

Fallah, M.P. and S.H. Ali. 2022. When maximizing profit endangers our humanity: vaccines and the enduring legacy of colonialism during the COVID-19 pandemic. *Studies in Political Economy*. 103, 1: 94–102. https:// doi.org/10.1080/07078552.2022.2047475.

Fallah, M.P., L.A. Skrip, S. Gertler, D. Yamin, and A.P. Galvani. 2015. Quantifying Poverty as a driver of Ebola transmission. *PLoS Neglected Tropical Diseases*. 9, 12: e0004260.

Fallah, M., S. Lavalah, T. Gbelia, M. Zondo, M. Kromah, L. Tantum, G. Nallo, J. Boakai, K. Sheriff, L. Skrip, and S. H. Ali. 2022. Contextualizing mobility during the Ebola epidemic in Liberia. *PLoS Neglected Tropical Diseases*. 16, 4: 1–17.

Fallah, M.P., L.A. Skrip, and J. Enders. 2018. Preventing rural to urban spread of Ebola: lessons from Liberia. *The Lancet*. 392, 10144: 279–80. https://doi.org /10.1016/S0140-6736(18)31435-1.

Fanelli, C. and H. Whiteside. 2020. COVID-19, capitalism and contagion. *Alternate Routes: A Journal of Critical Social Research*. 31, 1: e22506.

Fang, J. 2020. The 2003 SARS outbreak fueled anti-Asian racism. Coronavirus doesn't have to. *The Washington Post*, 4 February. https://www.washingtonpost .com/outlook/2020/02/04/2003-sars-outbreak-fueled-anti-asian-racism -this-pandemic-doesnt-have/.

Farmer, P. 2001. *Infections and Inequalities: The Modern Plague*. Los Angeles: University of California Press.

Farmer, P. 2020. *Fevers, Feuds, and Diamonds: Ebola and the Ravages of History*. New York: Farrar, Straus and Giroux.

Fidler, D.P. 2004a. Germs, governance, and global public health in the wake of SARS. *Journal of Clinical Investigation*. 113, 6: 799–804.

Fidler, D.P. 2004b. *SARS, Governance and the Globalization of Disease*. New York: Palgrave.

Fidler, D.P. 2004c. SARS: political pathology of the first post-Westphalian pathogen. In S. Knobler, A. Mahmoud, S. Lemon, et al., eds. *Learning from SARS: Preparing for the Next Disease Outbreak: Workshop Summary*. Washington, DC: National Academies Press. https://www.ncbi.nlm.nih.gov /books/NBK92470/.

Fidler, D. 2020. The World Health Organization and pandemic politics. *Think Global Health*, 10 April. https://www.thinkglobalhealth.org/article/world -health-organization-and-pandemic-politics.

Finn, B.M. and L.C. Kobayashi. 2020. Structural inequality in the time of COVID-19: urbanization, segregation, and pandemic control in sub-Saharan Africa. *Dialogues in Human Geography*. 10, 2: 217–20.

Florida, R. 2002. *The Rise of the Creative Class: And How It's Transforming Work, Leisure, Community and Everyday Life*. New York: Basic Books.

Florida, R. 2020. The geography of Coronavirus. *CityLab*. https://www.citylab.com/equity/2020/04/coronavirus-spread-map-city-urban-density-suburbs-rural-data/609394.

Florida, R., A. Rodríguez-Pose, and M. Storper. 2021. Cities in a post-COVID world. *Urban Studies*. https://doi.org/10.1177/00420980211018072.

Flusty, S. 2004. *De-Coca-Colonization: Making the Globe from the Inside Out*. London: Routledge.

Flynn, A. 2020. Municipal power and democratic legitimacy in the time of COVID-19. In C.M. Flood, V. MacDonnell, J. Philpott, S. Theriault, and S. Venkatapuram, eds. *Vulnerable: The Law, Policy and Ethics of COVID-19*. Ottawa: University of Ottawa Press.

Ford, T. 2012. Liberia's hasty forest sell-off risks more conflict. *The Guardian*, 5 July. https://www.theguardian.com/global-development/2012/jul/05/liberia-forest-sell-off-risks-conflict.

Friedmann, J. 1995. Where we stand: a decade of world city research. In P.L. Knox and P.J. Taylor, eds. *World Cities in a World System*. Cambridge: Cambridge University Press, 21–47.

Friedmann, J. 2002. *The Prospect of Cities*. Minneapolis: University of Minnesota Press.

Friendly, A. 2020. Insurgent planning in pandemic times: the case of Rio de Janeiro. *International Journal of Urban and Regional Research*. 46, 1: 115–25.

Frisina Doetter, L., B. Preuß, and H. Rothgang. 2021. Taking stock of COVID-19 policy measures to protect Europe's elderly living in long-term care facilities. *Global Social Policy*. 21, 3: 529–49.

Fudge, C., M. Grant, and H. Wallbaum. 2020. Transforming cities and health: policy, action, and meaning. *Cities & Health*. 4, 2: 135–51.

Gandy, M. 2004. Rethinking urban metabolism: water, space and the modern city. *City*. 8, 3: 363–79.

Gandy, M. 2006. The bacteriological city and its discontents. *Historical Geography*. 34: 14–25.

Gandy, M. 2022a. Urban political ecology: a critical reconfiguration. *Progress in Human Geography*. 46, 1: 21–43.

Gandy, M. 2022b. The zoonotic city: urban political ecology and the pandemic imaginary. *International Journal of Urban and Regional Research*. 46, 2: 202–19.

Garrett, L. 1994. *The Coming Plague: Newly Emerging Diseases in a World out of Balance*. London: Penguin.

GaWC (Global and World Cities). 2004. Globalization and World Cities Research Network. http://www.lboro.ac.uk/gawc.

REFERENCES | 215

Gebrekidan, S., K. Bennhold, M. Apuzzo, and D.D. Kirkpatrick. 2020. Ski, party, seed a pandemic: the travel rules that let Covid-19 take flight. *The New York Times*, 30 September. https://www.nytimes.com/2020/09/30/world/europe/ski-party-pandemic-travel-coronavirus.html.

Gee, M. 2020. Differing COVID-19 rates around Toronto underline enduring gaps in well-being. *The Globe and Mail*, 5 June. https://www.theglobeandmail.com/canada/toronto/article-differing-covid-19-rates-around-toronto-underline-enduring-gaps-in/.

Gill, S.R. and R.B. Benatar. 2020. Reflections on the political economy of planetary health. *Review of International Political Economy*. 27, 1: 167–90.

Glaeser, E. 2011. *Triumph of the City: How Our Best Innovation Makes Us Richer, Smarter, Greener, Healthier and Happier*. New York: Penguin.

Global Parliament of Mayors. 2021. Global Parliament of Mayors Summit Position Paper. [Summit Paper]. Global Parliament of Mayors Summit, Palermo, Italy. https://globalparliamentofmayors.org/positionpapers-gpm-summit-2021/.

Goh, K. 2021. *Form and Flow: The Spatial Politics of Urban Resilience and Climate Justice*. Cambridge, MA: MIT Press.

Golubchikov, O. and G. DeVerteuil. 2021. Urban inequalities and the lived politics of resilience. In P. Filion, B. Doucet, and R. Van Melik, eds. *Global Reflections on Covid-19 and Urban Inequalities. Vol. 4: Policy and Planning*. Bristol: Bristol University Press, 69–80.

Gonsalves, G. 2021. Covid Year 2: about suffering the old masters were never wrong. *The Nation*, 25 November. https://www.thenation.com/article/society/covid-deaths-endemic/.

Goodnough, A. and J. Hoffman. 2021. The wealthy are getting more vaccinations, even in poorer neighborhoods. *The New York Times*, 2 February. https://www.nytimes.com/2021/02/02/health/white-people-covid-vaccines-minorities.html.

Gostin, L.O. and E. Friedman. 2014. Ebola: a crisis in global health leadership. *The Lancet*. 384, 9951: 1323–5.

Gottschalk, R. 2016. Risk communication and generic preparedness: from agent-based to action-based planning – a conceptual framework. *British Journal of Medicine & Medical Research*. 13, 10: 1–5.

Goumenou, M., D. Sarigiannis, A. Tsatsakis, O. Anesti, A. Docea, D. Petrakis, D. Tsoukalas, R. Kostoff, V. Rakitskii, A. Demetrios, M. Spandidos, D. Aschner, and C. Mol. 2020. COVID-19 in northern Italy: an integrative overview of factors possibly influencing the sharp increase of the outbreak. *Molecular Medicine Reports*. 22, 1: 20–32.

Gover, A.R., S.B. Harper, and L. Langton. 2020. Anti-Asian hate crime during the COVID-19 pandemic: exploring the reproduction of inequality. *American Journal of Criminal Justice*. 45, 4: 647–67.

Graham, S. 2010. When infrastructures fail. In S. Graham, ed. *Disrupted Cities: When Infrastructure Fails*. New York: Routledge, 1–26.

Graham, S. and S. Marvin. 2001. *Splintering Urbanism: Networked Infrastructures, Technological Mobilities and the Urban Condition*. London: Routledge.

Grant, J.L. 2020. Pandemic challenges to planning prescriptions: how COVID-19 is changing the ways we think about planning. *Planning Theory & Practice*. 21, 5: 659–67. https://doi.org/10.1080/14649357.2020.1853408.

Grant, K. 2020. These two northwest Toronto neighbourhoods have COVID-19 positivity rates above 10 per cent, newly released data show. *The Globe and Mail*, 20 October. https://www.theglobeandmail.com/canada/article-toronto-reveals-rates-of-positive-covid-19-tests-by-neighbourhood/.

Güney, K.M., R. Keil, and M. Üçoğlu, eds. 2019. *Massive Suburbanization: (Re)Building the Global Periphery*. Toronto: University of Toronto Press.

Haggett, P. 1994. Geographical aspects of the emergence of infectious diseases. *Geografiska Annaler. Series B, Human Geography*. 76, 2: 91–104.

Halabi, S.F., L.O. Gostin, and J.S. Crowley, eds. 2017. *Global Management of Infectious Disease after Ebola*. Oxford: Oxford University Press.

Hamel, P. 2022. Governing cities in a post-suburban era: new challenges for planning? In R. Keil and F. Wu, eds. *After Suburbia*. Toronto: University of Toronto Press, 203–23.

Hamidi, S., S. Sabouri, and R. Ewing. 2020. Does density aggravate the COVID-19 pandemic? *Journal of the American Planning Association*. 86, 4: 495–509.

Harrison, P. 2014. Making planning theory real. *Planning Theory*. 13, 1: 65–81.

Harrison, P. 2020. Johannesburg and its epidemics: can we learn from history? *Gauteng City-Region Observatory*. November. https://cdn.gcro.ac.za/media/documents/GCRO_Occasional_Paper-Epidemics.pdf.

Hartt, M. 2020. COVID-19: a lonely pandemic. *Cities & Health*. 5, 1: 580–2.

Hassett, B. 2017. *Built on Bones: 15,000 Years of Urban Life and Death*. London: Bloomsbury.

Hellowell, M. and P. Nayna Schwerdtle. 2022. Powerful ideas? Decolonisation and the future of global health. *BMJ Global Health 2022*. 7, 1: e006924.

Helmuth, L. 2020. Nine important things we've learned about the coronavirus pandemic so far. *Scientific American*, 4 August. https://www.scientificamerican.com/article/nine-important-things-weve-learned-about-the-coronavirus-pandemic-so-far/.

Herhalt, C. and C. Wilson. 2021. COVID-19 outbreak reported at Amazon warehouse as Brampton Transit suspends service on route. *CP24 News Online*, 9 March. https://www.cp24.com/news/covid-19-outbreak-reported-at-amazon-warehouse-as-brampton-transit-suspends-service-on-route-1.5339526.

Hermer, J. 2021. Homeless encampment violence in Toronto betrays any real

hope for police reform. *The Conversation*, 27 July. https://theconversation
.com/homeless-encampment-violence-in-toronto-betrays-any-real-hope-for
-police-reform-165039#:~:text=The%20violence%20used%20to%20forcibly
,a%20cynical%20public%20relations%20ploy.

Herrick, C. 2014. Healthy cities of/from the South. In S. Parnell and S. Oldfield, eds. *The Routledge Handbook on Cities of the Global South*. London: Routledge, 556–69.

Hertel, S. and R. Keil. 2020. After isolation: urban planning and the COVID-19 pandemic. *Ontario Professional Planners Institute Blog*, 27 April. https:// ontarioplanners.ca/blog/planning-exchange/may-2020/after-isolation-urban -planning-and-the-covid-19-pandemic.

Heymann, D. 2017. Ebola: transforming fear into appropriate action. *The Lancet*. 390, 10091: 219–20.

Heymann, D.L. 2004. The international response to the outbreak of SARS in 2003. *Philosophical Transactions of the Royal Society B: Biological Sciences*. 359, 1447: 1127–9.

Heymann, D.L. and G. Rodier. 1997. Reemerging pathogens and diseases out of control. *The Lancet*. 349, 9068: S8–S9.

Heynen, N., M. Kaika, and E. Swyngedouw. 2006. Urban political ecology: politicizing the production of urban natures. In N. Heynen, M. Kaika, and E. Swyngedouw, eds. *In the Nature of Cities: Urban Political Ecology and the Politics of Urban Metabolism*. London: Routledge, 1–21.

Hill, D. 2021. The suburbs as they are, and could be. *Architecture AU*, 2 November. https://architectureau.com/articles/the-suburbs-as-they-are-and-could-be/.

Hoffman, B. 2014. How increased meat consumption in China changes landscapes across the globe. *Forbes*, 26 March. https:// www.forbes.com/sites/bethhoffman/2014/03/26/how-increased-meat-consumption-in-china-changes-landscapes-across-the-globe/#599c26666448.

Hooker, C. and S.H. Ali. 2009. SARS and security: health in the new normal. *Studies in Political Economy*. 84, 1: 101–28.

Horton, R. 2020a. *The COVID-19 Catastrophe: What's Gone Wrong and How to Stop it Happening Again*. Cambridge: Polity.

Horton, R. 2020b. Offline: COVID-19 is not a pandemic. *The Lancet*. 396, 10255: 874.

Houston, D. and K. Ruming. 2014. Suburban toxicity: a political ecology of asbestos in Australian cities. *Geographical Research*. 52, 4: 400–10.

Howard, A.M. 2017. Ebola and regional history: connections and common experiences. In I. Abdullah and I. Rashid, eds. *Understanding West Africa's Ebola Epidemic: Towards a Political Economy*. London: Zed Books, 19–46.

Huang, X., Q. Yang, and J. Yang J. 2021. Importance of community containment measures in combating the COVID-19 epidemic: from the perspective of urban planning. *Geo-Spatial Information Science*. 24(3): 363–71. https://doi .org/10.1080/10095020.2021.1894905.

Hynie, M. 2018. Refugee integration: research and policy. *Peace and Conflict: Journal of Peace Psychology*. 24, 3: 265–76.

Inside Logistics Online Staff. 2021. Peel Region Covid closures mount. *Inside Logistics: Canada's Supply Chain Magazine*, 4 May. https://www.insidelogistics .ca/business-operations/peel-region-covid-closures-mount-175654/.

Jackson, P. 2008. Fleshy traffic, feverish borders: blood, birds and civet cats in cities brimming with intimate commodities. In S.H. Ali and R. Keil, eds. *Networked Disease: Emerging Infections in the Global City*. Oxford: Wiley-Blackwell, 281–96.

Jackson, P. and A.H. Neely. 2015. Triangulating health: toward a practice of a political ecology of health. *Progress in Human Geography*. 39, 1: 47–64.

Jamieson, W. 2022. Logistical virulence, migrant exposure, and the underside of Singapore's model pandemic response. In H.B. Shin, M. Mckenzie, and D.Y. Young, eds. *COVID-19 in Southeast Asia: Insights for a Post-Pandemic World*. London: LSE Press, 131–40.

Johnson, R., M. Kandeh, A. Jalloh, G. Nelson, and T. Thomas. 2013. Sierra Leone. In A. Jalloh, T.S. Nelson, T.R. Zougmore, and H. Roy-Macauley, eds. *West African Agriculture and Climate Change: A Comprehensive Analysis*. Washington, DC: International Food Policy Research Institute, 323–52.

Johnston, C. 2008. Beyond the clearing: towards a dwelt animal geography. *Progress in Human Geography*. 32, 5: 633–49. https://doi.org/10.1177 /0309132508089825.

Jon, I. 2020. A manifesto for planning after the coronavirus: towards planning of care. *Planning Theory*. 19, 3: 331.

Jon, I. 2021. The city we want: against the banality of urban planning research. *Planning Theory & Practice*. 22, 2: 321–8.

Kaika, M., R. Keil, T. Mandler, and Y. Tzaninis, eds. 2022. *Turning Up the Heat: Urban Political Ecology for a Climate Emergency*. Manchester: Manchester University Press.

K'Akumu, O.A. and W.H.A. Olima. 2007. The dynamics and implications of residential segregation in Nairobi. *Habitat International*. 31, 1: 87–99.

Kaufman, J. 2006. SARS and China's health-care response: better to be both red and expert! In A. Kleinman and J.L. Watson, eds. *SARS in China: Prelude to Pandemic*. Stanford: Stanford University Press, 53–68.

Kaup, B.Z. 2018. The making of Lyme disease: a political ecology of ticks and tick-borne illness in Virginia. *Environmental Sociology*. 4, 3: 381–91.

Kaup, B.Z. 2021. Pathogenic metabolisms: a rift and the Zika virus in Mato Grosso, Brazil. *Antipode*. 53, 2: 567–86.

Kearns, R. and G. Moon. 2002. From medical to health geography: novelty, place and theory after a decade of change. *Progress in Human Geography*. 26, 5: 605–25.

Keesmaat, J., K. McKenzie, and R. Florida. 2020. Canada's new normal begins in our cities. *The Globe and Mail*, 23 May. https://www.theglobeandmail.com/opinion/article-canadas-new-normal-begins-in-our-cities/.

Keil, R. 2018a. Extended urbanization, "disjunct fragments" and global suburbanisms. *Environment and Planning D: Society and Space*. 36, 3: 494–511.

Keil, R. 2018b. *Suburban Planet: Making the World Urban from the Outside In*. Cambridge: Polity.

Keil, R. 2020a. The life of technology and the technologies of living. *disP: The Planning Review*. 56, 2: 4–7.

Keil, R. 2020b. The density dilemma: there is always too much and too little of it. *Urban Geography*. 41, 10: 1284–93.

Keil, R. 2020c. The spatialized political ecology of the city: situated peripheries and the capitalocenic limits of urban affairs. *Journal of Urban Affairs*. 42, 8: 1125–40.

Keil, R. Forthcoming. Covid, contagion and comparative urban research. In P. Le Gales and J. Robinson, eds. *The Routledge Handbook of Comparative Urban Studies*. London: Routledge.

Keil, R. and S.H. Ali. 2006. Multiculturalism, racism and infectious disease in the global city. *Topia: Canadian Journal of Cultural Studies*. 16, 16: 23–49.

Keil, R. and S.H. Ali. 2007. Governing the sick city: urban governance in the age of emerging infectious disease. *Antipode*. 39, 5: 846–73.

Keil, R. and S.H. Ali. 2008. Racism is a weapon of mass destruction: SARS and the social fabric of urban multiculturalism. In S.H. Ali and R. Keil, eds. *Networked Disease: Emerging Infections in the Global City*. Oxford: Wiley-Blackwell, 152–66.

Keil, R. and S.H. Ali. 2011. The urban political pathology of emerging infectious disease in the age of the global city. In E. McCann and K. Ward, eds. *Mobile Urbanism: Cities and Policymaking in the Global Age*. Minneapolis: University of Minnesota Press, 123–35.

Keil, R. and S. Hertel. 2020. COVID-19: climate emergency, COVID-19, Black Lives Matter: urban planning's insurgent moment. *Public Policy Institute. The University of Western Australia*. https://www.news.uwa.edu.au/archive/2020070112198/uwa-public-policy-institute/covid-19-climate-emergency-covid-19-black-lives-matter-urb/.

Keil, R. and M. Üçoğlu. 2021. Beyond sprawl? Regulating growth in southern Ontario: spotlight on Brampton. *disP: The Planning Review*. 57, 3: 100–18.

Keil, R., S. Biglieri, and L. De Vidovich. 2022. A heuristic device, not an actual map … revisiting the urban periphery. *Cities & Health*. https://doi.org/10.1080/23748834.2021.2016284.

Keil, R., P. Hamel, J.-A. Boudreau, and S. Kipfer, eds. 2017. *Governing Cities Through Regions: Canadian and European Perspectives*. Waterloo: Wilfrid Laurier University Press.

Kelly, R. 2006. *The Great Mortality: An Intimate History of the Black Death, the Most Devastating Plague of All Time*. New York: HarperCollins.

Kennedy, B. 2021. Toronto announces plan to combat disproportionate impact of COVID-19 on Black communities. *The Toronto Star*, 3 February. https://www.thestar.com/news/gta/2021/02/03/toronto-announces-plan-to-combat-disproportionate-impact-of-covid-19-on-black-communities.html.

Kieh, G. 2008. *The First Liberian Civil War: The Crises of Underdevelopment*. New York: Peter Lang.

Kieh, G. 2012. *Liberia's State Failure, Collapse and Reconstitution*. Cherry Hill: Africana Homestead Legacy.

Kieh, G. 2017. The political economy of the ebola epidemic in Liberia. In I. Abdullah and I. Rashid, eds. *Understanding West Africa's Ebola Epidemic: Towards a Political Economy*. London: Zed Books, 85–111.

King, B. 2010. Political ecologies of health. *Progress in Human Geography*. 34, 1: 38–55.

King, N.B. 2002. Security, disease, commerce: ideologies of postcolonial global health. *Social Studies of Science*. 32, 5–6: 763–89.

Kipfer, S. and J. Mohamud. 2021. The pandemic as political emergency. *Studies in Political Economy*. 102, 3: 268–88.

Kirby, A. 1993. *Power/Resistance. Local Politics and the Chaotic State*. Bloomington: Indiana University Press.

Kirby, A. 2019. Sustainability, adaptation and the local state: an overview. *Journal of Sustainability Research*. 1: e190012.

Kneebone, E. and E. Garr. 2010. The suburbanization of poverty: trends in metropolitan America, 2000 to 2008. *Metropolitan Policy Program at Brookings*. https://www.brookings.edu/wp-content/uploads/2016/06/0120_poverty_paper.pdf.

Knobler, S., A. Mahmoud, S. Lemon, et al., eds. 2004. *Learning from SARS: Preparing for the Next Disease Outbreak: Workshop Summary*. Washington, DC: National Academies Press.

Kock, R., W. Karesh, F. Veas, T. Velavan, D. Simons, L. Mboera, O. Dar, L.B. Arruda, and A. Zumla. 2020. 2019-nCoV in context: lessons learned? *The Lancet Planetary Health*, 6 February. https://doi.org/10.1016/S2542-5196(20)30035-8.

Koh, S.Y. 2022. Emergent bordering tactics, logics of injustice, and the new hierarchies of mobility deservingness. In H.B. Shin, M. Mckenzie, and D.Y. Young, eds. *COVID-19 in Southeast Asia: Insights for a Post-Pandemic World*. London: LSE Press, 183–92.

Kotsila, P. 2017. Health dispossessions and the moralization of disease: the case of diarrhea in the Mekong Delta, Vietnam. *Journal of Political Ecology.* 24, 1: 87.

Krauss, C. 2003. A respiratory illness: new cases; exposure of church group to disease raises chance of its spread in Toronto. *The New York Times,* 16 April. https://www.nytimes.com/2003/04/16/world/respiratory-illness-new-cases -exposure-church-group-disease-raises-chance-its.html.

Kreisel, D. 2020. The unraveling of "the unraveling of America." *Medium,* 8 August. https://medium.com/@deannakaykreisel/the-unraveling-of-the -unraveling-of-america-db63ed82fa25.

Krugman, P. 2021. The durable myth of urban hellholes. *The New York Times,* 12 July. https://www.nytimes.com/2021/07/12/opinion/covid-big-cities.html.

Kunzmann, K.R. 2020. Smart cities after Covid-19: ten narratives. *disP: The Planning Review.* 56, 2: 20–31.

Kushner, L. and G. Lindsay. 2021. The dark side of 15-minute grocery delivery. *Bloomberg CityLab,* 7 December. https://www.bloomberg.com/news /articles/2021-12-07/what-instant-delivery-services-could-do-to-cities?sref =Y5NzbMHF.

Lahai, J.I. 2017. *The Ebola Pandemic in Sierra Leone: Representations, Actors, Interventions and the Path to Recovery.* Cham: Springer International.

Lambin, E.F., A. Tran, S.O. Vanwambeke, C. Linard, and V. Soti. 2010. Pathogenic landscapes: interactions between land, people, disease vectors, and their animal hosts. *International Journal of Health Geographics.* 9, 1: 54.

Lancione, M. and C. McFarlane. 2016. Life at the urban margins: sanitation infra-making and the potential of experimental comparison. *Environment and Planning A: Economy and Space.* 48, 12: 2402–21.

Laporta, G.Z. 2014. Landscape fragmentation and Ebola outbreaks. *Memórias do Instituto Oswaldo Cruz.* 109, 8: 1088.

Laurent, L. 2020. Good Covid-19 news from Italy … and Sweden. *The Washington Post,* 5 August. https://www.washingtonpost.com/business/good -covid-19-news-from-italyand-sweden/2020/08/04/6e456656-d61d-11ea -a788-2ce86ce81129_story.html.

Leach, M. 2015. The Ebola crisis and post-2015 development: Ebola and post-2015 development. *Journal of International Development.* 27, 6: 816–34.

Leavitt, J.W. 2003. Public resistance or cooperation? A tale of smallpox in two cities. *Biosecurity and Bioterrorism: Biodefense Strategy, Practice, and Science.* 1, 3: 185–92.

Lefebvre, H. 1991. *The Production of Space.* Oxford: Blackwell.

Lefebvre, H. 2003. *The Urban Revolution.* Minneapolis: University of Minnesota Press.

Lehmann, S. 2021. Growing biodiverse urban futures: renaturalization and rewilding as strategies to strengthen urban resilience. *Sustainability*. 13, 5: 2932. https://doi.org/10.3390/su13052932.

Li, P. 2003. *Destination Canada: Immigration Debates and Issues*. Toronto: Oxford University Press.

Loftus, A. 2006. The metabolic processes of capital accumulation in Durban's waterscape. In N. Heynen, M. Kaika, and E. Swyngedouw, eds. *In the Nature of Cities: Urban Political Ecology and the Politics of Urban Metabolism*. Abingdon: Routledge, 173–90.

Loreto, N. 2021. *Spin Doctors: How Media and Politicians Misdiagnosed the COVID-19 Pandemic*. Halifax: Fernwood.

Lorimer, H. 2006. Herding memories of humans and animals. *Environment and Planning D: Society and Space*. 24, 4: 497–518.

Low, D.E. 2003. SARS: lessons from Toronto. In S. Knobler, A. Mahmoud, S. Lemon, A. Mack, L. Sivitz, and K. Oberholtzer, eds. *Learning from SARS: Preparing for the Next Disease Outbreak*. Washington, DC: National Academies Press, 63–70.

Lusk, K. 2021. Cities were radically reimagined during COVID-19. Can they stay that way? *Fast Company*, 2 April. https://www.fastcompany.com/90621038 /cities-were-radically-reimagined-during-covid-19-can-they-stay-that-way ?partner=rss&utm_source=rss&utm_medium=feed&utm_campaign=rss+ fastcompany&utm_content=rss.

Luxemburg Foundation. 2020. *A Window of Opportunities for Leftist Politics*. https://www.rosalux.de/fileadmin/rls_uploads/pdfs/LUXEMBURG/RLS _LUX_Mini_CORONA_EN_FINAL.pdf.

Lynch, K., E. Nel, and T. Binns. 2020. "Transforming Freetown": dilemmas of planning and development in a West African city. *Cities*. 101: 102694.

MacDougall, C. 2014. Liberian government's blunders pile up in the grip of Ebola. *Time.com*, 2 September.

MacGillis, A. 2021. *Fulfillment: Winning and Losing in One-Click America*. London: Scribe.

MacIntyre, C.R. 2020. Global spread of COVID-19 and pandemic potential. *Global Biosecurity*. 1, 3. https://doi.org/10.31646/gbio.55.

Madden, D. 2021. Red London in Tory Britain. *Jacobin*, 26 January. https:// jacobinmag.com/2021/01/london-urbanism-municipalism.

Magnusson, W. 2011. *Politics of Urbanism: Seeing Like a City*. London: Routledge.

Mariette, A. and L. Pitti. 2021. Covid-19 in Seine-Saint-Denis: when the pandemic entrenches health inequalities. *Metropolitics*, 17 September. https:// metropolitics.org/Covid-19-in-Seine-Saint-Denis-1-2-When-the-Pandemic -Entrenches-Health.html.

Mattern, S. 2021. *A City is Not a Computer: Other Urban Intelligences*. Princeton: Princeton University Press.

Matthew, R.A. and B. McDonald. 2006. Cities under siege: urban planning and the threat of infectious disease. *Journal of the American Planning Association.* 72, 1: 109–17.

Maxmen, A. 2021. Inequality's deadly toll. *Nature,* 28 April. https://www.nature .com/immersive/d41586-021-00943-x/index.html.

Mayer, J.D. 2000. Geography, ecology and emerging infectious diseases. *Social Science & Medicine.* 50, 7–8: 937–52.

McCarthy, S., L. Lew, W. Zheng, E. Xie, and P. Zhang. 2020. Coronavirus: how Disease X, the epidemic-in-waiting, erupted in China. *South China Morning Post,* 27 February. https://multimedia.scmp.com/infographics/news/china /article/3052721/wuhan-killer/index.html.

McFarlane, C. 2021. Repopulating density: COVID-19 and the politics of urban value. *Urban Studies.* https://doi.org/10.1177%2F00420980211014810.

McGuirk, P., R. Dowling, S. Maalsen, and T. Baker. 2020. Urban governance innovation and COVID-19. *Geographical Research.* 59, 2: 188–95.

McInnes, C., A. Kamradt-Scott, K. Lee, D. Reubi, A. Roemer-Mahler, S. Rushton, O.D. Williams, and M. Woodling. 2012. Framing global health: the governance challenge. *Global Public Health.* 7, 2: S83–S94.

McKinney, K.R., Y.Y. Gong, and T.G. Lewis. 2006. Environmental transmission of SARS at Amoy Gardens. *Journal of Environmental Health.* 68, 9: 26–30.

McMichael, A.J. 2001. Human culture, ecological change and infectious disease: are we experiencing history's fourth great transition? *Ecosystem Health.* 7, 2: 107–15.

Meth, P. and S. Charlton. 2020. Seeing in the suburbs. *Transformation: Critical Perspectives on Southern Africa.* 104: 113–24.

Misik, R. 2021. The revolt against reason. *Social Europe,* 6 December. https:// socialeurope.eu/the-revolt-against-reason.

Mitchell, D. 1996. *The Lie of the Land: Migrant Workers and the California Landscape.* Minneapolis: University of Minnesota Press.

Monstadt, J. 2009. Conceptualizing the political ecology of urban infrastructures: insights from technology and urban studies. *Environment and Planning A: Economy and Space.* 41, 8: 1924–42.

Moore, M., P. Gould, and B.S. Keary. 2003. Global urbanization and impact on health. *International Journal of Hygiene and Environmental Health.* 206, 4–5: 269–78.

Moos, M. and A. Skaburskis. 2007. The characteristics and location of home workers in Montreal, Toronto and Vancouver. *Urban Studies.* 44, 9: 1781–1808.

Moos, M., A. McCulley, and T. Vinodrai. 2020. COVID-19 and urban density: evaluating the arguments, discussion report. *University of Waterloo.* https://uwaterloo.ca/environment/sites/ca.environment/files/uploads/files /densityhousing_1_arguments_moosmcculleyvinodrai.pdf.

Morens, D.M. and A.S. Fauci. 2013. Emerging infectious diseases: threats to human health and global stability. *PLoS Pathogens.* 9, 7: e1003467.

Morris, L. and L. Beck. 2020. As Germany awaits vaccine, mass vaccination centers are built in less than a week. *The Washington Post,* 12 December. https://www.washingtonpost.com/world/europe/germany-mass-vaccination -centers/2020/12/11/efdb9b08-3951-11eb-aad9-8959227280c4_story .html.

Morse, S.S. 1993. Examining the origins of emerging viruses. In S.S. Morse, ed. *Emerging Viruses.* New York: Oxford University Press, 10–28.

Morse, S.S. 1995. Factors in the emergence of infectious diseases. *Emerging Infectious Diseases.* 1, 1: 7–15.

Muggah, R. and R. Florida. 2020a. Megacity slums are incubators of disease – but coronavirus response isn't helping the billion people who live in them. *The Conversation,* 14 May. https://theconversation.com/megacity-slums-are -incubators-of-disease-but-coronavirus-response-isnt-helping-the-billion -people-who-live-in-them-138092?utm_source=twitterandutm_medium= bylinetwitterbutton.

Muggah, R. and R. Florida. 2020b. COVID-19 will hit the developing world's cities hardest. Here's why. *World Economic Forum,* 27 May. https://www .weforum.org/agenda/2020/05/covid-19-will-hit-the-developing-worlds -cities-hardest-heres-why/.

Mukherjee, S. 2021. The Covid conundrum: why does the pandemic seem far deadlier in some countries than in others? *The New Yorker,* 1 March. https:// www.newyorker.com/magazine/2021/03/01/why-does-the-pandemic-seem -to-be-hitting-some-countries-harder-than-others.

Mulligan, K., S.J. Elliott, and C. Schuster-Wallace. 2012. The place of health and the health of place: Dengue fever and urban governance in Putrajaya, Malaysia. *Health & Place.* 18, 3: 613–20. https://doi.org/10.1016/j.healthplace.2012.01 .001.

Mullis, D. 2021. Peripheries, politics, centralities: geographies of COVID-19. Reflections from a German perspective on and beyond Biglieri et al. *Cities & Health.* https://doi.org/10.1080/23748834.2021.1964909.

Munster, V.J., D.G. Bausch, E. de Wit, et al. 2018. Outbreaks in a rapidly changing Central Africa: lessons from Ebola. *New England Journal of Medicine.* 379, 13: 1198–1201.

Murray, M. 2006. The epidemiology of SARS. In A. Kleinman and J.L. Watson, eds. *SARS in China: Prelude to Pandemic.* Stanford: Stanford University Press, 17–30.

NACSPH (National Advisory Committee on SARS and Public Health). 2003. *Learning from SARS: Renewal of Public Health in Canada.* Ottawa: Health Canada.

Nading, A.M. 2014. *Mosquito Trails: Ecology, Health, and the Politics of Entanglement*. Oakland: University of California Press.

Napier, D. and E.F. Fischer. 2020. The culture of health and sickness. *Le Monde Diplomatique*, 4 July. https://mondediplo.com/2020/07/04uganda.

Nasser, S. 2020a. Brampton has emerged as one of Ontario's COVID-19 hotspots, but experts urge caution on where to lay blame. *CBC News*, 14 September. https://www.cbc.ca/news/canada/toronto/brampton-coronavirus-covid-19 -south-asian-1.5723330.

Nasser, S. 2020b. Early signs suggest race matters when it comes to COVID-19. So why isn't Canada collecting race-based data? *CBC News*, 17 April. https:// www.cbc.ca/news/canada/toronto/race-coronavirus-canada-1.5536168.

Nathan, M. 2021. The city and the virus. *Urban Studies*. https://doi.org/10.1177 /00420980211058383.

Nathan, M. and H. Overman. 2020. Will coronavirus cause a big city exodus? *Environment and Planning B: Urban Analytics and City Science*. 47, 9: 1537–42.

Neuman, M., L. Chelleri, and T. Schuetze. 2021. Post-pandemic urbanism: criteria for a new normal. *Sustainability*. 13, 19: 10600. https://doi.org/10 .3390/su131910600.

Ng, M.K. 2008. Globalization of SARS and health governance in Hong Kong under "one country, two systems." In S.H. Ali and R. Keil, eds. *Networked Disease: Emerging Infections in the Global City*. Oxford: Wiley-Blackwell, 70–85.

Ni, Z., E.R. Lebowitz, Z. Zou, et al. 2021. Response to the COVID-19 outbreak in urban settings in China. *Journal of Urban Health*. 98, 1: 41–52.

Njoh, A.J. 2010. Europeans, modern urban planning and the acculturation of "racial others." *Planning Theory*. 9, 4: 369–78.

Normile, D. 2005. Researchers tie deadly SARS virus to bats. *Science*. 309, 5744: 2154–5.

Novacevski, M. 2021. Pestilence in planning: why Camus is a beacon for our times. *Planning Theory & Practice*. 22, 2: 329–35.

O'Connell, M. 2018. Why Silicon Valley billionaires are prepping for the apocalypse in New Zealand. *The Guardian*, 15 February. https://www.theguardian .com/news/2018/feb/15/why-silicon-valley-billionaires-are-prepping-for -the-apocalypse-in-new-zealand.

Onoma, A.K. 2016. Rites of mobility and epidemic control: Ebola virus disease in the Mano River Basin. *Governance in Africa*. 3, 1.

Ow, C.H. 1984. Singapore: past, present and future. In P.S. You and C.Y. Lim, eds. *Singapore: Twenty-Five Years of Development*. Singapore: Nan Ynag Xing Zhou Lianhe Aaobao, 366–85.

Pallister, D. 2006. Mittal accused of creating a state within a state in Liberia. *The Guardian*, 2 October. https://www.theguardian.com/business/2006/oct/03 /money.

Paolini, M. 2020. Manifesto for the reorganisation of the city after COVID-19: an open letter to the mayor of Barcelona. *degrowth*, 18 May. https://www.degrowth.info/en/2020/05/manifesto-for-the-reorganisation-of-the-city-after-covid-19/.

Parizeau, K. 2015. Urban political ecologies of informal recyclers' health in Buenos Aires, Argentina. *Health & Place*. 33: 67–74.

Pelley, L. 2020. Half of Scarborough ICU patients have COVID-19 as vulnerable workers, families bear brunt of pandemic. *CBC News*, 15 December. https://www.cbc.ca/news/canada/toronto/half-of-scarborough-icu-patients-have-covid-19-as-vulnerable-workers-families-bear-brunt-of-pandemic-1.5841390.

Perng, S.Y. 2020. Ignorance, exclusion, and solidarity in human–virus co-existence during and after COVID-19. *Dialogues in Human Geography*. 10, 2: 150–3.

Petersen, A.H. 2021. The topography of wellness. *Culture Study*, 8 December. https://annehelen.substack.com/p/the-topography-of-wellness.

PHAC (Public Health Agency of Canada). 2021. *CPHO Sunday Edition: The Impact of COVID-19 on Racialized Communities*. https://www.canada.ca/en/public-health/news/2021/02/cpho-sunday-edition-the-impact-of-covid-19-on-racialized-communities.html.

Phelps, N.A. and F. Wu, eds. 2011. *International Perspectives on Suburbanization: A Post-Suburban World?* Basingstoke: Palgrave Macmillan.

Pitter, J. 2020a. Urban density: confronting the distance between desire and disparity. *Azure Magazine*, 17 April. https://www.azuremagazine.com/article/urban-density-confronting-the-distance-between-desire-and-disparity/.

Pitter, J. 2020b. A call to courage: an open letter to Canadian urbanists. *The Canadian Urban Institute*, 10 June. https://canurb.org/citytalk-news/a-call-to-courage-an-open-letter-to-canadian-urbanists/.

Plageman, N., J.A. Hart, and T. Yeboah. 2020. Urban planning needs to look back first: three cities in Ghana show why. *The Conversation*, 14 September. https://theconversation.com/urban-planning-needs-to-look-back-first-three-cities-in-ghana-show-why-144913.

Pleyers, G. 2020. The pandemic is a battlefield: social movements in the COVID-19 lockdown. *Journal of Civil Society*. 16, 4: 295–312.

Popal, A. 2021. The duality of Amazon in Scarborough: from delivering jobs to packaging community relations. *Spacing*, 1 March. http://spacing.ca/toronto/2021/03/01/the-duality-of-amazon-in-scarborough-from-delivering-jobs-to-packaging-community-relations/.

Preston, R. 1994. *The Hot Zone: A Terrifying True Story*. New York: Anchor Books.

Quammen, D. 2012. *Spillover: Animal Infections and the Next Human Pandemic*. New York: W.W. Norton.

Quammen, D. 2014. *Ebola: The Natural and Human History of a Deadly Virus*. New York: W.W. Norton.

Ren, X. 2020a. Pandemic and lockdown: a territorial approach to COVID-19 in China, Italy and the United States. *Eurasian Geography and Economics*. 61, 4–5: 423–34.

Ren, X. 2020b. The quarantine of a megacity: China's struggle over the coronavirus epidemic. *International Journal of Urban and Regional Research*, 4 February. https://www.ijurr.org/the-urban-now/the-quarantine-of-a-megacity/.

Ren, X. 2022. Urban China and COVID-19: how Chinese Cities responded to the pandemic. In D. Goodman and C. Ergenc, eds. *Handbook of Local Governance in China*. Cheltenham: Elgar.

Ren, X. and R. Keil, eds. 2017. *The Globalizing Cities Reader*. London: Routledge.

Reuschke, D. and A. Felstead. 2020. Changing workplace geographies in the COVID-19 crisis. *Dialogues in Human Geography*. 10, 2: 208–12.

Richards, P. 2016. *Ebola: How a People's Science Helped End an Epidemic*. London: Zed Books.

Richards, P., J. Amara, M.C. Ferme, P. Kamara, E. Mokuwa, A. Sheriff, et al. 2015. Social pathways for Ebola virus disease in Rural Sierra Leone, and some implications for containment. *PLoS Neglected Tropical Diseases*. 9, 4: e0003567.

Richardson, E.T. 2020. *Epidemic Illusions: On the Coloniality of Global Public Health*. Cambridge, MA: MIT Press.

Robbins, P. 2004. *Political Ecology: A Critical Introduction*. Malden: Blackwell.

Robbins, P. 2012. *Political Ecology: A Critical Introduction*. 2nd edn. Malden: Wiley-Blackwell.

Robinson, J. 2006. *Ordinary Cities: Between Modernity and Development*. London: Routledge.

Rose, J. 2021. Life after death: how the pandemic has transformed our psychic landscape. *The Guardian*, 7 December. https://www.theguardian.com/society/2021/dec/07/life-after-death-pandemic-transformed-psychic-landscape-jacqueline-rose.

Rose-Redwood, R., R. Kitchin, E. Apostolopoulou, L. Rickards, T. Blackman, J. Crampton, U. Rossi, and M. Buckley. 2020. Geographies of the COVID-19 pandemic. *Dialogues in Human Geography*. 10, 2: 97–106.

Roth, K.H. 2022. *Blinde Passagiere: Die Coronakrise und ihre Folgen*. Munich: Antje Kunstmann.

Roy, A. 2020. The pandemic is a portal. *Financial Times*, 3 April. https://www.ft.com/content/10d8f5e8-74eb-11ea-95fe-fcd274e920ca.

Rubin, M. 2020. Urban density, governance and COVID-19: perspectives from South Africa. [Workshop]. Governing the Pandemic in Large Cities: From the BRICS and Beyond, University of Witwatersrand, 22 October.

Rudan, I. 2020. A cascade of causes that led to the COVID-19 tragedy in Italy and in other European Union countries. *Journal of Global Health*. 10, 1. https://doi.org/10.7189%2Fjogh-10-010335.

Rushton, S. and J. Youde, eds. 2014. *The Routledge Handbook of Global Health Security*. Abingdon: Routledge.

Saich, T. 2006. Is SARS China's Chernobyl or Much Ado About Nothing? In A. Kleinman and J.L. Watson, eds. *SARS in China: Prelude to Pandemic*. Stanford: Stanford University Press, 71–104.

Saiyed, S., N. Khaderoo, and G. Kocialek. 2012. Meeting freight challenges through effective regional planning and partnerships. [Paper presentation]. Transportation Planning Conference, 2012 TAC Annual Conference, New Brunswick, Canada.

Sala, G. 2020. COVID-19: the cities leading a greener and fairer recovery. *World Economic Forum*, 11 September. https://www.weforum.org/agenda/2020/09/recipe-for-green-just-recovery-covid-19-pandemic/.

Salehi, R. and S.H. Ali. 2006. The social and political context of disease outbreaks: the case of SARS in Toronto. *Canadian Public Policy/Analyse de Politiques*. 32, 4: 373–85.

Sample, I. and J. Gittings. 2003. In China the civet cat is a delicacy – and may have caused SARS. *The Guardian*, 24 May. https://www.theguardian.com/world/2003/may/24/china.sars.

Sander, M. 2021. Stadt in China führt Corona-Pranger ein. *Neue Zürcher Zeitung*, 31 December.

Sanderson, D. 2020. Coronavirus an "existential threat" to Africa and her crowded slums. *The Conversation*, 9 April. https://theconversation.com/coronavirus-an-existential-threat-to-africa-and-her-crowded-slums-135829?utm_source=twitterandutm_medium=bylinetwitterbutton.

Sandset, T. 2021. The necropolitics of COVID-19: race, class and slow death in an ongoing pandemic. *Global Public Health*. 16, 8–9: 1411–23.

Sanford, S. and S.H. Ali. 2004. The new public health hegemony: response to Severe Acute Respiratory Syndrome (SARS) in Toronto. *Social Theory and Health*. 3: 105–25.

Sanyal, B. 2018. A planners' planner: John Friedmann's quest for a general theory of planning. *Journal of the American Planning Association*. 84, 2: 179–91.

Sarasin, P. 2020. Understanding the coronavirus pandemic with Foucault? *Foucault Blog*, 31 March. https://doi.org/10.13095/uzh.fsw.fb.254.

Sassen, S. 1991. *The Global City: New York, London, Tokyo*. Princeton: Princeton University Press.

Sassen, S. 2000. *Cities in a World Economy*. 2nd edn. Thousand Oaks: Pine Forge Press.

Saunders, D. 2020. The urban cure: how cities seize opportunity from the pandemic crisis to change how they operate for the better. *The Globe and Mail*, 14 November. https://www.theglobeandmail.com/opinion/article-the-urban -cure-how-cities-seize-opportunity-from-the-pandemic-crisis/.

Saunders, D. 2021. Jane Jacobs's afterlife: revisiting *The Death and Life of Great American Cities*, 60 years later. *The Globe and Mail*, 7 August. https://www .theglobeandmail.com/opinion/article-jane-jacobss-afterlife-revisiting-the -death-and-life-of-great-american/.

Schaible, J. 2021. Die geistig-moralischen Wände der Pandemie. *Der Spiegel*, 1 February. https://www.spiegel.de/politik/deutschland/corona-und-die -machtlosigkeit-die-geistig-moralischen-waende-der-pandemie-a-3ef7dca2 -a43a-4822-ac29-2bbbae2dbffb.

Schermer, M. 2020. The after time: the future of civilization after COVID-19. *The American Scholar*, 31 August. https://theamericanscholar.org/the-after -time/#.X0-ygZNKhcs.

Schneider, K. 2022. The *good luck with that* pandemic. *Curbed*, 29 April. https:// www.curbed.com/2022/04/good-luck-with-that-covid.html.

Schorung, M., H. Buldeo Rai, and L. Dablanc. 2022. Flink, Getir, Cajoo … Les "dark stores" et le "quick commerce" remodèlent les grandes villes. *The Conversation*, 3 May. https://theconversation.com/flink-getir-cajoo-les-dark -stores-et-le-quick-commerce-remodelent-les-grandes-villes-182191.

Schrieber, L. and J. Widner. 2017. *The Hunt for Ebola: Building a Disease Surveillance System in Liberia, 2014–2015*. [Case study]. Innovations for Successful Societies. Princeton University. https://successfulsocieties.princeton.edu/publications /ebola-building-disease-surveillance-system-liberia.

Scott, A. 2000. *The Cultural Economy of Cities*. London: Sage.

Scott, A.J. and M. Storper. 2015. The nature of cities: the scope and limits of urban theory. *International Journal of Urban Theory*. 39: 1–15.

Scudellari, M. 2020. How the pandemic might play out in 2021 and beyond. *Nature*. 584, 7819: 22–5.

Seoni, R. 2020. COVID-19: a neighbourhood view for the city of Toronto. *Environics Analytics Blogs*, 7 July. https://environicsanalytics.com/en-ca /resources/blogs/ea-blog/2020/07/07/covid-19-a-neighbourhood-view-for -the-city-of-toronto.

Shabi, R. 2021. Stronger communities are emerging out of the wreckage of the pandemic. *The Guardian*, 8 September. https://www.theguardian.com /commentisfree/2021/sep/08/pandemic-mutual-aid-politics-food-banks -welfare-state.

Sharifi, A. and A.R. Khavarian-Garmsir. 2020. The COVID-19 pandemic: impacts on cities and major lessons for urban planning, design, and management. *Science of the Total Environment*. 749. https://doi.org/10.1016 /j.scitotenv.2020.142391.

Sheller, M. 2018. *Mobility Justice: The Politics of Movement in an Age of Extremes.* London: Verso.

Shin, H.B., M. Mckenzie, and D. Young Oh, eds. 2022. *COVID-19 in Southeast Asia: Insights for a Post-Pandemic World.* London: LSE Press.

Sims, L.D., T.M. Ellis, K.K. Liu, K. Dyrting, H. Wong, M. Peiris, Y. Guan, and K.F. Shortridge. 2003. Avian influenza in Hong Kong 1997–2002. *Avian Diseases.* 47, S3: 832–8.

Sisson, P. 2020. How the "15-minute city" could help post-pandemic recovery. *Bloomberg CityLab*, 15 July. https://www.bloomberg.com/news/articles/2020-07-15/mayors-tout-the-15-minute-city-as-covid-recovery.

Smith, D. and M. Timberlake. 2002. Hierarchies of dominance among world cities: a network approach. In S. Sassen, ed. *Global Networks, Linked Cities.* New York: Routledge, 93–116.

Smith, R.G. 2003. World city topologies. *Progress in Human Geography.* 27, 59: 561–82.

Spitzer, L. 1968. The mosquito and segregation in Sierra Leone. *Canadian Journal of African Studies / Revue Canadienne des Études Africaines.* 2, 1: 49–61.

Springer, S. 2020. Caring geographies: the COVID-19 interregnum and a return to mutual aid. *Dialogues in Human Geography.* 10, 2: 112–15.

Standring, A. and J. Davies. 2020. From crisis to catastrophe: the death and viral legacies of austere neoliberalism in Europe? *Dialogues in Human Geography.* 10, 2: 146–9.

Statistics Canada. 2017. Study: centre and peripheries: settlement patterns and social integration of the population with an immigrant background in the Toronto, Montréal and Vancouver metropolitan areas. *The Daily,* 8 May. https://www150.statcan.gc.ca/n1/daily-quotidien/170508/dq170508a-eng.htm.

Sultana, F. 2021. Climate change, COVID-19, and the co-production of injustices: a feminist reading of overlapping crises. *Social & Cultural Geography.* 22, 4: 447–60.

Swyngedouw, E. 2005. Governance innovation and the citizen: the Janus face of governance-beyond-the-state. *Urban Studies.* 42, 11: 1991–2006. https://doi.org/10.1080/00420980500279869.

Swyngedouw, E. 2006. Circulations and metabolisms: (hybrid) natures and (cyborg) cities. *Science as Culture.* 15, 2: 105–21.

Taylor, D.B. 2021. Timeline of the coronavirus pandemic. *The New York Times,* 17 March. https://www.nytimes.com/article/coronavirus-timeline.html.

Taylor, P.J. 2004. *World City Network: A Global Urban Analysis.* London: Routledge.

Teo, P., B. Yeoh, and S.N. Ong. 2008. Surveillance in a globalizing city: Singapore's battle against SARS. In S.H. Ali and R. Keil, eds. *Networked*

Disease: Emerging Infections in the Global City. Oxford: Wiley-Blackwell, 86–101.

Teo, S.S. 2021. Shared projects and symbiotic collaborations: Shenzhen and London in comparative conversation. *Urban Studies.* https://doi.org/10.1177 /00420980211048675.

Thompson, N. 2020. Spread of COVID-19 in Brampton linked to systemic factors. *Plant: Canada's Manufacturing Magazine,* 30 November. https:// www.plant.ca/general/spread-of-covid-19-in-brampton-linked-to-systemic -factors-experts-198893/.

Tong, M., A. Hansen, S. Hanson-Easey, et al. 2015. Infectious diseases, urbanization and climate change: challenges in future China. *International Journal of Environmental Research and Public Health.* 12, 9: 11025–36.

Toronto Public Health. 2020. Toronto Public Health releases new socio-demographic COVID-19 data. https://www.toronto.ca/news/toronto -public-health-releases-new-socio-demographic-covid-19-data/.

Toronto Public Health. n.d. COVID 19: ethno-racial identity and income. https://www.toronto.ca/home/covid-19/covid-19-pandemic-data/covid-19 -ethno-racial-group-income-infection-data/.

Treffers, S., S.H. Ali, R. Keil, and M. Fallah. 2021. Extending the boundaries of "urban society": the urban political ecologies and pathologies of Ebola virus disease in West Africa. *Environment and Planning E: Nature and Space.* https://doi.org/10.1177%2F25148486211054932.

Tzaninis, Y., T. Mandler, M. Kaika, and R. Keil. 2020. Moving urban political ecology beyond the "urbanization of nature." *Progress in Human Geography.* 45, 2: 229–52. https://doi.org/10.1177/0309132520903350.

UN Habitat. 2021. *Cities and Pandemics: Towards a More Green, Just and Healthy Future.* Nairobi: UN Habitat.

UNEP (United Nations Environment Programme). 2010. *Sierra Leone: Environment, Conflict and Peacebuilding Assessment.* https://wedocs.unep.org /20.500.11822/8202.

UNFPA (United Nations Population Fund). 2007. *UNFPA State of World Population 2007: Unleashing the Potential of Urban Growth.* https://www .unfpa.org/publications/state-world-population-2007.

Van Damme, W., R. Dahake, A. Delamou, et al. 2020. The COVID-19 pandemic: diverse contexts; different epidemics – how and why? *British Medical Journal Global Health.* 5: e003098.

Varia, M., S. Wilson, A. McGeer, E. Gournis, E. Galanis, and B. Henry. 2003. Investigation of nosocomial outbreak of Severe Acute Respiratory Syndrome (SARS) in Toronto, Canada. *Canadian Medical Association Journal.* 169: 285–92.

Vooren, C. 2021. Die zweite Seuche. *Die Zeit,* 6 December. https://

www.zeit.de/gesellschaft/zeitgeschehen/2021-12/corona-proteste-radikalisierung-politik-fehler?utm_referrer=https%3A%2F%2Ft.co%2F.

Wadhera, R.K., P. Wadhera, P. Gaba, J.F. Figueroa, K.E. Joynt Maddox, R.W. Yeh, et al. 2020. Variation in COVID-19 hospitalizations and deaths across New York City boroughs. *JAMA*. 323, 21: 2192–5.

Walcott, R. 2021. *On Property*. Windsor: Biblioasis.

Wald, P. 2008. *Contagious: Cultures, Carriers, and the Outbreak Narrative*. Durham, NC: Duke University Press.

Walker, P. and L. Fortmann. 2003. Whose landscape? A political ecology of the "exurban" Sierra. *Cultural Geographies*. 10: 469–91.

Wallace, R.G. and R. Wallace. 2016. Ebola's ecologies. *New Left Review*. 102: 1–13.

Wallace-Wells, D. 2021. How the West lost COVID: how did so many rich countries get it so wrong? How did others get it so right? *New York Magazine*, 15 March. https://nymag.com/intelligencer/2021/03/how-the-west-lost-covid-19.html.

Wang, F., S. Zou, and Y. Liu. 2020. Territorial traps in controlling the COVID-19 pandemic. *Dialogues in Human Geography*. 10, 2: 154–7. https://doi.org/10.1177/2043820620935682.

Wang, L.F., Z. Shi, S. Zhang, H. Field, P. Daszak, and B.T. Eaton. 2006. Review of bats and SARS. *Emerging Infectious Diseases*. 12, 12: 1834–40.

Westoll, N. 2021. Advocates, opposition slam Ontario government's move to strengthen minister's zoning power. *Global News*, 5 March. https://globalnews.ca/news/7680737/ministers-zoning-order-ontario-government-duffins-creek/.

White, J.A., A. Harmon, D. Ivory, L. Leatherby, A. Sun, and S. Almukhtar. 2022. How America lost one million people. *The New York Times*, 13 May. https://www.nytimes.com/interactive/2022/05/13/us/covid-deaths-us-one-million.html.

WHO (World Health Organization). 2009. *Cities and Public Health Crises: Report of the International Consultation, Lyon, France, 29–30 October 2008*. https://www.who.int/publications/i/item/WHO-HSE-IHR-LYON-2009-5.

WHO (World Health Organization). 2015. *Origins of the 2014 Ebola Epidemic*. https://www.who.int/news-room/spotlight/one-year-into-the-ebola-epidemic/origins-of-the-2014-ebola-epidemic.

WHO (World Health Organization). 2016. *Health as the Pulse of the New Urban Agenda: United Nations Conference on Housing and Sustainable Urban Development, Quito, October 2016*. https://apps.who.int/iris/handle/10665/250367.

WHO (World Health Organization). 2018. *Preparedness for Public Health Emergencies: Challenges and Opportunities in Urban Areas. High-Level*

Conference Report, Lyon, France, 3–4 December 2018. https://www.who.int/docs/default-source/documents/who-emergencies-in-urban-areas-web.

Wilkinson, A. 2020. Local response in health emergencies: key considerations for addressing the COVID-19 pandemic in informal urban settlements. *Environment and Urbanization*. 32, 2: 9.

Wilkinson, A. and M. Leach. 2015. Briefing: Ebola myths, realities, and structural violence. *African Affairs*. 114, 454: 136–48.

Wilson, K. 2021. Toronto launches initiative to support Black community disproportionately impacted by COVID-19. *CTV News*, 3 February. https://toronto.ctvnews.ca/toronto-launches-initiative-to-support-black-community-disproportionately-impacted-by-covid-19-1.5294064.

Witt, E. 2022. Letter from Los Angeles: can sustainable suburbs save Southern California? *The New Yorker*, 3 May. https://www.newyorker.com/news/letter-from-los-angeles/can-sustainable-suburbs-save-southern-california.

Wolf, M. 2016. Rethinking urban epidemiology: natures, networks and materialities. *International Journal of Urban and Regional Research*. 40, 5: 958–82.

Wood, C.L., A. McInturff, H.S. Young, et al. 2017. Human infectious disease burdens decrease with urbanization but not with biodiversity. *Philosophical Transactions of the Royal Society B: Biological Sciences*. 372, 1722. https://doi.org/10.1098/rstb.2016.0122.

Woolf, G. 2020. *The Life and Death of Ancient Cities: A Natural History*. Oxford: Oxford University Press.

Worthington, H. 2020. Urban planning sowed racial inequality in Minneapolis. Other North American cities must heed that warning. *The Globe and Mail*, 12 June. https://www.theglobeandmail.com/opinion/article-how-urban-planning-sowed-the-seeds-of-present-day-racial-inequality-in/.

Wu, T., C. Perrings, A. Kinzig, et al. 2017. Economic growth, urbanization, globalization, and the risks of emerging infectious diseases in China: a review. *Ambio*. 46, 1: 18–29.

Wylie, B. 2021. Democracy and the politics of salvage. *Bianca Wylie Medium*, 6 January. https://biancawylie.medium.com/democracy-and-the-politics-of-salvage-79803e629ef6.

Xiang, Z. 2020. COVID-19: on the epistemic condition. *Open Democracy*, 6 April. https://www.opendemocracy.net/en/can-europe-make-it/covid-19-epistemic-condition/.

Xu, Y. and Y. Ding. 2021. Responding to COVID-19 in the Liverpool City Region: Reopening after COVID-19 Lockdown: Insights from China. *Heseltine Institute Policy Briefing 036*. https://www.liverpool.ac.uk/media/livacuk/publicpolicyamppractice/covid-19/PB036.pdf.

Yang, G. 2022. *The Wuhan Lockdown*. New York: Columbia University Press.

Yong, E. 2018. The next plague is coming. Is America ready? *The Atlantic*, August. https://www.theatlantic.com/magazine/archive/2018/07/when-the -next-plague-hits/561734/?utm_source=twb.

Yong, E. 2020. How the pandemic defeated America. *The Atlantic*, September. https://www.theatlantic.com/magazine/archive/2020/09/coronavirus -american-failure/614191/.

Yong, E. 2021. How public health took part in its own downfall. *The Atlantic*, 23 October. https://www.theatlantic.com/health/archive/2021/10/how-public -health-took-part-its-own-downfall/620457/.

Yusuf, S. 2021. Is Amazon failing its warehouse workers? *York University Global Labour Research Centre*. https://glrc.info.yorku.ca/covid-19-and-the-world-of -work/covid-19-blog/is-amazon-failing-its-warehouse-workers/.

Zarate, L. 2020. Pandemic lessons, progressive politics: right to the city and new municipalism in times of COVID-19. *Minim*, 19 May. https://minim -municipalism.org/magazine/pandemic-lessons.

Zhan, M. 2005. Civet cats, fried grasshoppers, and David Beckham's pajamas: unruly bodies after SARS. *American Anthropologist*. 107, 1: 31–42.

Zhang, L. 2021. *The Origins of Covid-19: China and Global Capitalism*. Stanford: Stanford University Press.

Index ————————————————————

Page numbers in *italics* denote a figure.